HELPING SOPHOMORES SUCCEED

HELPING SOPHOMORES SUCCEED

Understanding and Improving the Second-Year Experience

Mary Stuart Hunter, Barbara F. Tobolowsky,
John N. Gardner, Scott E. Evenbeck,
Jerry A. Pattengale, Molly A. Schaller,
Laurie A. Schreiner, and Associates

JOSSEY-BASS
A Wiley Imprint
www.josseybass.com

National Resource Center for
The First-Year Experience®
& Students in Transition
UNIVERSITY OF SOUTH CAROLINA

Published by Jossey-Bass
A Wiley Imprint
989 Market Street, San Francisco, CA 94103-1741—www.josseybass.com

Jossey-Bass books and products are available through most bookstores. To contact Jossey-Bass directly call our Customer Care Department within the U.S. at 800-956-7739, outside the U.S. at 317-572-3986, or fax 317-572-4002.

Jossey-Bass also publishes its books in a variety of electronic formats. Some content that appears in print may not be available in electronic books.

Library of Congress Cataloging-in-Publication Data
Helping sophomores succeed : understanding and improving the second-year experience / Mary Stuart Hunter . . . [et al.].
    p. cm.
  Includes bibliographical references and index.
  ISBN 978-0-470-19275-7 (cloth)
  1. College sophomores–United States. 2. College students–United States. I. Hunter, Mary Stuart.
  LA229.H42 2010
  378.1'98–dc22

                                 2009029082

Printed in the United States of America

FIRST EDITION
HB Printing   10 9 8 7 6 5 4 3 2 1

THE JOSSEY-BASS HIGHER AND ADULT

EDUCATION SERIES

The University of South Carolina's National Resource Center for The First-Year Experience and Students in Transition was established in 1986 with a small grant from the South Carolina State Commission on Higher Education and has grown into a multi-faceted center providing professional development, research, and practitioner-focused publications for an international community of higher educators. The Center's scholarship and advocacy on behalf of college students in transition has garnered significant world-wide attention and impacted student success initiatives across the globe.

The Center's stated mission is to support and advance efforts to improve student learning and transitions into and through higher education. The Center achieves this mission by providing opportunities for the exchange of practical and theory-based information and ideas through the convening of conferences, institutes, workshops and other professional development events; publishing monographs, a peer-reviewed journal, an electronic newsletter, guides, and books; generating and supporting research and scholarship; hosting visiting scholars; and administering a robust Web site and numerous electronic listservs.

Although the Center is perhaps best known for its leadership in the first-year experience movement, other significant student transitions are central to the center's efforts and advocacy. National attention on the sophomore, or second-year, experience has been facilitated by the Center through information sharing at its annual National Conference on Students in Transition, the publication of two monographs on the sophomore year, the administration of two national surveys on sophomore programming, and national dialogue via an electronic listerv. This volume, *Helping Sophomores Succeed: Understanding and Improving the Second-Year Experience*, will provide an even wider audience of higher educators with resources and ideas to assist them as they strive to improve the second-year experience for students at institutions far and wide.

CONTENTS

LIST OF TABLES AND EXHIBIT

Tables

Exhibit

ACKNOWLEDGMENTS

Like the beginning of a new growing season, starting a new project is always a time for excitement and anticipation. That was certainly the case with this project. What we didn't anticipate at the beginning was how much we would learn as a result of planting the seed of an idea and then cultivating the development of the project. As we now approach the harvest, it is with grateful appreciation to David Brightman at Jossey-Bass for accepting our proposal to undertake the venture in the first place. We have been skillfully guided and gently pushed by his colleague, Erin Null, through each step of the manuscript development process. She pruned where necessary, fertilized when needed, and helped us see the potential when we felt wilted. Her guidance, flexibility, patience, and professionalism are much appreciated.

We owe special thanks to our colleagues at the National Resource Center for the First-Year Experience and Students in Transition at the University of South Carolina for their support during this project and for the very fact that the center's work has provided the landscape upon which much of the new work related to the sophomore year has been nurtured and developed in American higher education. The center's cultivation of national conversations, new survey research, and ground-breaking scholarship on the second college year enabled us to undertake this book. We are especially grateful to Tracy Skipper, editorial projects coordinator, and to Emily Mullins, graduate assistant, for their careful reviews of the manuscript drafts and their helpful suggestions.

We are indebted to our project team, including Scott Evenbeck, Jerry Pattengale, Molly Schaller, and Laurie Schreiner. Our early conversations with them conceptualizing the book and then identifying and inviting potential chapter contributors helped shape the volume you now hold in your hands. Their chapter contributions to this book are central to the book's breadth and depth. And to each of the chapter contributors, we are ever so grateful for your important contributions from the field, from Hawaii to the east coast, that have made this book possible.

And finally, we also acknowledge the thousands of higher educators who share our interest in the undergraduate experience and who are planting new and cultivating existing programs for second-year students on college and university campuses everywhere. As a result of your attention and interest, may sophomore students thrive for years to come!

Mary Stuart Hunter
Barbara F. Tobolowsky
John N. Gardner

AUTHORS AND CONTRIBUTORS

Edward K. Chan is associate professor of English at Kennesaw State University (Georgia). From 2003 to 2007 he also directed the Year 2 Kennesaw program and worked on sophomore issues at KSU and with colleagues across the country. He was a panelist on the national teleconference "The Forgotten Student: Understanding and Supporting Sophomores" (National Resource Center on The First-Year Experience and Students in Transition, March 9, 2006) and the national audio conference "Strategies for Sophomore Year Success" (PaperClip Communications, December 7, 2006). In 2007, he cofacilitated a sophomore workshop at the Fourteenth National Conference on Students in Transition. Edward Chan has also worked as a research fellow for the Center of Inquiry in the Liberal Arts at Wabash College studying out-of-class engagement and with the National Survey of Student Engagement Institute on the Documenting Effective Educational Practices project. He currently codirects KSU's Interdisciplinary Studies degree.

Mary Crowe is the director, Office of Undergraduate Research (OUR) at the University of North Carolina at Greensboro. OUR is dedicated to supporting and promoting undergraduate research, creative expression, and other scholarly experiences. She is a coprincipal investigator on two multiyear National Science Foundation funded grants focused on undergraduate research. She is a member of Project Kaleidoscope, a councilor in the Undergraduate Research Program Director division of the Council for Undergraduate Research, and on the Board of Governors of the National Conferences for Undergraduate Research. She earned her Ph.D. in biology from Northern Illinois University, and while a faculty member at Coastal Carolina University directed the research projects of over thirty students, including four who coauthored peer-reviewed articles on the behavioral ecology of crabs.

Scott E. Evenbeck is professor of psychology and dean of University College at Indiana University-Purdue University at Indianapolis (IUPUI). He joined the faculty of IUPUI in psychology in 1972, after completing his Ph.D. degree in social psychology at the University of North Carolina at Chapel Hill. Evenbeck has been involved for many years in the design, implementation, and assessment of programs for first-year college students and has given many presentations and written numerous articles and chapters on serving entering students. He serves as a Policy Center Advisor in the Foundations of Excellence in the First College Year and as a board member of the American Conference of Academic Deans. Evenbeck is a resource faculty member at the Summer Quality Academy of the Institute for Higher Education Policy. He served as a member of the Advisory Board for the National Resource Center for The First-Year Experience and Students in Transition from 2004 to 2008.

Robert W. Franco is professor of Pacific Islands Anthropology and director of the Office for Institutional Effectiveness at Kapiolani Community College, University of Hawaii. As a recognized expert on contemporary Samoan, Polynesian, and Pacific Islander demographic, ecological, health, and cultural issues, he has published scholarly research on contemporary Samoan political and cultural change, among other topics. He currently serves as the college's liaison to the Accrediting Commission for Community and Junior Colleges/WASC, Association of American Colleges and Universities, American Council on Education, Community College Survey of Student Engagement, and the Carnegie Foundation for the Advancement of Teaching (Community Engagement Classification). At Campus Compact, where he serves as senior faculty fellow for community colleges, he conducts trainings on service-learning, reducing the minority academic achievement gap, strengthening the liberal arts, and workforce development and civic missions of community colleges as "America's democracy colleges."

Jimmie Gahagan currently serves as assistant vice provost for student engagement at the University of South Carolina, where he also teaches a University 101 class for first-year student success. He has presented and published widely on such topics as residential learning initiatives, the first-year experience, academic advising, leadership development, the sophomore year, spirituality, and student retention. He has a B.A. in political science from the University of Richmond, an M.A. in student affairs administration, and a Ph.D. in higher education administration (anticipated May 2009) from the University of South Carolina.

Ann M. Gansemer-Topf is the associate director of research for the Office of Admissions at Iowa State University and a lecturer in the Department of Educational Leadership and Policy Studies at Iowa State University. Prior to her position in the Office of Admissions, she was the associate director of Institutional Research at Grinnell College focusing on departmental and campuswide assessment efforts. She has also been an academic advisor and taught and coordinated learning communities in the College of Design at Iowa State University and worked in residence life and campus ministry. She received her Ph.D. in educational leadership and policy studies from Iowa State University, M.S. in higher education from Iowa State University, and her B.A. in psychology from Loras College in Dubuque, Iowa. She was the recipient of a Research Excellence award from Iowa State University and recognized as Outstanding Academic Advisor from the College of Design at Iowa State University.

John N. Gardner is the senior fellow of the National Resource Center for The First-Year Experience and Students in Transition, and Distinguished Professor Emeritus of Library and Information Science at the University of South Carolina. He is also executive director of the Policy Center on the First Year of College, funded by grants from the Pew Charitable Trusts, the Atlantic Philanthropies, Lumina Foundation for Education, Winthrop Rockefeller Foundation, and USA Funds. Gardner had authored or coauthored numerous articles and books, including multiple annual editions of *Your College Experience* (1992–2009, with A. Jerome Jewler and Betsy O. Barefoot); *Step by Step to College and Career Success* (2005, 2007, and 2009, with A. Jerome Jewler and Betsy O. Barefoot); *The Freshmen Year Experience* (1989, with M. Lee Upcraft); *The Senior Year Experience* (1998, with Gretchen Van der Veer); *Challenging and Supporting the First-Year Student* (2005 with M. Lee Upcraft, Betsy O. Barefoot, and Associates); and *Achieving and Sustaining Institutional Excellence for the First Year of College* (2005 with Betsy O. Barefoot and Associates).

Virginia N. Gordon is dean emeritus and adjunct associate professor at the Ohio State University. She has extensive experience in teaching, administration, advising, and counseling in higher education settings. Her bibliography includes books, monographs, book chapters, and journal articles on many topics associated with higher education. Her latest publications are *Selecting a College Major: Exploration and Decision Making* (2009) and *Academic Advising: A Comprehensive Handbook* (2009). She has received national acclaim and numerous awards, the most fitting of which is NACADA's (National Academic Advising Association) naming of its award for outstanding contributions to the field of academic advising the *Virginia N. Gordon Award*.

Paul A. Gore, Jr. is an associate professor and student success special projects coordinator at the University of Utah in Salt Lake City. In addition to his academic and student support roles, Paul serves as the director of institutional analysis. He holds a Ph.D. in counseling psychology from Loyola University–Chicago, and master's degrees in counseling and applied biopsychology. Prior to arriving in Utah, Paul served as the director of the Career Transitions Research Department at ACT, Inc. in Iowa City, where he helped develop instruments, programs, and services in support of students' academic and career transitions. He has authored over forty peer-reviewed journal articles and book chapters. He is the past-chair of the Society for Vocational Psychology and serves on the editorial boards of several journals that focus on higher education, student development, and vocational psychology.

Sharon J. Hamilton, Chancellor's Professor Emerita of Indiana University-Purdue University Indianapolis (IUPUI) has been involved with enhancing student learning for over four decades. Formerly associate vice chancellor and associate dean of the faculties at IUPUI, and a founding member of the faculty of University College, Hamilton has written extensively about collaborative learning, general education, electronic portfolios, and the importance of literacy. Her memoir, *My Name's Not Susie: A Life Transformed by Literacy*, and her play, *My Brother Was My Mother's Only Child*, underscore the capacity of literacy to cope with complex life challenges such as those faced by sophomore students. Hamilton began teaching in a one-room, eight-grade schoolhouse on the Canadian prairies and was thereby introduced very early in her career to the vastly differing needs of students of varied backgrounds and intellectual experiences.

Mary Stuart Hunter is assistant vice provost at the University of South Carolina (USC). Stuart's work centers on providing educators with resources to develop personal and professional skills while creating and refining innovative programs to increase undergraduate student learning and success. She is a frequent speaker at conferences, symposia, and training events. Her recent publications include *Academic Advising: New Insights for Teaching and Learning in the First Year (2007)*, "The First-Year Experience: An Analysis of Issues and Resources" in AAC&U's *Peer Review (2006)*, and "The Second-Year Experience: Turning Attention to the Academy's Middle Children" in *About Campus (2006)*. She serves on national advisory boards of the National Society of Collegiate Scholars, the United States Department of Education's Network Addressing Collegiate Alcohol and Other Drug Issues, and the editorial board for the *Journal of Learning Communities Research*. She was honored in 2001 as the Outstanding Alumnae by USC's Department of Higher Education and Student Affairs and in 2006 as the Outstanding Campus Partner by USC's University Housing division.

Steven G. Jones is the associate provost for civic engagement and academic mission at the University of Scranton. Prior to moving to Scranton, he was the coordinator of the Office of Service Learning in the Center for Service and Learning at Indiana University-Purdue University, Indianapolis. Prior to that he was the associate director of the Integrating Service with Academic Studies project at Campus Compact from 2002 to 2004. Jones received a Ph.D. in political science from the University of Utah in 1995 and was an associate professor of political science at the University of Charleston from 1995 to 2002, where he also served as the director of the Robert C. Byrd Institute for Government Studies. He edited the second edition of Campus Compact's *Introduction to Service Learning Toolkit* and is a coauthor of two other Campus Compact monographs, *The Community's College: Indicators of Engagement at Two-Year Institutions* and *The Promise of Partnerships: Tapping into the Campus as a Community Asset*. He is also coeditor, with Jim Perry, of *Quick Hits for Educating Citizens*, which was published by Indiana University Press (2006).

Kirsten Kennedy is director of University Housing at the University of South Carolina. Previously she held positions in residential life at University of Missouri–Columbia and Bloomsburg University, as well as the position of adjunct assistant professor in the Department of Educational Leadership and Policy Analysis at University of Missouri–Columbia. Kennedy received her B.S.B.A. degree in management (1987) and her M.B.A. degree (1988) from Bloomsburg University of Pennsylvania. She earned her Ph.D. in Educational Leadership and Policy Analysis (2005) at University of Missouri–Columbia. Kennedy has published on topics including faculty participation in residential learning communities, today's college students, and assessing cost effectiveness in student affairs. Other research interests include parental influence on college student development, the history of higher education, and financial management of higher education and student affairs.

Stephanie L. Leslie is the director of study abroad at Indiana University-Purdue University Indianapolis (IUPUI). She is responsible for creating international opportunities with faculty members from all disciplines and coordinating the overseas experiences for IUPUI students. Leslie is the facilitator of the campus study abroad committee, which works to infuse study abroad throughout the campus. She is a founding member of the Indiana Re-Entry Conference that brings together returned study-abroad students from across the state to reflect deeply on their study abroad experiences and help them imagine how they can keep what they learned abroad active in their lives. She serves as the NAFSA: Association of International Educators Region VI Education Abroad representative. Her educational background includes a master of science degree in higher education administration–college student personnel, and bachelor's degrees in psychology and anthropology from Purdue University.

Jennifer A. Lindholm is special assistant to the vice provost for undergraduate education and associate director of the Center for Educational Assessment at the University of California, Los Angeles (UCLA). She is also director of the Spirituality in Higher Education Project. Formerly she served as visiting professor of higher education and organizational change at UCLA's Graduate School of Education and Information Studies and as associate director of the Cooperative Institutional Research Program at the Higher Education Research Institute (HERI). While at HERI, Jennifer also directed the institute's Triennial National Faculty Survey. In addition to the spiritual development of undergraduate students, Jennifer's research focuses primarily on the structural and cultural dimensions of academic work; the career development, work experiences, and professional behavior of college and university faculty; and issues related to institutional change within colleges and universities.

Jerry A. Pattengale is a leading voice for *purpose-guided education*™ and his recent books include *Why I Teach* and *The Purpose-Guided Student* (McGraw-Hill, 2008 and 2009). Pattengale also co-edited *Visible Solutions for Invisible Students: Helping Sophomores Succeed* published by the National Resource Center for The First Year Experience and Students in Transition, and served on its advisory board. His *Virtual Advising Link* (VAL) system was a NACADA award recipient (1999). Jerry received two Professor of the Year awards while teaching at Azuza Pacific University (CA) and an NEH award to study in Greece. He currently serves on the Governor's Council on Faith Based Initiatives (IN), the boards for the Collegiate Employment Research Institute (Michigan State University), and Veriana Networks, Inc. (a new media group). Pattengale is the assistant provost for scholarship and public engagement at Indiana Wesleyan University (approximately 15,500 students), one of the Founding Institutions of the *Foundations of Excellence* program.

Molly A. Schaller is an associate professor and coordinator of the College Student Personnel Program and a Fellow in the Ryan C. Harris Learning Teaching Center at the University of Dayton. Prior to her faculty position she worked for ten years in student affairs administration. She holds a bachelor's degree in psychology from the Ohio State University, master's degree from Miami University in college student personnel, and a Ph.D. in higher education administration from Ohio University. Her research focus is on college student development, with special emphasis on sophomore students. She has consulted with numerous institutions as they have worked to develop their sophomore programs. Schaller also researches the relationship between physical space, pedagogy, and learning on college campuses.

Laurie A. Schreiner is professor and chair of Doctoral Higher Education at Azusa Pacific University (CA). After receiving her Ph.D. in community psychology from the University of Tennessee, she has taught for the past 26 years in liberal arts colleges and universities. She is co-author of *StrengthsQuest: Discover and Develop Your Strengths in Academics, Career, and Beyond*, in addition to the *Student Satisfaction Inventory*, an instrument used by over 1,600 colleges and universities nationally, and *Visible Solutions for Invisible Students: Helping Sophomores Succeed*. A recipient of two federal grants for first-year programming and campuswide strengths-based approaches to retention, she is also a senior research associate with the Gallup Organization; is on the advisory board of the National Resource Center for The First-Year Students and Students in Transition; and directs a national project on assessment and retention for a consortium of 100 faith-based liberal arts colleges.

Susan Buck Sutton is associate vice president of International Affairs for Indiana University with specific responsibilities for IU's urban campus, Indiana University-Purdue University Indianapolis (IUPUI). At IUPUI, she leads campus efforts in all aspects of internationalization, from international student admissions and services to curriculum internationalization. She serves on the Executive Committee of the Association of International Education Administrators and is the chair of the International Education Leadership Knowledge Community of NAFSA. Sutton is also Chancellor's Professor of Anthropology and the past president of the General Anthropology Division of the American Anthropological Association. She also teaches a service-learning course on the anthropology of modern Greece on the island of Paros every summer. Sutton received her B.A. from Bryn Mawr College and Ph.D. from the University of North Carolina and has published four books and nearly 50 articles on both internationalization and anthropology

Julie Tetley is the director of First-Year and Sophomore Studies and Advising at the Colorado College. In her role, she has developed a program specifically for second-year students entitled the *Sophomore Jump*. She has several years of experience in teaching and advising and has given numerous presentations at the local, state, and national level. In addition, she served as the Commission Chair for NACADA's Small Colleges and Universities Commission from 2006 to 2008. She is currently enrolled in a doctoral program in the School of Education and Human Development at the George Washington University and her dissertation focuses on promoting self-authorship through a learning partnership academic advising program.

Barbara F. Tobolowsky is associate director of the National Resource Center for The First-Year Experience and Students in Transition at the University of South Carolina. In this position, she supervises the center's research, conferences, and publication efforts. Tobolowsky also is a clinical assistant professor in the Department of Educational Leadership and Policies, and teaches graduate seminars in the Higher Education and Student Affairs Program (HESA). She earned her doctorate from the University of California, Los Angeles, in higher education and organizational change.

M. Lee Upcraft is a senior research scientist at the Center for the Study of Higher Education, assistant vice president emeritus for student affairs, and professor emeritus of higher education at Penn State University and a senior scholar diplomate of the American College Personnel Association. He is the author or editor of 125 books, monographs, book chapters, and refereed journal articles on topics such as assessment in student affairs, the first-year experience, student persistence, academic advising, alcohol and other drug abuse, professional ethics, residence halls, student development theory, and higher education administration.

Kathryn J. Wilson is assistant vice chancellor for research at Indiana University-Purdue University Indianapolis (IUPUI). She founded the IUPUI Center for Research and Learning and served five years as its executive director. She is the principal investigator (PI) and director for the IUPUI Ronald E. McNair Program and the PI for a multi-institutional National Science Foundation research project to develop an electronic research portfolio to document intellectual gains experienced by students during participation in faculty-mentored research experiences. She serves on the Board of Governors of the National Conferences on Undergraduate Research (NCUR) and is a divisional councilor of the Council on Undergraduate Reserach (CUR). She is an associate professor of biology with a Ph.D. in plant science from Indiana University, Bloomington. Prior to campuswide positions she served 12 years as associate dean for research and graduate studies in the IUPUI School of Science, where she founded the school's undergraduate research program and had primary responsibility for promotion and support of faculty research and graduate programs.

HELPING SOPHOMORES SUCCEED

INTRODUCTION

John N. Gardner, Jerry A. Pattengale,
Barbara F. Tobolowsky, and Mary Stuart Hunter,

As higher educators, even though we may have differing educational philoso-
phies and find ourselves in different types of institutions in terms of mission
and student characteristics, our collective overreaching goal is student success.
Although we may quibble over definitions of student success (such as GPA, timely
graduation, and so forth), our hopes are for students to attend the best institution
for them to accomplish their personal goals, whether that is earning a bachelor's
or associate's degree or acquiring needed job skills to help them in their future
lives or both. To that end, we offer initiatives, programs, and supports along the
way to help students achieve their goals. For the past three decades, efforts in
the first year have received renewed attention, because one of the first leaks in
the higher education pipeline comes when students begin their first year of study.
Those first-year efforts (for example, first-year seminars) have often led to many
students making better grades, persisting to graduation, being more satisfied with
their collegiate experiences, and a host of other positive outcomes (Tobolowsky,
Mamrick, & Cox, 2005).

Although there is now extensive scholarship on the first-year and senior-
year transitions, fewer scholars and practitioners have turned their attention
to year two even though there is strong evidence that there is another serious
pipeline leak during this crucial time (Tobolowsky & Cox, 2007a). Students in
the second year too often feel invisible on their campuses (as highlighted in the
titles of two publications from the National Resource Center for The First-Year

Experience and Students in Transition dedicated to looking at the sophomore experience: *Visible Solutions for Invisible Students: Helping Sophomores Succeed* (Schreiner & Pattengale, 2000) and *Shedding Light on Sophomores: Explorations into the Second College Year* (Tobolowsky & Cox, 2007a). Too often these students no longer qualify for the supports offered to first-year students and they have not yet found comfort in a disciplinary home. Feeling lost, at the very least, can lead to frustration, and at its worst, to dropping out. Research suggests that students do experience these negative reactions, with the second-highest attrition occurring in the sophomore year (Almanac Issue, *Chronicle of Higher Education,* 2007–2008). This book hopes to shine a light on this too often neglected population to provide strategies for educators to help reverse this trend.

As authors, we can immediately anticipate a variety of possible reactions to this new work including

1. Why a book on another college "transition"? Is there sufficient substance to this transition to require this sort of attention?
2. How interesting. I am curious to see why this is a significant transition for students.
3. At last, someone has focused on the second year, because it confirms my long-held belief that something unique happens to students in the second year . . . and it isn't good.

Our hope is that by the end of the book, any doubters will agree that the second-year experience is unique and challenging for many students, and those with curiosity or an innate belief about the sophomore experience will have evidence to support those attitudes.

As we shall present, this work follows a long body of research, innovation, and applied practice to identify and improve student success in other critical college student "transitions." Those works provided insight and inspiration as we tackled this less understood transition. In addition to those models, the following questions guided the development of this book.

1. What is the second year of college?
2. Does the second year differ substantially from the first year of college? If so, how?
3. What are some of the lessons learned from successful first-year and senior programs that could be applied to second-year improvement efforts?
4. Is the second year of undergraduate study a distinct period of personal and academic growth and learning for a significant number of students?

5. Is there empirical support for the archetypal notion of the "sophomore slump"? Is retention an issue in the second year?

6. What kind of a literature base is there to justify this work?

7. What are the central challenges to student learning and success in the second year?

8. What are the components for an academic rationale for such interventions?

9. If a campus wanted to intentionally improve its efforts to promote success in the second year, what might be academic and programmatic options for consideration? What can be learned from campuses already engaged in efforts aimed at the second year?

10. How might this experience and period in college be different for students in two-year institutions compared to four-year institutions? How might each sector respond accordingly?

We hope these are questions our readers will also consider and, after reflection, lead them to appropriate action.

History and Context Underlying Current Work on the Sophomore-Year Experience

The efforts to improve the first year are well documented in the literature. But the particular efforts to focus on the first year, it is generally agreed, began with the efforts of the University of South Carolina with its first-year seminar course, University 101, in the mid-1970s. This course provided the foundation for a series of conferences on (what is now known as) the first-year experience, where higher educators gather annually to share their experiences, insights, and research on new student support efforts. Accompanying these conference activities has been the creation and growth of a literature base, which now permeates many academic journals, launched by the National Resource Center for The First-Year Experience and Students in Transition at the University of South Carolina. The center's expanded mission to advocate for a broader focus on "students in transition" led to a call for attention to efforts to improve the senior year, transfer transitions, and the second or sophomore year. In 2000, the center's publication of *Visible Solutions for Invisible Students*, edited by Laurie Schreiner and Jerry Pattengale, marked the first book-length treatment of the second college year in America.

Both the senior-year and the sophomore-year conversations and campus efforts are outgrowths of the earlier focus on the first year. On many campuses the same faculty and academic and student affairs administrators that initiated attention to the first year are also driving this second-year focus. In fact, there is direct carry-over and convergence of these lines of work. Thus, although distinct, nevertheless, the efforts are interconnected. All evidence suggests that the more educators learned from the first-year student focus, the more they were inspired to reach out to address the needs of other students in transition.

Many educators (and organizations) have contributed to efforts to improve student success throughout the undergraduate experience. Especially influential have been campus-based practitioners who have adopted, replicated, altered, refined, and institutionalized these lines of work on hundreds of campuses. This volume is a direct result all of these efforts.

Lessons from the First-Year and Senior-Year Movements

An obvious place to begin this exploration is with a brief look at other student transitions. Although the first-year transition is much more established in both the practice and literature of higher education than the senior year, enough is known about both for meaningful comparisons to other transition improvement efforts. A recapitulation of that literature belongs in other books. Suffice it to say here that, though distinct, the first-, senior-, and now sophomore-year efforts are interconnected. These connections become apparent when comparing these three primary transition efforts.

Retention as the Primary Driver

Although we wish we could report that the overwhelming reasoning behind why colleges and universities ought to pay more attention to second-year students was the prized educational outcomes that might thereby be enhanced, alas, both the first-year and the sophomore-year foci seem to be driven by "retention," and hence a revenue and business model. There are some elite institutions where this may not be the case, but these would be the exceptions. Most certainly, proponents of more attention for this transition do offer educational and humanistic arguments. However, in terms of winning necessary support from resource allocators, the case still is being driven by the search for the fiscal Holy Grail: increased revenue by means of enhanced retention and graduation rates.

On the surface, retention does not play the same role in our focus on senior students. There the arguments appear primarily to be educational and humanistic in nature, such as providing intellectual capstone experiences; lending more integration and coherency to the curriculum; and providing more support for students as they (and their families) deal with the transition stresses of leaving college. Yet even in this transition there are elements of a financial and business model. As Gardner argued in *The Senior Year Experience* (Gardner, Van der Veer, & Associates, 1998), those who advocate for alumni development and cultivation before students actually leave college are part of the driving force behind a focus on seniors. In other words, it is hoped that attention on seniors will ultimately increase long-term financial-giving prospects.

Transition Efforts Reveal Varying Degrees of Intellectual Focus

Although all three transition efforts have an intellectual focus, it is more prominent in the sophomore and the senior years. One of the criticisms frequently made about the support strategies for first-year students is that they lack sufficient academic content and rigor and, in fact, are often (or even primarily) not delivered by educators with faculty status. It is our observation and experience that the efforts in the sophomore and senior years appear to have more focus on what's happening to students in the major in terms of academic decision making than first-year initiatives.

Non-Faculty Members Have an Original and Disproportionate Influence

Faculty involvement is intimately connected to the intellectual focus of these three transition efforts; however, many of these programs were driven initially by non-faculty. It would be argued by many that this has been a mixed blessing and that the espousal by student affairs professionals for more attention to these transitions may have inhibited or discouraged faculty from becoming engaged sooner. Nevertheless, the contributions of legions of student affairs professionals and academic advisors to the needs of these students in transition should be acknowledged. It is our contention that the majority of initiatives within all three lines of work are faculty-owned and driven, regardless of how they may have started out, particularly with respect to the first-year work dating to the 1970s.

Varying Degrees of Stress Characterize These Transitions

The first-year and senior-year transitions are periods of higher stress for students and their families than the sophomore-year period. The beginning and ending transitions are periods of greater uncertainty and perceived higher stakes than the second year. However, this perception does not square with the realities for many students who make critical decisions (such as choosing a major or deciding not to remain in this college or any other college) during this collegiate period.

Family Involvement Varies During the Three Transition Periods

Families are much more likely to be engaged in decisions surrounding the first-year and senior-year transitions because the issues revolve around these questions: Where is my child/spouse going to college? What does she/he need to get off to a good start? What is my child/spouse going to do after college? Because the challenges of adjustment and the consequences of decision making do not appear either so apparent or significant in the sophomore year, it seems there might be a lower level of family engagement. Nevertheless, in the era of "helicopter parents" and families communicating via text, e-mail, and cell phones on a constant basis, families do remain significantly engaged during the second year and could be considered as potential partners for campus-based efforts to improve student performance.

There Is Less Attention Paid to the Second Year

To date, more attention is paid to issues associated with the beginning and end of college than the sophomore year. Of course, one of the purposes of this book is to redress this difference and to argue for attention to all three in a more balanced, seamless continuum.

Defining the Sophomore Year Is More Challenging than Defining Other Transitions

Perhaps one reason there has been less attention paid to the second college year is that it is more difficult to define. It is much easier to define the beginning and the ending periods of college, because they are more distinct, pronounced, and therefore amenable to redress. There is a greater ambiguity about when the second year begins both developmentally and academically. Is it a matter of time in college, number of credits earned, level of commitment and investment by the student, or degree of certainty about major and purpose?

The book editors considered these definitions and decided to take a broad view and focus on the second year a student is in college, recognizing that the examples shared within this book may, in fact, be based on a somewhat different, institution-specific group. The belief is that the differences are nuanced. The book editors felt that whether a student has crossed the credit threshold to be a sophomore or not, when they begin their second college year they are likely to face similar issues.

Greater Attention Is Paid to Decision Making for the Major

One of the critical decisions in the second year is regarding the selection of academic major. Often in the first year students are allowed to defer this issue and address more pressing developmental needs (such as the transition to college itself). But this particular decision must be paramount in the second year; therefore, the amount of attention paid to academic advising and career planning is greater than during the first year and even the senior year.

The Role of General Education Is Less Significant Beyond the First Year

Students are spending less curricular and classroom time in general education courses in the second-year and senior-year transitions than in the first year. This has enormous implications for teaching and advising students in the second year, class size, student motivation, and student perception of the relevance of academic requirements and work. This factor also increases the centrality of the student's academic home unit in a successful second year.

The Possibilities for Pedagogies of Engagement Increase Beyond the First Year

It is possible, depending on institutional size and type, that class size may be smaller in the second year. Students may be more likely to be taught by full-time faculty, who may be more likely to use pedagogies of engagement. It should be an aspirational objective to maximize this potential for interactive classroom settings and hands-on learning opportunities so as to increase student engagement and satisfaction.

Primary Objectives in the Second Year

The primary goal of this book is to expose the unique challenges of the second year that make it such a vulnerable period for students on their higher education journey. Those challenges have a direct connection to the overriding tasks of the sophomore year: (a) selecting an appropriate, achievable major and (b) developing purpose. It is often at the end of the second year that students on four-year campuses must declare their majors and that students on two-year campuses will need to make decisions about where and how to continue their higher education. Selections of majors are bound up with students' agonizing about deciding on a career, and these decisions lead students to an investigation of purpose.

A qualitative study of sophomores and juniors at a private institution in the Midwest explored perceptions of the sophomore year and found that some issues of major and life purpose were heightened in the second year (Gansemer-Topf, Stern, & Benjamin, 2007). For example one second-year student in the study stated, "It definitely felt like, you're 20, you're a sophomore, you have to declare your major. I definitely felt like I had to figure out the next 10 years" (p. 36). Another student commented, "There's quite a good deal of discussion among people generally . . . about what exactly they want to do with their lives. I think it's probably something to do with the whole having to declare your major" (Gansemer-Topf et al., p. 36). Therefore, many of these students felt great pressure to address questions such as, What do I want to do when I grow up? What is my life going to be about?

The Role of Purpose in the Second Year

Undeniably, the dialogue on finding one's life purpose is challenging for people at all ages and circumstances. Parker Palmer (1998) brought the discussion of purpose to the attention of many academic circles by looking at educators. His message on purpose or personal alignment states in brief that

> Many of us were called to teach by encountering not only a mentor, but also a particular field of study. We are drawn to a body of knowledge because it shed light on our identity as well as on the world. We did not merely find a subject to teach—the subject also found us. (Palmer, p. 25)

Palmer's notion of finding one's identity and place in the world is at the very heart of true student success (Pattengale, 2006). Concomitantly, researchers are also finding that for the traditional student the main intersection with this sense of purpose occurs during the second year (Reynolds, Gross, & Millard, 2005).

The complexity of dealing with a student's search for purpose manifests itself both in the variety of approaches described in the following chapters and, unfortunately, in a noticeable silence in higher education scholarship. There are a few exceptions. *Why I Teach: And Why It Matters to My Students* (Pattengale, 2008),

The Path to Purpose: Helping Our Children Find Their Calling in Life (Damon, 2008), and *The Purpose-Guided Student: Dream to Succeed* (Pattengale, 2009) are three of the more recent books that approach student success through this focus on purpose. The latter reports findings from a study on a purpose-guided curriculum conducted by Indiana Wesleyan University and Indiana University and funded by the Lumina Foundation, which had positive results (Reynolds et al., 2005). It found that various cohort groups of "undecided students," those often labeled as "at-risk" or more likely to leave college, persisted at higher rates than students not taking a curriculum focused on purpose (all odds ratios were positive for the various cohorts, n = 1,700). Most of these undecided students found clarity and focus during their second year. Although this study is limited to a specific four-year campus, it supports the notion that a focus on purpose helps students navigate the rough waters of higher education.

However, it is important to note that issues for second-year students are not limited to the four-year sector. Though it is easier to define students as being in their "second" year when they are traditional-aged at a four-year campus, the changing demographic tells us that today's college student is as likely to be older, married, and attending a two-year campus as he or she is to be an 18–22-year-old student living on four-year residential campus. For this reason, we have asked the authors included in this book to provide examples, where possible, of approaches, programs, and initiatives for second-year students on two-year campuses to attempt to capture the diversity of institutions and students.

Organization of the Book

With these goals in mind, this book is divided into three sections. The first section provides a comprehensive look at the foundational underpinnings of the second-year experience by first presenting a review of the literature on second-year students and their experiences in college, followed by a more focused consideration of recent research on this student population and theoretical insights into second-year students' development. The second section focuses on various examples of programs that engage sophomores. Taken together, this section offers a road map to a comprehensive approach to assisting second-year students. Authors focus on academic and career advising, academic support, faculty development, pedagogy, and programmatic efforts such as service-learning, study abroad, and undergraduate research, which are specifically geared to this population. In the final section, the chapters provide step-by-step guides to implementation and assessment, concluding with recommendations for educators interested in improving second-year student success.

This work reflects our belief that it is important to encourage educators to consider the development of a comprehensive, intentional, academic, and cocurricular approach to the second year on their campuses. We have seen how providing only a first-year seminar or another single initiative in the first year is never as effective as offering a comprehensive, coherent, integrated range of efforts for students based on an overall plan for student success, inside and outside the classroom. An explicit, intentional, comprehensive, well-articulated, and coordinated approach to the second year communicates to sophomores that they are as valued by the institution as students in other periods. Only when students have a sense of being valued will they no longer feel and be "invisible."

PART ONE

FOUNDATIONS

What is the sophomore-year experience? Who are second-year students and what are their issues and concerns? Does the second-year experience differ dramatically from the first? Is there actually a sophomore slump? These were some of the initial questions that guided the development of this book and are addressed in Part One.

As we enter this relatively new territory, it is critical that we begin with a solid foundation based on prior research and theory. By building on what is already known we can make deeper meaning of the information in the subsequent sections of the book. In Chapter One, Molly A. Schaller explores the unique experiences of different subpopulations of second-year students and their specific needs and challenges. In Chapter Two, Kirsten Kennedy and M. Lee Upcraft review the limited research that has been done to date on this special population and investigate the existence of the sophomore slump. Laurie A. Schreiner shares the findings from one of the few studies conducted with sophomores from 26 public and private four-year institutions in Chapter Three. Molly A. Schaller in Chapter Four offers a theoretical grounding to sophomore development.

CHAPTER ONE

UNDERSTANDING THE IMPACT OF THE SECOND YEAR OF COLLEGE

Molly A. Schaller

What is the rationale for a focus on sophomores? Is the sophomore-year experience different from any other college year? Clearly the authors and editors of this book argue that the sophomore year, whether defined by credit hours or the actual second year of college, is a unique and important developmental period when students are examining their life purpose. The sophomore year is a time for turning inward and for exploring how one fits into college life and the world at large. Gardner, Pattengale, and Schreiner (2000) assert that the most compelling reason for attending to sophomores is the possibility of students dropping out during or after their second year. They also contend that prolonged indecisiveness, poor academic course selection, low levels of academic and cocurricular engagement and integration, behavioral problems, and increased time to degree completion all can manifest themselves in the sophomore year.

The purpose of this chapter is to examine how the structure of the college experience affects sophomores in a unique way; it emphasizes the relationship between the institution and the student by looking at issues of persistence, engagement, satisfaction, and major choice, including academic self-efficacy and motivation.

The Development of Sophomore Programs

Questions focused on the second-year experience have not been raised broadly in higher education. In fact, limited literature, even descriptive research, exists regarding the sophomore year. This lack may be due to the fact that research strategies on four-year institutions have focused on the magnitude of change seen in college students over the entire four years of the college experience, thus research designs often call for measurements in the first and senior years of college. The diverse enrollment patterns at community colleges, which may range from one term to many years, complicates research further. Therefore, an empirically based understanding of the second college year remains illusive. (For more information on available research, see Chapter Two.)

Although research is sparse, sophomore-year programs do exist throughout the country in focused academic programs, which support sophomore students in specific majors or from specific service areas such as residence life, student leadership development, career development, or even campus ministry. However, more comprehensive programs, across academic divisions or beyond single offices, are few and far between. Liberal arts colleges seem to have been the first to respond specifically to the needs of second-year students. Beloit College's sophomore-year experience program is one of the first of its kind in providing a unified program for sophomores, which focuses on the academic and social integration of sophomore students. Colgate University, Colorado College, and others have followed in the development of sophomore-year experience programs that involve multiple departments and, therefore, offer a more comprehensive approach. These institutions recognize that sophomore students have unique needs that are not being served, perhaps because these students tend to be placed in cohorts, beginning the college experience together and moving as a class to the sophomore year.

Do sophomores at liberal arts colleges differ from those at other types of institutions or are faculty and student affairs professionals at smaller institutions more likely to be in relationships with students that allow them to notice when students have concerns? The reality is likely much more complex than this simple question; however, the underlying question remains: What are the issues that our students face at various times during their academic experience? How do we find ways to notice and respond to these issues as they arise? Issues of persistence, academic success, student engagement, and satisfaction when coupled with the unique developmental experience of many sophomores make for a complex time in college life.

The First-Year Experience Sets the Stage

The first-year experience movement, which began in the late 1970s (Hunter, 2006), in many ways has set the stage for the questions we ask about the sophomore year. First-year programs were developed to support students in making the transition from high school to college by focusing on the academic and social transitions that new students negotiate (Tinto, 1987). In many ways, these programs are designed to bridge the gap between the K–12 experience and the postsecondary experience. Higher education has designed transition programs for the first year of college because this connection is not provided in high school (McDonough, 2004).

Programs and initiatives designed to address first-year issues are now commonplace. In a national survey of curricular first-year programs, researchers found that 96 percent of institutions had a new student orientation program, 89 percent offered first-year English classes with 25 or fewer students, 62 percent offered faculty development programs on teaching first-year students, more than 60 percent of institutions collect and report midterm grades for first-year students, 80 percent of four-year and 62 percent of two-year institutions offer first-year seminars (Barefoot, 2005). As institutions across the country identify programs that support first-year students, those approaches quickly become identifiable as best practices. Relatively new initiatives in higher education, such as learning communities, Supplemental Instruction, or service-learning programs are found in more than one quarter of institutions (Barefoot, 2005). However, Barefoot asserts, many of the programs that exist throughout the country do so without a coherent, purposeful strategy. On many campuses, first-year programs are not intentionally woven into the fabric of campus life or the curriculum.

The student experience of the first year remains a key focus and rightly so. Numerous theories and models have provided a framework for understanding the experience of college students and have assisted in focusing institutional attention on key areas (Bean & Metzner, 1985; Cabrera, Castaneda, Nora, & Hengstler, 1992; Tinto, 1975, 1987). Academic preparation, financial burdens, academic and social integration, involvement, faculty contact, time away from campus, institutional commitment, and other factors have been identified and studied. However, there is no reason to believe that students who survive the first year of college are suddenly successful in their second year.

Implications for the Second Year

Students' experiences during the first year of college have been transformed on many campuses. In reaction to the enrollment boom that followed World

War II, first-year students were often warehoused in massive, impersonal classes with little additional support. Today, first-year students may still have some large classes but they may also have access to faculty in first-year seminars, first-year interest groups, and learning communities. Students were once left on their own to respond to the academic rigors of college. Today, institutions provide tutoring, Supplemental Instruction, developmental coursework, and other supports (Barefoot, 2005). First-year orientation, welcome week activities, and the other programmatic additions make the first-year experience a time filled with structure and opportunity.

What then, is the experience of those students who return for the second year of college? One of the unintentional consequences of enhanced first-year initiatives may be a sense of abandonment in the sophomore year (Flanagan, 1991; Schreiner & Pattengale, 2000). Although first-year experience programs are pervasive (Barefoot), few of these initiatives extend to the second year (Gahagan & Hunter, 2006). This fact alone is not a reason to develop second-year programs, but it does provide a powerful argument for truly comprehensive institutional responses across academic years that are related to the developmental and academic needs of students.

One challenge facing institutions is that there is little known about how sophomores may differ from first-year students. Although the literature on the first-year experience is extensive, major gaps exist with regard to persistence beyond the first year (Nora, Barlow, & Crisp, 2005). Furthermore, Graunke and Woosley (2005) warn that we need to be cautious in applying what is known about first-year students to students in other years, because student issues vary dramatically during particular college years. Their text identifies the complex differences that exist between the two years and how those differences affect students in unique ways during this time.

Retention and Persistence

In an examination of students beginning college in the 1995–1996 academic year, Berkner, He, and Forrest (2002) found only 51 percent of students who began at four-year institutions successfully completed a degree within six years at their original institution. When transfer students are included, the six-year graduation rate rises to 58 percent. While first- to second-year retention is followed closely, there is less attention paid to retention beyond the first year. For students who intend to complete a four-year degree, at least as many students leave after the second year as do the first year (Berkner et al., 2002).

Why do students drop out? In their meta-analysis of research of four-year college student performance and persistence, Robbins and others (2004) concluded that factors such as academic self-efficacy, academic goals, and academic skills are the most salient factors once students have attended college. Although precollege academic markers, such as high school grade point average and scores on standardized tests, remain important in predicting retention to the sophomore year, academic success in the first year (Allen, Robbins, Casillas & Oh, 2008) is most likely to predict persistence beyond the second year.

In the second year of college, first-generation students face the highest risk for departure (Ishitani, 2006). Risk factors include enrolling part-time, delaying entry, not having a regular high school diploma, having children, being a single parent, being financially independent, and working full time (Berkner et al., 2002). First-generation students who delay entry are 81 percent more likely to depart in the second year.

Braxton, Hirschy, and McClendon (2004) revised Tinto's student departure theory and in the process identified 16 propositions to consider when examining departure from commuter institutions. While many of the propositions are related tangentially to the sophomore year of college, others may be of primary concern to persisting students. Ongoing accumulation of debt or the evaluation of the worth of continued enrollment, motivation to make steady progress toward degree completion, students' ability and need for control in daily life, general self-efficacy, affiliation needs, participation in learning communities, and academic integration may have an impact on the persistence of students during or after the sophomore year.

Student Issues in the Sophomore Year

Tinto (1987) suggests that the decision to persist is a series of recommitments to personal goals that are mediated by factors both internal and external to the institution. Though first-year initiatives frequently have academic and social integration as a goal, it is a mistake to suggest that such integration is fully achieved within the first year. This section examines the issues that contribute to students' academic and social integration in the sophomore year of college. When considering academic integration, issues such as major selection, academic self-efficacy, career development, connections with faculty, motivation, and financial viability each play a role in the sophomore experience.

The Major and Academic Self-Efficacy

Most four-year institutions require that students select a major near or at the end of the second year of college. Whereas some programs and institutions emphasize earlier major selection, only 8 percent of colleges require students to select a major upon entry (Barefoot, 2005). Thirty-six percent of liberal arts institutions do not allow first-year students to officially declare a major, and more than half of all institutions report allowing students to declare a major but do not force or strongly encourage students to declare in their first year (Barefoot, 2005). As students accumulate credit hours, coursework selection is increasingly directed by one's interests and majors. As students explore academic interests, they evaluate their ability to be successful in their major(s) of interest.

Academic self-efficacy is best defined as the self-evaluation of one's ability or chance for success or both in the academic environment (Chemers, Hu, & Garcia, 2001; Robbins et al., 2004). Academic self-efficacy beliefs are a poor predictor of academic success in the first semester of college but are a good predictor at the end of the first year (Gore, 2006). This suggests that as students gain awareness of the college setting and of their own abilities in this setting, academic self-efficacy is based upon more accurate understanding of one's abilities. The impact of having a strong belief in one's ability to succeed is clear. Academic self-efficacy remains the best psychosocial predictor of grade point average (Robbins et al., 2004). It has been found to moderate the effect of stressors on perceived stress (Zajacova, Lynch, & Espenshade, 2005). However, academic self-efficacy may be of concern in the sophomore year for those students who have faced difficult academic challenges in the first year, for those who have not been selected into majors of their choice, or for those who decide to change academic focus areas from their college entry plans. There is some evidence that academic self-efficacy can be increased by enrollment in a study skills course (Boysen & McGuire, 2005). Programs that help to build student's academic self-efficacy and study skills are often focused on first-year students as they make the transition into college. However, as students begin to narrow options for their majors or enroll in more challenging courses, the connection between course selection, major selection, and one's sense of success becomes clearer.

The selection of the major is a complex process requiring students to have the academic ability for the specific coursework, awareness and understanding of available options, and decision-making skills particularly in balancing interests with future career or life goals. Galotti (1999) found that between winter of the first year and winter of the second year, the number of major alternatives under consideration by students dropped. Declaring a major requires that sophomores have an attachment and commitment to ideas, interests, and a group of faculty members at a time when they may well be continuing to separate from their original plans and family (Margolis, 1989). In the community college setting, over 50 percent of enrolled students are in terminal occupational programs (Townsend &

Wilson, 2006). Students enrolled in occupational programs or professional schools may find major changes particularly difficult as they accumulate credit hours.

The positive impact of being decided or clear about one's major cannot be understated. Sophomores with higher degree of certainty in their major had higher grade point averages (Graunke & Woosley, 2005). Some research indicates that undecided students have lower academic performance and lower persistence rates than those who are decided (Leppel, 2001). Therefore, even though we cannot posit categorically that undecided students will have lower persistence rates, this must be considered on an individual institutional basis. Reverse transfer, or transferring from a four-year to a two-year institution, may be more likely for those second-year students who do not select a major (Hillman, Lum, & Hossler, 2008).

Career Development

A great deal has been written about the impact of prolonged adolescence on college students (Howe & Strauss, 2000). One concern is that students are not prepared to make decisions about a career direction during the college years because there is little societal pressure for students to take responsibility for their own or family members' lives. It is interesting that students who are more autonomous are more decided in their career direction (Guay, Ratelle, Sevécal, Larose, & Deschênes, 2006). With college students showing signs of strong connections to their parents (Howe & Strauss, 2000), developing autonomy and separating from parents may be a particular challenge. Still, undecided students can be characterized in two distinct ways: (a) those who are developmentally undecided, whose status as undecided will shift as they become more self-aware and develop a sense of purpose and life direction or (b) those who are chronically undecided and do not seem to improve their career or major decision-making skills. Chronically undecided students have low levels of autonomy; developmentally undecided students show signs of increased self-efficacy during early college years (Guay et al., 2006). Sophomore students who remain undecided at the end of the academic year face particular challenges. These students may choose to either withdraw from school or to select a major that allows for career decision making later. Major selection and career decision making do not always go hand in hand. In some cases, students move far enough along in coursework that finishing the degree of study may take precedence over a true commitment to a career path. Older students seem to exhibit greater career maturity; however, they may also face more life pressures in their decision-making process (Luzzo, 1999). (For more on career issues, see Chapter Six.)

Faculty Contact

Student contact with faculty is one of the strongest predictors of retention, persistence, engagement, and academic success. In the sophomore year, students may find it particularly difficult to build relationships with faculty as the student changes majors, leaves the first-year academic advisor, or enrolls in large classes. In a study of nearly 4,000 students in the first and second year of college, Fischer (2007) found that student connections with faculty were related to higher grades for all types of students. Furthermore, another study found that the quality of faculty interaction is a predictor of sophomore success (Graunke & Woosley, 2005).

Many majors are structured in ways that have the highest student-faculty contact in the junior and senior years. Although many first-year experience programs have increased faculty interaction with first-year students, second-year students are often completing general education or foundation courses in larger classes and with non-major faculty or with adjuncts. As one engineering faculty member suggests, there may be a need to adjust the curriculum to increase faculty contact in the first two years (Dym, 2006). And in the sophomore year, substantive, educationally meaningful student-faculty interaction will not just automatically happen; instead, it will need to be expected, nurtured, and supported (Kuh et al., 2005). (For more on faculty development, see Chapter Eight.)

Student Motivation

Student motivation to attend college may be quite different from the motivation to persist in college. Although there are a variety of motivational descriptors, one thing is clear: students who do not have defined goals may lack the motivation to make the types of decisions necessary for persistence in college (Hull-Blanks et al., 2005). Côté and Levine (1997) identified five motivators for college attendance: (a) careerism or a desire to enter a specific career area, (b) personal development, (c) humanitarian interests or a desire to help others, (d) parental or societal expectations, and (e) default motivation or going to college because there is no other perceived choice. Phinney, Dennis, and Osario (2006) studied a more diverse population and subsequently added three additional motivators: (a) a desire to help one's family, (b) the encouragement of others, and (c) a desire to prove oneself. In their study, they found that career, personal, and humanitarian motives were positively related to college self-efficacy, college commitment, and confidence in one's ability to accomplish degree goals. Attending college to avoid less desirable options, holding what Côté and Levine (1997) called a default motivation, was negatively related to these measures (Phinney et al., 2006). Helping one's family is important for some students, but meeting parental expectations is also important to the success of students.

Parents' lack of educational expectations may have an impact on the student's view of the college experience. First-generation students whose parents do not have specific educational expectations are most likely to depart in the second year of college (Ishitani, 2006). When these students are unsure about their own educational expectations, they are 1.3 times more likely to leave their first college in the second year (Ishitani, 2006).

Yet in a study of sophomores at one institution, commitment to a specific major or career was not related to degree completion (Graunke, Woosely, & Helms, 2006). Rather, higher levels of student commitment to completing their degree at the specific institution and commitment to obtain a bachelor's degree were significant predictors of degree completion (Graunke et al., 2006). Students from higher socioeconomic classes who aspire to complete advanced degrees are more likely to persist in college, suggesting that their long-term goals are motivators (and also they have the economic means to do so without financial problems becoming a disruptive variable) (Paulsen & St. John, 2002). However, Paulsen and St. John found that students from lower socioeconomic backgrounds who aspired to complete an advanced degree were less likely to persist in college or were more likely to stretch out the costs of college by enrolling sporadically. Costs, then, play a mitigating role in terms of persistence for many students.

Students' Values

Students' values about work and career goals are complicated. While there are no studies of sophomore student values, Duffy and Sedlacek's (2007) research does provide a model for understanding what second-year students may face. They described four types of values: (a) *intrinsic,* such as autonomy and interests, (b) *social,* such as working with people and making a contribution to society, (c) *extrinsic,* such as money and job security, and (d) *prestige-related,* such as careers that are highly respected. In recent studies, men were most likely to describe extrinsic values such as career and financial success; women were most likely to describe social values or prestige-related goals (Duffy & Sedlacek; Hull-Blanks et al., 2005). Women's goals were found to be more directly related to persistence, were longer range, and were more specific than extrinsic goals (Hull-Blanks et al., 2005). Duffy and Sedlacek found that students from households with a median parental income described intrinsic values, whereas students from low and high parental income households described extrinsic values. In a sample of more than 3,500 first-year students, 29 percent were seeking careers consistent with their interests; 47 percent were seeking careers consistent with their values or desired career outcomes.

A connection between interests and major is an important consideration. Tracey and Robbins (2006) found that individuals who were in majors similar to their interest profile had higher grade point averages than those with lower interest-major match. However, having a match between major and interest was not a predictor of persistence for all students. Students who are less able to identify a set of interests seem to be particularly sensitive to an environmental mismatch. These findings suggest a dynamic and complicated relationship between interests and major.

Financial Issues

As noted above, cost, motivation, and persistence are related for many college students. The impact of loans on persistence and degree attainment is complicated by the conditions that surround loan taking (Dowd & Coury, 2006). One important question is the financial return on investment. Students who struggle to pay or who perceive themselves as having less of an ability to pay may fail to develop a sense of social integration (Braxton et al., 2004). Students risk losing scholarships when they earn a low grade point average, do not continuously enroll full-time, or decide to transfer institutions. In addition, there is a complex relationship among race, socioeconomic status, type of financial aid, and persistence in the first year of college (St. John, Paulsen, & Carter, 2005). Beyond the first year of college, there is little research to explain how financial aid affects persistence (Pascarella & Terenzini, 2005). Loss of one-time grants and scholarships in the second year, loss of scholarships due to academic difficulty, understanding potential earning power, and the increasing pressure to find meaning in the college experience all come into play in the sophomore year.

Social Integration and Involvement

Institutions put numerous resources into encouraging involvement for first-year students. Organizational fairs and social opportunities are structured to assist students in developing a social and emotional connection to the people at the institution. One the one hand, Fischer (2007) found that becoming involved in formal organizations or activities on campus is related positively to academic success in college. On the other hand, developing more informal friendships on campus may reduce the likelihood of leaving college (Fischer, 2007). Social integration, first identified by Tinto (1987), is related to students' entering characteristics and ability to pay, initial level of institutional commitment, proactive social adjustment strategies, and psychological engagement (Braxton et al., 2004). Braxton, Hirschy, and McClendon (2004) suggest that students become committed to their institution when they perceive that the institution has integrity, has a commitment to the welfare of students, and that there is a potential social community at the institution.

Involvement in extracurricular activities is important for all groups, but especially for minority students. For these students, such involvement reduces the likelihood of leaving college by at least 83 percent (Fischer, 2007). Graunke and Woosley (2005) found that institutional commitment and involvement in student activities were not predictors of grade point average in sophomores. Although Foubert and Grainger's (2006) study had a low effect size, they found that involved sophomores exhibited greater development in academic autonomy and lifestyle planning than less involved students. This developmental difference was not seen in the senior year between involved and uninvolved students, thus suggesting that involvement may have a greater positive effect on the development of students early in the college experience. Whereas social integration has been viewed as important for persistence, it is also contributes positively to student development. In the sophomore year, students may well have lost their informal contacts from the first year of college because of changes in living arrangements, discontinued learning communities, and enrollment in larger classes outside the major.

Satisfaction

Students' satisfaction with the college experience at their institution is a frequent research outcome. Satisfaction indicates not that students are pleased with the amenities of the college setting, but that they are making academic progress and developing a sense of belonging and mastery over the environment. In an analysis of data from the National Longitudinal Survey of Freshmen, Fischer (2007) found that for most students high school grade point average has a significant impact on satisfaction in college. Formal involvement in organizations or support programs and informal social ties are also related to satisfaction. Formal social ties seem to be especially powerful in increasing African American student satisfaction. Racial climate, if negatively perceived, has a negative relationship to satisfaction for all groups. For all students, higher levels of college satisfaction reduced the likelihood of leaving college (Fischer, 2007).

In her analysis of the satisfaction of students, Juillerat (2000) found that sophomores at public institutions value an institutional system that works well, is easy to negotiate, and is responsive to students. These students also identify approachable faculty and excellent instruction as a value. Sophomore students at private colleges tend to have higher expectations than students in any other class. Juillerat suggested that this may be related to the special attention paid to first-year students and students' perception that the junior and senior years are filled with more positive experiences.

Academic Engagement

If the sophomore year produces any type of slump, boredom, or lack of interest (Gardner et al., 2000; Margolis, 1976; Wilder, 1993) then certainly academic engagement is an important factor for sophomore students. Margolis (1989) suggested that one of the real issues of the sophomore year is that there are not as many challenges built into the roles of sophomore students and thus excitement gives way to boredom. Student engagement has two key components that contribute to student success (Kuh, Kinzie, Schuh, Whitt, & Associates, 2005). The first component is the amount of time and effort students put into their studies and other activities that lead to the experiences and outcomes that constitute student success. The second factor is the way institutions allocate resources and organize learning opportunities and services to entice students to participate in and benefit from such activities.

Kuh and colleagues (2005) found that students who write more papers, read more books, meet more frequently with faculty and peers, and use informational technology appropriately show greater gains in critical thinking, problem solving, effective communication, and responsible citizenship. Sophomore students may be less likely to engage in these behaviors. Wilder (1993) compared students whose grade point average (GPA) declined in the sophomore year with those whose GPA did not. They found that absenteeism was a significant factor for those whose grade-point average declined in the sophomore year compared to those that did not. In their examination of the experiences of more than 50,000 full-time students enrolled from 1990 to 1998, Hu and Kuh (2002) found that the largest percentage of both first-year and sophomore students were in the disengaged group with smaller fractions in the engaged group. In their examination of learning productivity indicators of an even larger sample, Kuh and Hu (2001) reported two key findings that are important to the sophomore-year experience. First, they found that the amount of effort and student-reported learning and personal gains increased in a linear way from the first through the senior year. However, sophomores had statistically lower scores from seniors on six key indicators: (a) cooperation among students, (b) reading and writing, (c) the total amount of effort they reported putting into college, (d) their self-reported gains from college, (e) active learning, and (f) faculty contact. Scores on these final two indicators decreased from the first-year to the sophomore year.

Student Diversity

When considering designing programs or initiatives for any student population, it is important to recognize the specific challenges and opportunities that different students experience. Whereas there is little research about specific populations in the sophomore year, there are clear concerns and needs for many identifiable groups on our campuses. This section takes a brief look at gender, socioeconomic status, racial and ethnic diversity, age, sexual orientation, and academic ability because each of these characteristics affect students in the sophomore year in important ways.

Gender Issues

The selection of majors continues to be influenced by gender. Women are more likely to persist if their majors are education, health, and humanities or liberal arts and are less likely to persist if their major is business, even with high academic performance levels (Leppel, 2001). Men, on the other hand, are more likely to persist if business is their major and are less likely to persist if education is their major even when they performed well academically (Leppel, 2001). In making major and career decisions, women are most influenced by specific career paths and long-range goals. Women may begin college with hopes of stepping into nontraditional (for women) majors (such as the hard sciences, math, engineering) and find the climate too uncomfortable, resorting back to more accepted majors by the sophomore year. At the same time, men seem to be under tremendous pressure to be successful and this pressure has an impact on their selection of major and career planning (Bellani, 2007).

At the University of Richmond, attrition of sophomore men is of greater concern to the institution than the attrition of first-year students (Bisese & Fabian, 2006). These men, even though they enter with similar SAT scores, are four times more likely than women to be placed on academic probation. In a survey of their male students, the university found that men tended to have significant concerns about their future, including worries about getting a job, getting into graduate school, and reaching their career plans. Those designing interventions for sophomore students should examine the experiences of men and women on their campuses in order to best meet students' unique needs.

Socioeconomic Status

Social class is an important factor in college selection and persistence and there-fore should be a consideration in the development of institutional policies and programs (Paulsen & St. John, 2002). Students from lower socioeconomic backgrounds may be most impacted in their transition by parental expectations and their own educational aspirations (Peng & Fetters, 1978). While there are some support programs for first-generation or lower socioeconomic status (SES) students, these support programs are often not sustained throughout the four years of college. Students from lower SES families are more likely to work while in school, attend part-time, live off campus, attend public institutions, and be cost conscious in their college selection (Paulsen & St. John, 2002). These characteristics suggest that academic and social integration (Tinto, 1987) may be a particular challenge for lower SES students. In the sophomore year, when institutions provide fewer support programs, this is of particular concern. In their study of third-year college retention, Allen, Robbins, Casillas, and Oh (2008) found that economically disadvantaged students are more likely to leave college prior to the junior year.

Upper- and middle-class students may not be challenged by cost issues in the same ways; however, their social class standings may suggest interesting challenges in the sophomore year. These students may come to college with vast life experiences, including studying abroad or international travel, exposure to foreign language, music lessons, and other opportunities. Career decision-making under these circumstances may be a particular challenge if students come to college with multiple notions of possible careers. These students may also feel pressure to be financially successful in their future careers and therefore find conflict between personal interests and a desire for career or financial success. The sophomore year is a critical time in decision making for future career direction. (See Chapter Six for more on career development.)

Racial and Ethnic Diversity

As we will see in Chapter Four, sophomore students often face identity development issues, a growing sense of self, and the need to make sense of self in a new environment. Although most students face these issues, diverse students, particularly those who are in the minority on their campuses, may find additional challenges on their campus and in their identity development process. The intersection between racial and ethnic diversity, social and academic integration, and persistence is well researched overall and while not explored specifically for sophomores, is an important consideration. For example, institutional contacts are particularly important for students from underrepresented groups (Fischer, 2007). Students who do not develop these contacts early in the college career may need additional supports in the second year of college. By contrast, maintaining connections off campus has a negative effect on grades for Caucasian and African American students but does not have this same effect for Asian and Hispanic students (Fischer, 2007). This suggests that different approaches may be needed in supporting students from a broad range of family or cultural values.

Career and major selection are often influenced by one's cultural values. For example, in one study African American sophomores in majors with economic potential such as health, business, engineering, or computer sciences were more likely to persist (St. John, Hu, Simmons, Carter, & Weber, 2004). Students' perceptions of worthy or acceptable majors are influenced by their culture of origin. Students' decisions are also influenced by their perception of barriers. African American women anticipate more career barriers than other college women (Lopez & Sujin, 2006). In addition, students' motivations for attending college are influenced by their cultural background. Understanding student experiences in the sophomore year requires that institutions to pay particular attention to the priorities, values, and challenges faced by students and to examine these issues by using race and ethnicity as one lens.

Age

Nontraditional age or adult students make up a significant portion of college students. Donaldson and Townsend (2007) reported that 43 percent of college students were over the age of 24. Hagedorn (2005) identified "four corners of friction" for adult students (p. 24). Access, success, retention, and institutional accommodation are challenges facing many of these students. Although access may not be an issue in the sophomore year, adult students face other issues regardless of the number of credit hours accrued. In a study of 5,000 nontraditional age students, these students reported that finding time for college, family responsibilities, and job responsibilities were obstacles to success (Hagedorn, 2005). As students continue into the second or sophomore year, maintaining endurance and focus may be particularly difficult for students who have multiple life demands. Structures, therefore, should be flexible, allowing for students to enroll and move through the academic program at their own pace (Kazis et al., 2007). As student populations diversify, it will become increasingly important for institutions to carefully study the obstacles to success for students on individual campuses and at multiple points throughout enrollment.

Sexual Orientation

As discussed previously, making sense of one's self in a new environment is a challenge for many college students. Few student groups are at more risk in the identity development process than gay, lesbian, and bisexual students. These students may come to college having negotiated their sexual orientation with appropriate support networks in place to move through this developmental period as other students do. However, many gay, lesbian, and bisexual students come to terms with their sexual orientation after college begins, when they are away from home and their communities of origin (D'Augelli, 1992). Often, these students are at particular risk during the college years because of societal views of their sexual orientation (D'Augelli, 1989). In the sophomore year, students are questioning their lives, their position in college, and their future. For students who are also dealing with the coming out process, the second year may be a particularly difficult time.

Academic Ability

Students arrive at college with a full range of academic abilities. Although the range is important in the college experience, students on either end of the continuum are of particular concern during the sophomore year. Honors students may find challenge in determining a career direction when there are multiple options. For these students, there may be a struggle to identify a single goal (Graunke et al., 2006). This may be a particular issue during the sophomore year when students are required to choose a specific direction.

On the other end of the continuum, students who enter college with academic deficits are becoming commonplace. According to Attewell, Lavin, Domina, and Levey (2006), 40 percent of traditional-aged undergraduate students take at least one remedial course (specifically: 58 percent of students at two-year colleges, 31 percent at non-selective four-year institutions, 14 percent at selective, and 2 percent at highly selective). What is even more striking is that 52 percent of students from the lowest socioeconomic quartile and 24 percent of students from the highest socioeconomic quartile take at least one remedial course. For students at four-year institutions, taking remedial coursework has a statistically significant negative effect of on a student's likelihood to graduate (Attewell et al., 2006). This negative effect was not found at two-year institutions. In the second year, students who enter taking remedial courses, particularly those taking multiple remedial courses, may not have earned enough credits to hold sophomore status. These students may be considered first-year students by the institution, depending on how it defines sophomores, while their classmates are sophomores. This leaves students feeling inadequate as they are unable to progress at the pace of their peers. In traditional four-year institutions, for students who have difficulty selecting a major and for those who face financial difficulties, this may be a period of heightened risk for withdrawal.

Summary

Students respond to their institutions and the demands of the sophomore year in unique ways. Increasing academic self-efficacy, student involvement, integration, engagement, and satisfaction; supporting students as they make major, career, and life purpose decisions; developing pedagogies and experiences outside the classroom that engage sophomores in relationships with faculty and staff; attending to financial and academic concerns; and responding to diverse needs of students are each important in the sophomore year. This text sets out to assist faculty and administrators in developing approaches that will recognize the importance of the sophomore year. While the literature on the second year is not yet robust, this chapter identified specific topics for concern for students and institutions in the sophomore year.

If, as Kuh and his colleagues (2005) suggest, institutions are to have an unshakeable focus on student learning, they must examine the experiences of sophomores. Specifically, institutions must use data to examine the departure rates, academic experiences, level of engagement, and satisfaction of sophomore students. Sophomore students must feel a "specialness about being a student here" (Kuh et al., 2005, p. 315). Focusing on sophomore student success does not need to be any different than focusing on students' success in general. Kuh and his partners provide us with a straightforward approach in designing such initiatives. They suggest that institutions must have many complementary policies and practices to academically and socially support sophomore students. Institutions must find ways to induce large numbers of sophomores to use programs and resources that will assist the sophomore student in becoming more engaged in the college or university environment and clearer about a career and life direction. And institutions must set and hold sophomores to standards that stretch them to perform at high levels, inside and outside the classroom.

CHAPTER TWO

KEYS TO STUDENT SUCCESS

A Look at the Literature

Kirsten Kennedy, M. Lee Upcraft

The keys to student success include a complex combination of factors beyond ability and motivation. Focusing on known success factors and applying what is known about student success to the second year of college is even more complicated. This chapter analyzes the research and literature on the sophomore year, including student success, sophomore academic performance, typical sophomore issues, the origins and redefinition of the "sophomore slump," and institutional interventions that promote sophomore student success. The chapter is not intended to be a comprehensive review, but rather a representative sampling of what the research and literature tells us about student success and, when available, sophomore student success. Our assumption is that when studies that focus on student success throughout the college years are cited, they included sophomores. Studies that included only first-year students were excluded from this review, as well as studies that were methodologically deficient. We have relied heavily on authors such as Pascarella and Terenzini (2005), who have reached conclusions about student success based on their comprehensive review of available literature and research, and studies based on national databases such as those by the National Survey of Student Engagement at Indiana University, the Department of Education Office of Educational Research and Improvement, and selected single institution studies.

Keys to Student Success

To frame our discussion of sophomore student success, we first take a look at the keys to student success in general, primarily because of the dearth of research specific to the sophomore year. Our definition of student success is that students earn grades sufficient to meet graduation requirements. Students may learn, grow, and develop substantially, but if they do not graduate, they are not deemed a "success" by most institutional standards.

While there are many models that attempt to explain student success, we have chosen Astin's (1977) Input-Environment-Outcome (I-E-O) model because it is the foundation for most other student success models. It is based on the commonsense notion that student success is a function of who students were before they entered college and what happened to them after they enrolled. Input variables typically include student demographics and characteristics prior to college. Environmental variables typically are divided into institutional characteristics and student academic and out-of-classroom experiences.

Student Input Variables

In general, successful students, compared to those who are not, have a prior record of earning good grades, score well on standardized admissions tests, have a strong commitment to obtaining a degree, have strong parental-family support, and come from higher socioeconomic levels. Men, racial and ethnic minorities (except Asians), and older students are generally less "successful" (Astin, 1993a; Pascarella & Terenzini, 2005).

Institutional Characteristics

Pascarella and Terenzini (2005) found that institutional characteristics that positively affected academic performance and persistence included attending a four-year institution, a single-sex institution, or a predominantly Black institution. They also reported availability of financial aid as a very powerful predictor of student success. Financial aid reduces (or eliminates) economic obstacles to obtaining a degree. In other words, financially aided students are slightly more likely than unaided students to persist and graduate. Similarly, St. John, Cabrera, Nora, and Asker (2000) discovered that finance-related factors (that is, student aid, tuition, and other costs) explained about half the variance in the persistence process. The type of aid also mattered; students who received a financial aid package made up of grants or with a higher ratio of grants to loans displayed a higher level of persistence (St. John, 1989, 1990). Nora, Barlow, and Crisp (2005) suggested that students who pay in-state tuition are more likely to re-enroll for their second and third years than are out-of-state students. Institutional size or type or both had mixed impacts on student success.

Pascarella and Terenzini (2005) concluded that "students' institutional commitments exert an important and positive effect in shaping their persistence decisions" (p. 426). They also state that a student's level of involvement in the academic and social systems of the institution is another important factor in a student's decision to stay at the institution. Both of these statements demonstrate a good institutional fit. Conversely, students who are not involved and integrated into their campus academic and social systems are less likely to experience a good institutional fit, thus resulting in their leaving the institution. The National Survey of Student Engagement (2008) lists a supportive campus environment as one of its benchmarks of educational practice that is essential to student success.

Students' Classroom-Related Experiences

One of the strongest predictors of student success is the quality of student effort. For example, Pascarella and Terenzini (2005) and Kuh et al. (2005) concluded that the greater a student's engagement in academic work, the greater his or her learning. Likewise, instructional strategies that increase students' active engagement in learning such as active and collaborative learning appear to have a positive impact on persistence, knowledge acquisition, general cognitive growth, grades, and intellectual and cultural openness.

Furthermore, according to Pascarella and Terenzini (2005) and Kuh and Hu (2001), interactions with faculty play independent and positive roles in persistence, development of career-relevant skills, career choice, general cognitive development, reflective thinking, general student development, and moral reasoning. Merely the perception that faculty members are accessible and concerned about student success can also have a positive effect (Pascarella & Terenzini, 2005). Lundquist, Spalding, and Landrum (2002–2003) reported specific faculty behaviors that contributed to persistence; they included being supportive of student needs, being approachable, and returning phone calls and e-mails in a timely fashion.

Teaching methods are also critical to student success. Pascarella and Terenzini (2005) reported that passive instructional techniques, such as lecturing, appear to be less effective in achieving learning outcomes than active learning techniques, such as collaborative learning, cooperative learning, small group learning, problem-based learning, case studies, peer tutoring, and others. The National Survey of Student Engagement (2008) identifies active and collaborative learning as one of its benchmarks of effective educational practice that contribute to student success.

Academic major appears to affect persistence and graduation, with students majoring in science, engineering, business, and health-related professions more likely to graduate than similar students in other majors, but the effects of major field appear to be less a matter of the discipline than of the attendant economic opportunities as well as the culture and climate within the academic department (Pascarella & Terenzini, 2005).

Students' Out-of-Classroom Experiences

Students' out-of-classroom experiences that positively influence student success include developing successful and supportive interpersonal interactions. For example, according to Pascarella and Terenzini (2005), interactions with student peers play a positive role in student persistence, racial and ethnic attitudes and relations, interpersonal relationships, major field of study, career choice, general cognitive development, and critical thinking. In addition, they found that peer interactions, in general, and the settings in which they occur are most likely to be influential. Astin (1993a) found that peer relations are critical for support, confirmation of one's identity, opportunity for socialization, and persistence. Astin suggested that the student's peer group is the single most important source of influence on growth and development during the undergraduate years.

There are many out-of-class variables that contribute to student success. Some of those include participating in extracurricular activities, working part-time, enrolling full-time, perceiving high student satisfaction, perceiving a supportive campus climate (especially for women and minorities), participating in service learning, using selected student services (particularly academic advising and counseling), and participating in intercollegiate athletics. It also has been found that students living in on-campus residence facilities, compared to those who live elsewhere, are more likely to persist and graduate, have more positive and inclusive racial-ethnic attitudes, be more open to diversity, have slightly greater cognitive growth and intellectual development, and show greater gains in knowledge acquisition and skill development (Pascarella & Terenzini, 2005; Upcraft, Gardner, & Barefoot, 2005).

However, student collegiate experiences that have a negative impact on student success include enrolling part-time, working full-time, abusing alcohol and other drugs, participating in Greek Life, interrupting enrollment such as stopping out, transferring vertically (from a two-year institution to a four-year institution), transferring horizontally (from one institution to another), and reverse transferring (transferring from a four-year institution to a two-year institution).

The evidence is mixed on the affects of age and major field on student success (Pascarella & Terenzini, 2005).

Overall, students' active involvement in their learning and educational experiences, both inside and outside the classroom, is the key to student success, and the extent to which institutions value and encourage such involvement through formal and informal interventions will determine student success (Kuh, Kinzie, Buckley, Bridges, & Hayek, 2007).

Sophomore Academic Performance

By far the most credible study of sophomore academic performance was done by Adelman (2006), who followed students and their attendance patterns from high school through college, *without regard for institution*. In his analysis, Adelman made the distinction between retention, which he defines as being limited to a specific institution, and persistence, which refers to the *"quality* of the student's record going forward" (p. 53). He found that 8 percent of entering students leave college (not just their current institution) during their sophomore year. From an individual institutional perspective, this number is likely to be higher. An important finding relevant to individual institutions is that, "by the end of students' second year, a significant range in credit generation, academic performance, and curricular participation has opened up between those who eventually completed bachelor's degrees and those who did not" (p. 61). Adelman also found that this academic record spread actually began earlier than the sophomore year, as evidenced by roughly one in five students entering their sophomore year not earning enough satisfactory progress toward a degree and one in six students carrying low GPAs. "The second academic calendar year offers students the opportunity to recapture any lack of momentum of the first. In this respect, the second year may be even more important than the first" (Adelman, 2006, p. 53). Bean (1985) found that the most powerful predictor of sophomore attrition was socialization-selection variables, including college grades, institutional fit, and institutional commitment.

College grades may well be the single best explanation for sophomore academic performance and degree completion (Pascarella & Terenzini, 2005). Adelman (1999) found both first-year grades and a measure of subsequent grade trends to be statistically significant, positive predictors of bachelor's degree completion beyond the effects of an array of other variables, including precollege characteristics. Having first-year grades in the top two quartiles increased a student's likelihood of degree completion by two to three times over students with grades in the bottom three quartiles.

Issues Facing Sophomores

Although sophomores face many of the same issues as their first-, third-, and fourth-year colleagues, they may have issues that are unique to their enrollment status. On the basis of interviews conducted with student affairs professionals, Pattengale (2000) divided sophomore issues into three basic categories: academic issues, developmental issues, and institutional issues.

Academic Issues

As previously noted (Adelman, 2006), one in six students entered the sophomore year either in poor academic standing or having failed to make satisfactory progress toward their degrees. Poor academic performance was one of the major academic issues sophomores face in determining whether to stay at their current college, transfer to a different college, or drop out altogether. The national data that exist on college student persistence produced by Adelman (2006) suggests that among students beginning in college, 89.7 percent persisted into the second calendar year at some institution. More specifically, 95.8 percent persisted into the sophomore year in four-year institutions, 84 percent in community colleges, and 71.5 percent in other subbaccalaureate institutions. Because institutional retention numbers are often much lower, these persistence statistics clearly show that not all student attrition from a single institution signals attrition from college.

Other than poor academic performance in the first year, what else accounts for sophomore attrition and academic underachievement? Other than the variables previously identified that impact all students, there is little research regarding sophomore academic performance. Gardner (2000), in a single institution study of 2,414 students, found that sophomores study the least out of all students. Whereas first-year students, juniors, and seniors spent 18 percent to 20 percent of their time studying outside of class, sophomores spent, on average, 15 percent of their time studying. Sophomores were also found to spend more time in social, leisure, and physical fitness activities than first-year students, juniors, and seniors.

Gardner (2000) also discovered that an incompatibility between students' dominant learning styles and instructors' course delivery methods resulted in students' attrition from the institution. "Unable to find a learning method that works for them, some students may opt to leave the university, usually after the sophomore year. The learning style incompatibility may be masked by bad grades and certainly a lack of connection to academics" (p. 70). Gardner also found that sophomores in particular were more prone to view an instructor as seldom or never interacting in class, even when the instructor reported that she or he "encouraged students in class or built upon student-generated ideas" (p. 71). Gardner also found that sophomores were less likely to participate in class and had less interaction with their fellow students. Furthermore, sophomores are less likely to have a close relationship with a faculty member (Coburn & Treeger, 1997).

Choosing a major and career is a second major academic issue facing sophomores. Pascarella and Terenzini (2005) found that choosing a career was heavily influenced by informal interactions with faculty, whether those were informal conversations, assisting with faculty research, or other out-of-classroom contact. Gardner (2000) stated that when sophomores did interact with faculty, the topic was most likely to be related to career issues. Sophomores had fewer conversations with their peers about majors compared to their first year, that is until such time that they declared a major (Gardner, 2000). Graunke and Woolsley (2005) identified commitment to an academic major as a significant predictor of grade point average. (See Chapters Five and Six for a more detailed discussion of major and career selection.)

Developmental Issues

Because there is little direct empirical evidence to indicate how many, or to what extent, sophomores confront developmental issues, we must rely on a combination of theory, opinions, and research. Among the developmental issues that negatively affect sophomore student success are struggles with identity confusion, personal relationship problems, lack of purpose, and dissatisfaction with college.

Some sophomore students may enter into an identity crisis created by a period of confusion and uncertainty (Furr & Gannaway, 1982). Coburn and Treeger (1997) found that some sophomores, as they struggle with their identity development, often do so at the expense of previous interpersonal relationships, as new ones develop. Some sophomores may face personal relationship problems (Richmond & Lemons, 1985). Margolis (1976) described sophomores engaged in an identity crisis that involves their social, academic, and personal self. Thus, they may have difficulty processing their thoughts and feelings associated with confusion over all of the available choices (Furr & Gannaway, 1982).

Based on Chickering's (1969) vectors of development, Lemons and Richmond (1987) identify developing purpose as a major developmental task of college sophomores. They may not be able to make decisions because they become paralyzed by the number of choices (Coburn & Treeger, 1997). They may also be at odds with their parents over career or major selection (Pattengale, 2000) and struggling with a period of spiritual exploration that includes questioning or confirming the values instilled by their parents, primarily by being exposed to many right answers, all backed up with logical, cogent arguments (Coburn & Treeger, 1997).

There is strong empirical evidence that sophomores may express dissatisfaction with their collegiate experience. Juillerat (2000) conducted an initial Student Satisfaction Inventory (SSI) study of 118,706 traditional undergraduate students, followed by a second study specifically examining sophomore retention issues. Consistent with other year-based cohort classes, sophomores expressed the least satisfaction with administrative practices associated with billing, financial aid, not getting the runaround, and adequate health care services. Sophomores, as well as other classes, were dissatisfied with "issues affecting their lives as students on campus, such as weekend activities, athletic programs, food services, parking, residence hall rules, and channels for expressing complaints" (p. 22). Juillerat found that sophomores are significantly more dissatisfied than other students with the approachability and concern of their advisors, the registration process, receiving timely feedback from faculty, and the caring nature of faculty members. These four items are also ones in which sophomores indicated were of great importance in the SSI.

Institutions that sophomores attend may in some cases negatively affect their success. Colleges and universities may create out-of-classroom environments that are not supportive of student success and that lack curricular integration and direct support for the sophomore year compared to the first year, all of which may result in a poor fit between the institution and the sophomore student (Pascarella & Terenzini, 2005).

Redefining the "Sophomore Slump"

Perhaps conspicuously absent from this review of the literature and research on the sophomore year so far is any consideration of the so-called "sophomore slump." Because it has become an often-used phrase to describe the sophomore year, it deserves some attention in this review. In sports, the "sophomore slump" refers to "a significant decline in competitive performance during an athlete's second (or sophomore) year at a given level of competition following an outstanding first (or rookie) season" (Taris, 2000, p. 57). This sports definition might lead educators to assume that a sophomore slump in college students could mean decreasing grades compared to the first year or increased student attrition during the sophomore year. Just what, if any, evidence supports the "sophomore slump"?

Feldman and Newcomb (1994) found only two previous studies that documented the sophomore slump phenomenon, neither of which included declining grades and dropping out of college. The first was Freedman's (1956) study that concluded: "Evidences of what has been called 'sophomore slump' are rare. Rather it appears that the inertia or disorganization implied by this term are [*sic*] more likely to occur in the second semester of the freshman year" (p. 22). The second was Baur's (1965) four-year study of student-college interactions, which concluded that the most prevalent issues that sophomores faced were boredom and apathy. Feldman and Newcomb (1994) analyzed four other studies: Birney, Coplin, and Grose's (1960) preliminary report of the class of 1959 at Amherst College; DiRenzo's (1965) report on student imagery at Fairfield University during 1963–64; Finnie's (1967) paper on student satisfaction at Harvard presented at the American College Health Association conference; and Whyte's (1963) unpublished doctoral dissertation on male Cornell students and their level of alienation from the college, all of which concluded that the most dissatisfied class was the sophomore class.

Subsequent studies on the sophomore slump have defined the phenomenon in various ways. However, Richmond and Lemons (1985) point out that the sophomore slump is difficult to define because "there seems to be no one problem that can be identified and ... it seems unwise to lump all the problems of individual students together" (p. 176). Many definitions of the sophomore slump focus on the issues and problems that sophomores face. Furr and Gannaway (1982) said that the "sophomore slump is a term frequently used by college educators to describe the period of confusion and uncertainty that occurs during the sophomore year" (p. 340), whereas Kramer, Taylor, Chynoweth, and Jenson (1987) stated,

> Compared to the freshman year, during the sophomore year students may feel less hopeful, less engaged, and less competent. It is a year of reflection on what they have achieved academically, and on what they want to accomplish in the future. (as cited in Gordon, Habley & Associates, 2000, p. 99)

Margolis (1976) described a situation in which three inter-related areas (academic, social, and self) accumulate into a sophomore identity crisis. Lemons and Richmond (1987) describe the sophomore slump as "a period of developmental confusion" (p. 18).

Perhaps the best empirically based evidence of the sophomore slump comes from the students themselves, as captured by Penn State Pulse (1998). Students in this study described their sophomore year as being caught between directions and not knowing what path to choose. They also relayed feelings of boredom generated from the same old routine, which made it difficult for those sophomores to stay motivated. They perceived the academic rigor of college being much tougher now, and they were feeling that they were failing their own high expectations. They felt invisible, as they were not getting as much attention as the first-year students on campus. All in all, sophomores at Penn State felt challenged but bored and unmotivated as well.

Although all of these studies identify the existence of a sophomore slump in some form, they do not establish the percentage of students who have these experiences. No doubt, students feel the effects of a sophomore slump, but how widespread or intense the phenomenon is remains unknown (Gump, 2007). While the current findings focus more on the issues and experiences of sophomores, an actual statistical sophomore slump could exist. Research that includes multiple institutions and examines both grade point averages and attrition rates for sophomores, taking into consideration first-year grades, should be conducted. Doing so would provide a broader, empirically supported perspective to the sophomores' academic and psychosocial development.

In light of these findings, it is evident that the so-called sophomore slump is *not* a regression from first-year academic and personal development. The sophomore slump may be redefined, however, as a multidimensional phenomenon, which could begin as early as the second semester of college and includes one or more of the following:

- *Academic deficiencies* such as failing to make satisfactory academic progress toward a degree and carrying a low grade point average into the second year
- *Academic disengagement* such as lacking academic motivation, failing to have meaningful interactions with faculty, not participating in class, feeling disconnected from their college major, and experiencing incompatibility between learning and teaching styles
- *Dissatisfaction with the collegiate experience* such as being unhappy with administrative processes, feeling that advisors and faculty do not care, not receiving timely faculty feedback, and feeling isolated from peers and the campus community
- *Major and career indecision* such as failing to meet the academic requirements for their desired major, experiencing anxiety about making career and major decisions, and taking extra time to graduate because of changing majors
- *Developmental confusion* such as struggling with one's identity, spirituality, beliefs and values, and life purpose

Institutional Interventions That Promote Sophomore Success

Unfortunately, most institutions provide services and programs targeted to first-year students but typically pay little attention to students in their sophomore year. According to Pattengale (2000), sophomores may be feeling let down from the extraordinary amount of attention paid to them during their first year. The result is that, according to Gump (2007), institutions may be simply delaying the attrition process by providing such invasive first-year interventions.

Earlier in this chapter, we suggested that the classroom environment, interactions with faculty, student use of student services, and participation in selected intentional institutional interventions positively affected student success. We further suggested that sophomores, as well as their first-, third-, and fourth-year colleagues, benefit from such institutional efforts. Sophomores, in particular, should benefit from these programs and services because they specifically address issues that are linked to the sophomore experience. However, the literature connecting these efforts specifically and directly to sophomores is sparse.

Academically Related Experiences

As reported earlier, classroom-related variables and faculty interactions enhance student success. Although studies specific to sophomores are limited in number, there are a few. For example, Nora, Barlow, and Crisp (2005) found that academic and social experiences that contribute to students being retained into the second and third years include collaborative learning experiences and engagement in classroom discussions. Also, sophomore satisfaction with faculty interactions was found to be a significant predictor of grade point averages (Graunke & Woosley, 2005). But on the whole, we must assume that the academically related variables that positively affect all student success also apply to sophomores. (For a more extensive discussion of the critical role of the classroom and faculty in sophomore success, see Chapters Seven and Eight.)

Academic Advising

As suggested earlier, the preponderance of research on academic advising suggests that advising programs are consistently effective in promoting student persistence, even when there are statistical controls for other factors (Pascarella & Terenzini, 2005). Kramer (2000) recommended explicit interventions for sophomores, essentially tailoring academic advising sessions with sophomores to meet their developmental needs. Specifically, Kramer suggests that advisors assist their sophomore students in reflecting on what they have achieved academically and also what they want to accomplish in the future. Kramer notes that "attention from advisors may be an important factor in overcoming [the sophomore slump]" (p. 99). Nealy (2005) found that advisement is the most important variable for sophomore-year retention. (For a more extensive discussion of the impact of academic advising, see Chapter Five.)

Participation in Undergraduate Research

Pascarella and Terenzini (2005) concluded that participation in undergraduate research has a positive influence on persistence and degree completion, independent of other factors. This effect was strongest for sophomores rather than first-year students. Participation in research programs elevate degree aspirations and the likelihood of enrolling in graduate school. (For a more extensive discussion of the impact of undergraduate research, including enhanced personal growth, revised career goals, increased motivation for further educational study, and gains in critical thinking and problem solving, see Chapter Eleven.)

As suggested earlier, all in all, the evidence to support the impact of specific services and programs on sophomore student success is limited. However, that is not to say that programs and services that positively impact all students are not effective in supporting sophomore student success. On the contrary, studies on the impact of these interventions that included sophomores may be said to have an indirect impact on them, including Supplemental Instruction, place of residence, learning communities, service-learning, study abroad, availability of financial aid, peer relations, and the many other variables identified earlier in this chapter.

Moreover, it is premature to offer any conclusions about the effectiveness of specific institutional interventions targeting sophomores, such as sophomore seminars, second-year programs, faculty mentoring, career fairs, sophomore orientation, Web sites devoted to sophomores, sophomore living-learning communities, academic support services, and others. However, early anecdotal accounts are promising. An excellent resource for such programs is the National Resource Center for The First-Year Experience and Students in Transition. The center's website (www.sc.edu/fye) lists institutions that have sophomore-specific programs, many of which are conducting assessments to determine the effectiveness of such interventions.

Perhaps the best summary of what institutions can do to promote student success are the benchmarks of effective educational practice, developed by the National Survey of Student Engagement (2008), based on its ten years of research with over 1,300 institutions. These benchmarks include the level of academic challenge, active and collaborative learning, student faculty interaction, enriching educational experiences, and supportive campus environments.

Conclusion

Readers should take note of several important caveats in interpreting this review of the literature and research on the sophomore year. First, this review is not intended to be comprehensive, but studies cited are generally representative of the genre of studies under review. Second, single institution studies must be viewed with some caution because they are not necessarily generalizable to all institutions. Third, there is no such thing as a perfect study. All of the studies cited have limitations, and the reader is encouraged to refer to the original work to evaluate these limitations. Fourth, the sophomore-year experience is very institution specific; thus, not all strategies will work at every institution. And fifth and perhaps most important, reviews of national and institutional studies can be instructive in helping institutions understand the second-year experience. They are not, however, intended to serve as the only guide to developing services and programs that promote sophomore student success. Institutions must develop initiatives consistent with their missions, resources, students, faculty, leadership, and other characteristics. Institutions must assess the effectiveness of efforts to improve student success in general, and sophomore success in particular, in order to establish as basis for sophomore-year policies, practices, and decisions.

The focus on the sophomore year is in its infancy. When the first-year experience began to emerge, practitioners were far ahead of research substantiating the effectiveness of intervention programs. The same can be said for the second-year experience in that many intervention programs have been initiated but the empirical research to confirm (or disprove) their effectiveness is lacking, as evidenced by the thin number of studies covered in this literature review. Furthermore, there is institutional anecdotal evidence that these interventions hold promise for having a positive impact on the second-year experience. We believe with ample time that the research will catch up with the practices to provide a research-substantiated basis for sophomore student success and institutional intervention effectiveness.

CHAPTER THREE

FACTORS THAT CONTRIBUTE TO SOPHOMORE SUCCESS AND SATISFACTION

Laurie A. Schreiner

Research on the sophomore experience has been sparse, despite increasing interest in the sophomore slump and the development of sophomore programs at a number of colleges and universities. In this chapter, the results of a large-scale survey focused on sophomores is highlighted as the basis for understanding which sophomore experiences lead to greater likelihood of success, satisfaction, and persistence. The chapter outlines five recommendations arising from an analysis of students' survey responses for institutions to improve the sophomore experience.

Most of the research that has been conducted on the sophomore experience thus far has been one of three types: (a) qualitative research on the lived experiences and developmental changes within individual sophomores on particular campuses (Schaller, 2005), (b) survey research on the types of programs and services offered to sophomores (Tobolowsky & Cox, 2007a), or (c) surveys of sophomores on particular campuses (Graunke & Woosley, 2005). Only one quantitative study of sophomores has been conducted across multiple institutions: Juillerat's (2000) study comparing the satisfaction patterns of dropouts versus persisters among sophomores at faith-based private institutions.

Juillerat's (2000) study collected sophomore responses to the *Student Satisfaction Inventory* (Schreiner & Juillerat, 1993) and then tracked those students one year later to determine whether they were still enrolled in the same institution.

A comparison of the satisfaction levels of those who persisted with those who left their institutions found that sophomores who did not return as juniors were clearly distinguishable from those who reenrolled, both in terms of what was most important to them and the areas where they were most dissatisfied. Specifically, sophomore dropouts did not have as high expectations as persisters about campus climate, caring faculty, spiritual fit, or intellectual growth but had significantly higher expectations of service excellence and student-centered policies on campus. These dropouts were significantly less satisfied in all these areas but were particularly dissatisfied with the campus climate, intellectual growth, and spiritual fit.

A follow-up to the Juillerat (2000) study was conducted among 1,705 sophomores at 31 of the same faith-based four-year institutions as previously studied (Schreiner, 2007b). This study used logistic regression analysis to determine the significant predictors of retention among these sophomores; it also compared predictors of sophomore attrition to those of first-year student attrition in the same institutions. Although this study has limitations (such as students who are not representative of students across all types of U.S. institutions), the results do provide preliminary insights into aspects of the sophomore experience that appear to be significant in students' decisions to remain enrolled. Specifically, there were four factors that increased the odds of sophomores' persistence to the junior year at these institutions and accounted for 12.4 percent of the total variation in persistence one year after they were assessed: being male, having a higher college GPA, and reporting greater satisfaction with the campus climate and the quality of instruction on campus. In addition, sophomore attrition patterns were characterized by significantly higher levels of dissatisfaction with institutional services than seen in first-year student attrition predictors.

Throughout the studies that have been conducted with sophomores to date there are three basic themes that permeate the results, whether the study was qualitative or quantitative. Those themes include the primacy of campus climate as predictive of sophomore persistence (Juillerat, 2000; Schreiner, 2007b), the importance of instructional effectiveness, intellectual growth, faculty interaction, and advising as sophomores engage in a focused exploration of their career and life goals (Graunke & Woosley, 2005; Juillerat, 2000; Schaller, 2005; Schreiner, 2007b), and the increased dissatisfaction with the institution and its services that is often experienced in the sophomore year (Gahagan & Hunter, 2006; Juillerat, 2000; Schreiner, 2007b). In order to expand our understanding of the sophomore experience to a larger sample that included multiple types of institutions, a survey was conducted in spring 2007 that incorporated considerable information about sophomores' experiences and satisfaction levels on 26 four-year private and public campuses, and also assessed their self-reported levels of thriving.

The concept of *thriving* was borrowed from developmental psychology literature and is based on the work of Keyes and Haidt (2003), who coined the term *flourishing* to describe adults in midlife and beyond who are actively and productively engaged with others. Emotional vitality and positive functioning are the hallmarks of flourishing individuals. Such persons rise to life's challenges and are hopeful for the future, engage in healthy relationships, are creative and productive in their work, and experience a sense of meaning and purpose in their lives. Building on these elements of flourishing, the concept of *thriving* as assessed in the *Sophomore Experiences Survey* adds elements of academic success and goal orientation (Schreiner, 2009).

The 2007 survey of sophomores is described in the next section. A more detailed description of the statistical analyses can be found in Appendix A.

The 2007 Sophomore Experiences Survey

In spring 2007, a request was sent to members of the sophomore listserv, hosted by the National Resource Center for The First-Year Experience and Students in Transition, asking for their help in collecting data from sophomores about their experiences. The Web-based instrument was designed to measure various aspects of the sophomore experience, in addition to levels of student thriving, which was conceptualized as academic self-efficacy, hope, mindset, engaged learning, and meaning in life. Twenty-six four-year institutions, 16 private and 10 public, surveyed their sophomores that spring. Most institutions sent the survey to all sophomores on campus, but a small handful targeted only their sophomore leaders or participants in their sophomore programs. These sampling limitations result in an inability to generalize the findings to all sophomores across all institutions but do provide a descriptive portrait of the largest group of sophomores in multiple institutions to date.

Of the 2,856 sophomores in the final sample, 932 (31 percent) were from public institutions and the remaining 1,924 were from private institutions. Complete demographic information about the student participants can be found in Table 3.1. The sample was predominantly female (71 percent) and Caucasian (84 percent) and reflected students who were mostly satisfied with their college experience. In interpreting the results of this survey, it is important to note its limitations. The sample is not representative of the total sophomore population nationally, as it contains a disproportionate number of women, Caucasian students, and student leaders on four-year campuses (41.7 percent of the sample). Because of these sampling limitations, the data were weighted by gender, race, and leadership status in order to gain a clearer picture of the sophomore experience.

TABLE 3.1. DEMOGRAPHIC CHARACTERISTICS OF THE STUDENT SAMPLE: THE SOPHOMORE EXPERIENCE SURVEY (N = 2,856)

Variable	Percentage
Gender	
Female	71.9%
Male	28.1%
Race/Ethnicity	
African-American	3.3%
American Indian/Alaskan Native	.6%
Asian-American/Pacific Islander	3.5%
Caucasian	84.1%
Hispanic	3.9%
Multiethnic	2.9%
Prefer not to respond	2.3%
Degree Goal	
None	.5%
Bachelor's degree	18%
Teaching credential	2.2%
Master's degree	47.2%
Doctorate	19.1%
Medical or law degree	12.3%
Other	.7%
Residence	
On-campus housing	66.7%
Off campus	33.3%
Athlete	
Yes	10.9%
No	89.1%
Choice of institution at enrollment	
First choice	73.7%
Second choice or lower	27.3%

Note: Participating institutions included Austin Peay State University, Azusa Pacific University, Baldwin Wallace College, Baylor University, Bethel University (MN), Brevard College, Clemson University, Cornerstone University, Indiana Wesleyan University, Lynn University, Monmouth College, Northwestern College (IA), Occidental College, Point Loma Nazarene University, Seton Hall University, Slippery Rock University, Southwestern College, SUNY-Cortland, Transylvania University, University of Central Arkansas, University of Cincinnati, University of Nevada-Reno, University of North Alabama, University of South Carolina, and Villa Julie College.

Public institutions were analyzed separately from private institutions so that the predictors of sophomore satisfaction and intent to reenroll that were specific to each type of institution could be clarified. The result is a preliminary glimpse into the experiences of sophomores in a variety of four-year institutions.

As a group, the sophomores who responded to this survey were most satisfied with the learning process and were least satisfied with their academic advising experiences as sophomores. Almost 63 percent of them reported their sophomore year as better than their first year, and 64 percent planned to re-enroll as juniors at the same institution. Complete information about the instrument can be found in Exhibit 3.1 and students' responses to each survey item are outlined in Table 3.2. In addition to responding to items about their sophomore experiences and levels of thriving, students were given the opportunity to respond to an open-ended question at the end of the survey. The question asked, "What one thing would you change about your sophomore year?" Students also were invited to provide any further comments they wished to make. A total of 463 students commented and some of those quotations will be used in the following sections to illustrate the major quantitative findings from the survey.

In order to analyze the results of the *Sophomore Experiences Survey*, we conducted a series of hierarchical multiple regression analyses. Because the type of institution was a significant predictor of many of the outcome variables, we conducted separate analyses for public institutions (10 institutions; 932 students) and private institutions (16 institutions; 1,924 students). The variables that were used as ultimate outcomes (criterion variables) in the study included intent to reenroll, intent to graduate, overall satisfaction with their college experience, the degree to which their sophomore year was better than their first year, and the perception that tuition would be worth it in the long run. Significance levels were set at $p < .05$ for all analyses. In conducting the analyses, we entered student thriving variables into each equation after controlling for students' background characteristics and then entered campus experiences and perceptions into the equation. By entering these variables sequentially in this manner, we could determine the degree to which each step added to our understanding of students' variation in each outcome. A more thorough description of the analyses can be found in Appendix A for readers who are interested in regression tables.

Sophomore Experiences Survey: Major Findings

There were seven major findings from the *Sophomore Experiences Survey*:

1. The statistical models created to predict the ultimate outcomes of intent to reenroll, intent to graduate, overall satisfaction, satisfaction with tuition value, and feeling that the sophomore year was better than the first year are strong models with significant predictors that have not been used to date in other studies of sophomores. We were able to explain from 17 percent (second year better than first) to 55 percent (overall satisfaction) of the variance in sophomores' outcomes. New information about sophomores was gained through this survey that helps us understand the second-year experiences in ways we have not before.

Exhibit 3.1. Psychometric Properties of the Instruments

Sophomore Experience Survey

The *Sophomore Experience Survey* was developed in 2007 in order to collect information about the sophomore experience and levels of student thriving across a number of different institutions in the United States via existing public domain and research scales. Thus, the instrument used the original response formats from each of the following scales:

- The *Academic Self-Efficacy Scale* (Chemers, Hu, & Garcia, 2001) consists of eight internally consistent items ($\alpha = 0.81$) that measure students' confidence in their ability to perform optimally on academic tasks. Predictive validity studies have connected students' scores to their cumulative GPA and persistence (Chemers, Hu, & Garcia, 2001).
- The *Engaged Learning Index* (Schreiner & Louis, 2006) consists of 15 internally consistent items ($\alpha = 0.91$) that measure meaningful processing, focused attention, and active participation in learning. Confirmatory factor analyses have established these three scales and predictive validity studies have connected students' scores to their satisfaction with learning, their learning gains while in college, and their intent to reenroll (Schreiner & Louis, 2008).
- The *Adult Trait Hope Scale* (Snyder et al., 1991) consists of eight internally consistent items (α ranges from 0.74 to 0.84 in previous studies) that measure two components of "agency" and "pathways" toward goals. Numerous predictive validity studies have connected students' levels of hope with their cumulative GPA and persistence to graduation (Snyder, Wiklund, & Cheavens, 1999).
- The *Meaning in Life Questionnaire* (MLQ; Steger, Frazier, Oishi, & Kaler, 2006) consists of 10 items with internal consistency ranging from 0.81 to 0.92 in various studies. There are two scales within the MLQ: a Presence scale that assesses the extent to which respondents feel they have found a purpose or meaning in life, and a Search scale that measures the extent to which students seek meaning as part of the personal development process. Convergent and discriminant validity of the subscales has been demonstrated through a multitrait-multimethod matrix (Steger, Frazier, Oishi, & Kaler, 2006).
- The *Mindset* scale (Levy, Stroessner, & Dweck, 1998), an eight-item scale measuring students' *fixed* or *growth* mindsets that affect how they approach the learning environment. Students with a fixed mindset believe their intelligence is set early in life and is unchangeable, whereas students with a growth mindset see their ability as malleable and are more likely to invest effort in the learning process as a result. Studies conducted by Levy, Stroessner, and Dweck have established the discriminant validity of implicit theories (mindset) as separate from cognitive abilities, self-esteem, optimism, or motivation.

Demographic Information: These items included information about the students' gender, race/ethnicity, transfer status, first-generation status, living arrangements, participation in intercollegiate athletics, degree aspirations, certainty of their major, number of hours worked on and off campus, number of courses dropped in the sophomore year, high school grades, college grades, whether their current institution was their first choice at enrollment, their extent of travel outside the United States during college, and in how many courses they have received a grade of C or lower.

Sophomore Experience Items: These items assessed students' level of participation in campus organizations and events, the frequency of and their satisfaction with interaction with faculty; their satisfaction with their peers; and their involvement in leadership, peer mentoring, service-learning courses, and learning communities. Students' overall satisfaction with their college experience, their satisfaction with the amount they were learning, and their satisfaction with advising were also ascertained. They were asked how their sophomore year compared to their first year of college and how their courses in the sophomore year compared to those in their first year. They were also asked to what extent they were confident that the money they were paying for college would be worth it in the long run and how concerned they were about the amount of debt they were incurring.

2. Students' satisfaction with their overall college experience was the strongest predictor of intent to reenroll and graduate, followed by their perception that tuition was a worthwhile investment. These findings underscore the importance of student satisfaction, as well as the sense that students have of the "value added" dimension of their college experience. Although many students commented on the high price of college, when they felt that their tuition dollars were a worthwhile investment they reported intending to reenroll the following fall and to graduate from the same institution.

3. The frequency of student-faculty interaction and students' satisfaction with that interaction were highly significant predictors of intent to reenroll, intent to graduate, and of students' perceiving their tuition as a worthwhile investment. These two variables were also significant contributors to all student outcomes in this study. Although substantial literature exists on the importance of student-faculty interaction, previous research has not examined this variable specifically with sophomores. Since more than a third of the sophomores in this study had never connected with faculty outside of class for any reason, exploring intentional ways for sophomores to have rewarding contact with faculty is an important implication of these findings.

4. Peer satisfaction was the strongest contributor to overall student satisfaction and was also significantly related to students' satisfaction with faculty. Although these findings need to be explored further, the contribution of peers

TABLE 3.2. SOPHOMORE EXPERIENCES SURVEY
SUMMARY OF RESULTS

Item	National Norms (N = 2,856)	
	Mean	SD
Engaged Learning Index: (5-point scale with 5 high)		
1. I am learning a lot in most of my classes.	4.14	.76
2. I often discuss with my friends what I'm learning in class.	3.74	.91
3. I regularly participate in class discussions in most of my classes.	3.63	1.01
4. I feel as though I am learning things in my classes that are worthwhile to me as a person.	3.89	.88
5. It's hard to pay attention in many of my classes.	2.78	1.00
6. I can usually find ways of applying what I'm learning in class to something else in my life.	3.67	.86
7. I ask my professors questions during class if I do not understand something.	3.59	.98
8. In the last week, I've been bored in class a lot of the time.	3.08	1.07
9. I find myself thinking about what I'm learning in class even when I'm not in class.	3.53	.89
10. Sometimes I am afraid to participate in class.	2.82	1.12
11. I feel energized by the ideas that I am learning in most of my classes.	3.34	.89
12. I usually think about how the topics being discussed in class might be connected to things I have learned in previous class periods.	3.77	.81
13. Often I find my mind wandering during class.	3.34	.98
14. When I am learning about a new idea in a class, I think about how I might apply it in practical ways.	3.47	.84
15. Sometimes I get so interested in something I'm studying in class that I spend extra time trying to learn more about it.	3.10	1.04
Mindset Items (5-point scale with 5 high)		
1. Your intelligence is something very basic about you that you can't change very much.	2.50	.98
2. You can always change basic things about the kind of person you are.	3.57	1.88
3. You can learn new things, but you can't really change how intelligent you are.	2.66	1.04
4. You are a certain kind of person, and there is not much that can be done to really change that.	2.43	.98
5. No matter how much intelligence you have, you can always change it quite a bit.	3.44	.89
6. You can do things differently, but the important parts of who you are can't really be changed.	3.08	1.02

TABLE 3.2. (*Continued*)

Item	National Norms (N = 2,856)	
	Mean	SD
7. You can substantially change how intelligent you are.	3.19	.95
8. No matter what kind of person you are, you can always change substantially.	3.56	.85

Academic Self-Efficacy Items (7-point scale with 7 high)

1. I know how to schedule my time to accomplish tasks.	5.37	1.49
2. I know how to take notes.	5.64	1.29
3. I know how to study to perform well on tests.	5.21	1.43
4. I am good at research and writing papers.	5.10	1.54
5. I am a very good student.	5.56	1.21
6. I usually do very well in school and at academic tasks.	5.69	1.16
7. I find academic work interesting and absorbing.	4.91	1.40
8. I am very capable of succeeding at this institution.	6.08	1.03

Adult Hope Scale Items (8-point scale with 8 high)

1. I can think of many ways to get out of a jam.	6.47	1.15
2. I energetically pursue my goals.	6.68	1.12
3. There are lots of ways around any problem.	6.54	1.12
4. I can think of many ways to get the things in life that are most important to me.	6.62	1.14
5. Even when others get discouraged, I know I can find a way to solve the problem.	6.33	1.18
6. My past experiences have prepared me well for my future.	6.80	1.23
7. I've been pretty successful in life.	6.86	1.12
8. I meet the goals that I set for myself.	6.56	1.18

Meaning in Life Questionnaire Items (7-point scale with 7 high)

1. I understand my lifes meaning.	5.12	1.45
2. I am looking for something that makes my life meaningful.	5.31	1.64
3. I am always looking to find my lifes purpose.	5.16	1.59
4. My life has a clear sense of purpose.	5.11	1.42
5. 5. I have a good sense of what makes my life meaningful.	5.60	1.29
6. I have discovered a satisfying life purpose.	5.16	1.44
7. I am always searching for something that makes my life feel significant.	4.83	1.67

(*Continued*)

TABLE 3.2. (*Continued*)

Item	National Norms (N = 2,856)	
	Mean	SD
8. I am seeking a purpose or mission in life.	5.03	1.62
9. My life has no clear purpose.	2.50	1.65
10. I am searching for meaning in life.	4.25	1.87
Faculty Interaction Frequency (5-point scale with 5 = frequently)		
1. Met with a professor during office hours	3.29	.95
2. Discussed career plans or goals with a professor	2.86	1.11
3. Met informally or socially with a faculty member outside of class or office hours	2.27	1.26
4. Discussed academic issues with a faculty member outside of class or office hours	2.39	1.25
5. Met with your academic advisor	3.56	.96
Satisfaction Levels (5-point scale with 5 = very satisfied)		
1. The amount you are learning in college so far	4.01	.82
2. The academic advising you have experienced this year	3.66	1.17
3. Your overall experiences on this campus so far	4.02	.92
4. The contact you have had with faculty this year	3.88	.91
5. Your experiences with your peers on this campus this year	4.05	.95

LEVELS OF STUDENT INVOLVEMENT

Type of Involvement	Not at All Involved	Occasionally or Somewhat Involved	Involved or Very Involved
1. Leadership of student organizations on campus	48.7%	26.2%	25.1%
2. Student organizations on campus	22.1%	40.6%	37.3%
3. Fraternity or sorority	83%	3.9%	13.2%
4. Community service	26.4%	46.6%	27.1%
5. Campus events and activities	14.9%	52.7%	32.3%
6. Student government	81.9%	12.7%	5.3%
7. Peer mentoring or leadership programs	59.9%	21.9%	18.3%
8. Religious activities that are not required	41%	25.9%	33.1%

ADDITIONAL ITEMS ABOUT THE SOPHOMORE EXPERIENCE

Item		Disagree or Strongly Disagree	Neutral	Agree or Strongly Agree
1.	I enjoy talking to my professors about what I'm learning in class.	19.1%	32.9%	48%
2.	I like to learn about myself.	3.3%	13.5%	83.1%
3.	I am confident that the amount of money I'm paying for college is worth it in the long run.	20.8%	23.9%	55.3%
4.	I know how to apply my strengths to achieve academic success.	6.7%	18.8%	74.6%
5.	I intend to re-enroll at this institution next year.	4.4%	4.0%	91.6%
6.	This is the institution I intend to graduate from.	4.1%	4.9%	91.0%
7.	I feel very discouraged about the amount of debt I'm incurring to pay my college bills.	33.4%	24.2%	42.4%

How Sure Are You of Your Major?

Very Unsure	Somewhat Unsure	Somewhat Sure	Very Sure
6.7%	5.2%	24.2%	63.9%

How Often Have You Participated in Service-Learning Courses in College?

Not at All	One Course	More Than One Course
64.1%	23.5%	12.3%

Have You Participated in a Learning Community in College?

Yes	No	Not Sure
27.3%	57.5%	15.3%

(Continued)

TABLE 3.2. (*Continued*)

How Many Courses Have You Dropped or Withdrawn from Since Beginning College?

None	One	Two or Three	Four or Five	Six or More
56.3%	27.9%	14.1%	1.2%	.4%

In How Many Courses Have You Received a Grade Below C Since Beginning College?

None	One	Two or Three	Four or Five	Six or More
69%	14.9%	12.9%	2.8%	.4%

Have You Traveled Outside the United States Since Beginning College?

No	For Two Weeks or Less	For More Than Two Weeks
63%	22.8%	14.2%

Compared to Your First Year of College, Has This Year Been:

Much Worse	Worse	About the Same	Better	Much Better
2%	11.6%	23.6%	42.9%	19.9%

Compared to Your First Year, Have Your Courses This Year Been:

Much Worse	Worse	About the Same	Better	Much Better
2%	12.3%	28%	42.8%	14.9%

to students' interaction and satisfaction with faculty is noteworthy. Sophomores who were more involved in campus activities were also those most likely to report high levels of peer satisfaction, so it could be that campus involvement functions as a mediating variable between peer and faculty satisfaction.

5. Engaged learning was the student-thriving variable with the greatest ability to predict student success, satisfaction, and retention. More important than individual levels of hope, sense of purpose and meaning in life, or academic self-efficacy, students' psychological engagement with the learning process holds

considerable potential as a framework for designing sophomore programs that can affect their satisfaction and retention.

6. Sophomores' experiences and levels of satisfaction differed significantly between public and private institutions. Sophomores attending private institutions were significantly more likely to enjoy talking to professors and to interact with them more in a variety of settings; they were also more likely to be involved in campus activities and to participate in community service and service-learning courses. They reported higher levels of satisfaction with virtually every aspect of their sophomore experience, including the perception that the sophomore year was a better experience than their first year. Their reported levels of engaged learning and meaning in life were significantly higher, but their levels of hope were significantly lower and there were no differences in academic self-efficacy across institutional type. Students in private institutions were more likely to be in their first-choice institution and more of them reported intending to pursue a graduate degree. Students from the public institutions in this sample were more likely to be first-generation college students, had lower self-reported GPAs, and had dropped more courses in the sophomore year.

Student background characteristics explained more of the variation in responses among the public institution sample than in the private institution sample, which means that not only are there more diverse types of students attending public institutions but also that this diversity contributes more to the differences in students' satisfaction and may affect the experiences they have as sophomores. In contrast, campus experiences accounted for more of the variance in student outcomes in private institutions than in public institutions. This finding means that private institutions may have even more potential for affecting the sophomore experience through programming and services than public institutions may have.

7. Despite these differences in public and private institutions, campus experiences were still the largest contributor to students' perceiving the sophomore year as better than the first year. If they perceived their courses were better, if they were satisfied with their peers on campus, and if they had participated in a learning community, they were likely to report the sophomore year as better than the first year. These are all features of the sophomore experience that can be influenced by programming and services, whether the institution is public or private.

The *Sophomore Experiences Survey* has a number of important limitations that should be taken into consideration when interpreting the results. Although sampling limitations were addressed by weighting demographic variables significantly related to each outcome, we did not include institutional characteristics beyond public-private typology in the analyses. For example, the size and selectivity of the institutions were not factored into the analyses. Further research should not only include such institutional variables but should also intentionally analyze their effect through a procedure such as hierarchical linear modeling.

Recommendations for Sophomore Success and Satisfaction

Several themes emerged from the *Sophomore Experiences Survey,* many of which were illustrated eloquently in students' comments. These five recommendations are listed in order of importance, as determined by the degree to which they are significantly predictive of sophomore success and satisfaction.

Connect Students to Faculty and Engage Them in the Learning Process

Sophomores' level of interaction and satisfaction with faculty was the only variable that significantly predicted every student outcome. It significantly predicted students' intent to reenroll and graduate, their overall satisfaction with their college experience, and their perception that tuition was worth it. It also was strongly related to students' involvement on campus and satisfaction with their peers. There was a powerful connection between faculty interaction and students' psychological engagement in the learning process. The more students interacted with faculty and were satisfied with that interaction, the more likely they were to report being highly engaged in the learning process—and vice versa.

Although this finding is not new, the particular dimensions of faculty-student interaction that are most salient for sophomores is new information. Previous research has demonstrated the connection between faculty-student interaction and academic success for all students, as evidenced in grade point average and self-reported learning gains (Fischer, 2007; Kuh & Hu, 2001; Pascarella & Terenzini, 2005). Research has also demonstrated that students' satisfaction with faculty interaction varies by race (Lundberg & Schreiner, 2004), with African American students being least satisfied, despite their higher frequency of interaction. Kuh and Hu confirmed an important link between student-faculty interaction and student satisfaction with the college experience; they also demonstrated that student-faculty interaction encourages students to invest greater effort in other "educationally purposeful activities" (p. 329). Although they found that higher-ability students interacted more frequently with faculty, they were not able to clarify whether students initiated this interaction or faculty invited it. Noel's (2007) grounded-theory study of high-achieving seniors provided a glimpse into this interaction by illuminating the process more fully: Students usually initiated the contact, but often reported that it was the faculty member's way of engaging them in class that led the student to seek further opportunities to interact outside of class.

Previous research with sophomores in particular has found the same linkages between student-faculty interaction and academic success (Graunke & Woosley, 2005), as well as intent to reenroll (Keup, 2002). What the study in this chapter adds to our knowledge is the importance of student-faculty interaction in affecting sophomores' perceptions that tuition will be worth it in the long run and the role that engaged learning and campus experiences play in the levels of student-faculty interaction and satisfaction. One of the strongest contributors to students' sense of their tuition being worth it in the long run is their perception of faculty. When students are connected to faculty in and out of class, when they are actively engaged with faculty in the learning process, and when they believe that faculty care about their learning and can help them connect to their future goals, they believe their tuition dollars are well spent. As one student noted, "I don't like how much it costs to go here, but I think it's worth it for the experiences I've had and the people I've met. I absolutely love the classes in my major and the way professors challenge me to become the person I want to be."

Sophomores tended to interact most with faculty by seeking them out during office hours (37 percent reported doing this regularly or frequently). Only one in five interacted with faculty informally or socially outside of class. Thirty-four percent of the sophomores never talked to faculty about academic issues and 35 percent never or rarely talked to faculty about their career plans or goals. Noel's (2007) study found that one of the most powerful aspects of the faculty-student relationship outside of class was that faculty were able to help students see a future for themselves they had never thought possible. Discussing career plans and goals could be a vital process, particularly for a sophomore who is still unsure of his or her major, yet these types of conversations are not happening frequently in the sophomore year.

Student comments about faculty interaction were poignant reminders of how important this issue is to the sophomore experience. Although half of the students in this sample were satisfied or very satisfied with their interaction with faculty, the other half were represented in such comments such as, "My professors don't even know who I am, let alone care about me or my life," and "If there was one thing I could change about my sophomore year, it would be my fear of approaching faculty." The fact that half of these sophomores were not satisfied with their interactions with faculty is a sobering finding, given the importance of student-faculty interaction in the learning process.

Because Noel (2007) had found that high-achieving students sought out interaction with faculty outside of class after being engaged in the classroom, it was important to explore students' comments about engaged learning, as well as the connection between their scores on the *Engaged Learning Index* and their satisfaction with faculty interaction. Engaged learning is defined as "a positive energy invested in one's own learning, evidenced by meaningful processing, attention to what is happening in the moment, and involvement in specific learning activities" (Schreiner & Louis, 2006, p. 6). The level of engaged learning that students reported was not only a significant predictor of their interaction and satisfaction with faculty but also of their perceptions that tuition would be worth it in the long run.

Even though 85 percent of the students agreed or strongly agreed that they are "learning a lot" in most of their classes, there are many indications that they are not psychologically engaged in the learning process much of the time. Almost 40 percent reported feeling bored "a lot" in their classes, 45 percent reported their mind wanders often during class, 28 percent said they often find it hard to pay attention in class, and almost half stated they are afraid to participate in class sometimes. About 60 percent of the students in this sample reported regularly participating in classes, asking questions, and thinking about what they are learning even when they are not in class. But only 45 percent reported feeling energized by the ideas they are learning in class.

Sophomores' comments about their classes provided further insight into this lack of engagement. One sophomore reported:

> The classes are mostly done by teachers reading PowerPoints and the students taking notes. There is no creativity or excitement in many of my professors' lectures. They are very boring classes that I feel are not preparing me for the future or giving me any real, new knowledge.

Another adds, "many professors are very knowledgeable but they are just not familiar with good teaching techniques that keep students attentive." Other comments included, "It seems like a lot of busy work, not much learning or new ideas relating to my major," and "I feel as if a lot of the material I was learning this year had no application and it was being taught just because. I was hoping to be able to apply what I was learning at this point but I can't say that I can." One student even gave some unsolicited advice to her institution:

> I would make it a rule that teachers be enthusiastic about what they're teaching so they can help the students want to learn it. Unenthusiastic teachers kill the learning atmosphere. That's what has made my year the hardest so far. . . .

The contrast to engaged students was striking. One reported, "I love this university! I also love the personal relationships given to the students by every professor. This creates, at least for me, a great environment to learn in." Another student wrote at length about a specific professor:

> I do need to say that Dr. Lisa is a wonderful instructor. She keeps the students' attention with her natural good humor and informative teaching.... She instructs with an enthusiasm I would hope all instructors teach with and challenges her students to learn. Initially, I had heard she was a hard instructor (meaning, you actually had to work at learning), but I can tell you from experience, she is worth every dollar when it comes to providing an education. I would like to be her student for life....

These comments and the data they represent confirm Lowman's (1994) assertion that the most effective faculty combine intellectual excitement with interpersonal rapport. Students who reported feeling energized in the classroom also were the ones who sought out faculty for further interaction outside the classroom. They reported that these faculty expressed an interest in them; as Kuh and Hu (2001) note, this connection encouraged students to invest greater effort in the types of activities that would lead to their academic success. Although many of these students were performing well in their classes, that was not the whole story. The analyses controlled for students' academic self-efficacy and college grades, yet still found a significant relationship between engagement in the classroom and frequency of faculty interaction. In addition, students who participated in service-learning courses or in learning communities not only reported more frequent interaction with faculty, as might be expected, but also reported significantly greater satisfaction with faculty. Thus, these types of courses can be an additional vehicle for facilitating satisfying student-faculty interactions.

Focus Sophomore Advising on Connecting Present and Future Identities

Although faculty interaction and engaged learning were the strongest contributors to most of the outcome variables in these studies, satisfaction with academic advising during the sophomore year was a strong predictor of many outcomes, as well. Specifically, sophomores' satisfaction with advising significantly predicted their overall satisfaction with their college experience, predicted their perception of tuition as a worthwhile investment, and contributed strongly to their satisfaction with faculty as a whole. These results seem to confirm Light's (2001) assertion that "good advising may be the single most underestimated characteristic of a successful college experience" (p. 81).

Some students who reported positive experiences with their advisor noted that it was helpful to have an advisor who had been specially trained to address sophomore-year issues. Others emphasized the importance of their advisor being a faculty member, commenting that "it's been helpful to have a professor as my advisor because their advice is more accurate and supportive than my family's or peers!" Yet others were frustrated with faculty advisors, with complaints such as, "it is impossible to meet with a faculty member without having an appointment a week in advance." Fewer than half of the students in this sample met with their advisor on a regular basis, but 60 percent were satisfied or very satisfied with the advising they received in their sophomore year. Although more than half the students were generally satisfied with their second-year advising experiences, these ratings were still the lowest satisfaction ratings of any college experience assessed in the survey. In addition, the negative student comments about advising far outweighed any positive comments. A number of sophomores had had experiences with receiving incorrect information, difficulty making appointments, and confusion over prerequisites and major requirements.

The role of advising becomes particularly important in helping students who are not yet sure of their major. In the *Sophomore Experiences Survey,* 64 percent of the students were very sure of their major, as might be expected at the end of the sophomore year. Yet 12 percent were somewhat or very unsure of their major, and many expressed anxiety about that. As one student noted,

> Sophomore year has been very hard in the sense that I have wanted to change my major to find something that fits for me and gives me a sense of significance, but I wish I had more time. There is a lot of pressure to declare a major and sometimes I feel like I'm not ready and I should take time off to find out who I am before I put my life into a box.

Another student added, "knowing what I want to do with the rest of my life is near impossible," and his feelings were echoed by one who expressed a lack of motivation: "I don't feel like working anymore since I don't know what I want to do after college, and since I'm not even sure of my major."

The issue of selecting a major that is a good fit is perhaps one of the most important issues for the sophomore year. Certainty of major was a significant predictor of intent to graduate. It also was significantly related to engaged learning and faculty satisfaction. When students have decided on a major that is a good fit for them, they tend to enjoy their classes more and have a greater desire to connect to faculty within their major. The advisor can play a helpful role in assisting the student in the decision-making process and exploring possibilities of majors that are congruent with the student's values, interests, and strengths.

The sophomore year is often "too late" to explore a major on many campuses, however. There is considerable pressure to enter the sophomore year with a declared major so that students can graduate on time. Yet it was clear from the student comments in this study that the exploration process may take longer than expected, does not flow smoothly, and remains a puzzle for some even at the end of the sophomore year. One student, whose true desire was to be a musician (which he noted "you don't go to college for"), concluded that he was in college "because that is what people do if they want to live comfortable lives." Having an advisor explore with a student the values, life goals, and reasons for being in college can help sophomores reach a decision that is more energizing to them than the "default" position of choosing a major that everyone else recommends for them.

One of the best ways for advisors to help sophomores who are still unsure of their major is to help them connect their interests, values, and life goals to a *future self,* or what Markus and Nurius (1986) refer to as a "possible self" (p. 954). Doing so focuses on students' sense of purpose and creates higher levels of hope, both of which were significantly connected in this study to engagement in the learning process. In a six-year study of college students that controlled for their entrance exam scores, those students with higher levels of hope had higher grades and were more likely to graduate (Snyder, Wiklund, & Cheavens, 1999). Students with high levels of hope are able to establish meaningful goals and then design specific steps they are motivated to take to reach those goals (Lopez et al., 2004). Advisors can teach students what Snyder and his colleagues (2002) call "hopeful thinking" (p. 824): setting goals, finding pathways to those goals, and learning how to motivate oneself.

Build Purpose and Peer Satisfaction Through Selective Involvement on Campus

Peer satisfaction was the largest contributor to sophomores' overall satisfaction with their college experiences and significantly predicted whether they perceived their second year as better than their first. Sophomores in this study reported settling into a more "solid" group of friends on whom they could depend. Those who were most satisfied also reported being more selective about their campus involvement, choosing organizations and activities that were congruent with their interests and values—and particularly with their major—rather than as a mechanism for getting to know others. One sophomore expressed it this way: "This year has been amazing for me. My freshman year I was ready to transfer but I got involved in different organizations and now I love it here!!! My one piece of advice would be to get involved!"

Sophomores who were struggling were not able to make these same connections. As one reported, "sophomore year is difficult because you either have a solid group of friends from freshman year or you are stuck with a bunch of immature freshmen." Many were surprised by how little the institution did to help sophomores get involved and make connections. One commented,

> There are a lot of activities geared toward freshmen and seniors, but I know I have felt more discouraged about staying in school this year than I was last year ... if there could be some programs established to support sophomores, encouraging us to stick it out, I think that would be incredibly helpful.

Another added, "It's tough learning to adjust to sophomore year versus freshman year because there is a lot less effort being put in by the institution for a sense of community. Everyone is more busy and has their set friends, and so sophomore year is lonelier."

Sophomore programs can play a helpful role for students who are struggling to find their purpose and place in the university. Many such programs are described elsewhere in this book, but common features that could make a difference in students' sense of belonging have been outlined by Stockenberg (2007) and include building a class identity, providing opportunities to interact more with faculty, creating active connections and involvement specifically for sophomores, facilitating structured exploration in their major and areas of interest, and enhancing students' social networking.

Empower Students to Navigate the Institution's Systems

One source of frustration for sophomores may be due to the fact that the institution has turned its collective attention to the incoming class, such that campus housing, course registration, and other important transaction points with the institution are more difficult to navigate than they expected. Previous studies of sophomore retention (Juillerat, 2000; Schreiner & Juillerat, 1993) had found that one of the clearest areas where sophomores were most dissatisfied is with the amount of "campus run around," which was defined as being sent from one office to another to resolve a problem. This dissatisfaction was echoed in the *Sophomore Experiences Survey,* as one student noted,

> you always hear about the run around, because everywhere you go they send you somewhere else, because they are not sure of the right answer. It would be nice to get complete answers for once. I hope this doesn't sound rude, but you wanted my opinion, right?

Bean (2005) points out that "the bureaucratic aspects of the academy are soulless, deadening students whose spirits should be lifted by their academic experiences" (p. 230). He suggests that these transactions could actually become learning experiences for students, asserting that students who feel not only helped but empowered by their exchanges with the institutional systems will be more likely to feel loyal to the school and remain enrolled. Cross-training personnel, providing service excellence training and examining all the transaction points in a student's education for what students need to know and be able to do, could help reduce the negative aspects of institutional bureaucracy.

Braxton, Hirschy, and McClendon (2004) point out that there are important ways for an institution to communicate to students its integrity and commitment to their welfare. Institutional integrity is expressed in how policies and rules are articulated and administered. In previous studies, sophomores who were struggling, along with sophomores who actually departed their institutions, were characterized by their frustrations with unfair policies and the lack of channels for complaints (Juillerat, 2000; Schreiner, 2007b). These students perceived their institution as not delivering on its promises—and that perception affected their motivation and decision to leave. An institution's commitment to students' welfare and the perception that it values students is not only communicated through policies but also through student participation in the decision-making process about such policies. Such participation by sophomores could help an institution see more clearly the types of decisions that are affecting the sophomore experience most. Including sophomores on campus committees, inviting them to participate in focus groups to give feedback about the level of campus services or how to shape a particular policy, could have a positive impact on sophomores' perceptions of institutional integrity and commitment to their welfare.

Help Sophomores Connect Their Strengths to Academic Success

One of the most interesting findings in the *Sophomore Experiences Survey* was the predictive ability of the item, "I know how to apply my strengths to achieve academic success." This item was included in the survey because a number of the participating institutions had developed strengths-based programs in the first year in order to help students experience greater levels of success. Although it can be argued that it is impossible to know what students meant when they responded to this item, particularly on campuses where there was no strengths-based programming, the fact that it was a significant predictor of intent to graduate, overall satisfaction, faculty satisfaction, and perception of tuition as worthwhile makes it an important variable to explore further.

Although highly correlated ($r = 0.56$) with academic self-efficacy, this variable still contributed in uniquely significant ways to the understanding of students' satisfaction, institutional commitment, and perceptions of tuition value. After controlling for academic self-efficacy, students who responded positively to this item were also significantly more likely to engage in class and were more satisfied with the learning process and with faculty. They were more likely to interact with faculty around career issues and during office hours, they met with their academic advisor more, were more likely to take on peer leadership roles, and were more involved in student government and the leadership of student organizations.

Thus helping sophomores connect their strengths to academic success could be a fruitful avenue to explore in our attempts to improve the second-year experience. When students are able to identify the assets they already have within them and see what they are able to contribute to the learning environment, they are more confident in their ability to succeed. When an advisor or faculty member helps the student develop and connect those strengths to the academic tasks expected of them, the student not only feels more competent but actually has specific new tools and strategies for achieving academic success. These new tools and strategies provide a greater sense of academic control, which Perry, Hall, and Ruthig (2005) have demonstrated is an important precursor to learning. This confidence and perceived competence increases the motivation to invest the time and effort needed to be successful (Ryan & Deci, 2000). Such an emphasis on applying students' strengths to academic tasks could be used in advising programs (Schreiner & Anderson, 2005) and first-year seminars (Louis, 2008), but it could also be woven into any sophomore-level course. A strengths-based approach can equip students for the unknown complexity of a rapidly changing society by providing a coherent sense of who they are and what they have to offer, while encouraging them to explore who they can become.

Helping students identify their strengths and reflect on specific ways they can apply them to the learning experience builds the sense of being a vital contributor to a community of learners. Advising questions or journaling assignments can help students identify their strengths, but instruments also can be of value as a springboard to that discussion. The *Clifton StrengthsFinder*™ (Gallup Organization, 1999) is an online instrument that provides students with their top five "signature themes" of talent that can be productively applied to achieve success. Psychometric studies specifically with college students have found the instrument to be reliable and valid for use in strengths development programs on college campuses (Schreiner, 2006), and there is a student textbook and Web site that outlines a strengths-based approach to the college experience (Clifton, Anderson, & Schreiner, 2006). The *VIA Classification of Strengths* (Peterson & Seligman, 2002) is also a reliable and valid online measure that provides respondents with their top five "signature strengths" expressed as character virtues. The primary difference between the two instruments lies in their definition of strengths. The *Clifton StrengthsFinder*™ conceptualizes strengths as developed talents that lead to excellence, while the *VIA Classification of Strengths* views strengths as elements of personal character that lead to the development of universally valued virtues.

Conclusion

From the large-scale *Sophomore Experiences Survey*, clues to improving the sophomore experience have emerged that should be helpful to colleges and universities. Focusing on the sophomore experience through programs designed to help sophomores navigate this new stage of their educational career is an important start, but even without such programs there are steps an institution can take. Many of these steps are long-term investments in student success: helping faculty connect to students and engage them in the learning process, training advisors to help sophomores connect to their strengths and their future, providing service excellence training across the campus, and reexamining policies for their impact on student learning. But some steps can be taken immediately: seeking out sophomores and listening to their perspectives on institutional policies, identifying the key transactions sophomores have with the institution and transforming them into learning opportunities, and targeting sophomores for campus involvement that is congruent with their major or interest areas. With each step, an institution signals its commitment to sophomores, their learning, and their growth as whole persons who are an important part of the academic community.

CHAPTER FOUR

COLLEGE SOPHOMORES

The Journey into Self

Molly A. Schaller

Theoretical models that illuminate the developmental experiences of students in late adolescence support our work with college students. Many of these models focus on the cumulative growth seen over four years. The intent of this chapter is to examine the sophomore-year experience for traditional-age students attending private, four-year institutions, specifically. Nevertheless, the findings may provide some insight into the experience of non-traditional students at different types of institutions. The chapter is organized chronologically, as if following students into college, through the sophomore year, and beyond. Although most developmental experiences are not strictly age-related, examining student experiences from the beginning of college into the sophomore year provides us with a better understanding of the evolution of traditional students' development.

The stories of traditional-aged students at three four-year institutions are used here to describe the developmental challenges facing sophomores. The students were participants in three different qualitative studies conducted with sophomores at private four-year institutions. All students were asked questions about their experience during the second year of college. Quotes from the study participants are presented throughout the chapter, with pseudonyms, as a means of illustrating the developmental experiences of second-year students. The studies involved 46 sophomore students. The original study (see Schaller, 2000; and Schaller 2005) involved 19 students at a moderately selective, private, religiously affiliated institution. An additional nine students from this same institution participated in a second study focused on resident assistants (RAs) (Schaller & Wagner, 2007). Eight students from a nonselective, private institution and ten students from a highly selective private institution have also participated in qualitative studies designed to understand how students make sense of the sophomore-year experience. In each of the studies, I served as the principal investigator and conducted all of the interviews using a phenomenological methodology (Van Manen, 1990) designed to understand the sophomore-year experience or the experience of sophomore RAs. All participants were asked questions regarding their experience of the sophomore year, particularly as it related to academics, relationships, and view of the self. The experiences of sophomore students at public institutions, those enrolled in two-year colleges, or nontraditional students are not reflected here and, therefore, research on these populations is needed.

Theoretical Framework

The sophomore year of college is a time of transition. Frequently, students start the year without a clear academic focus, but by the end of the year most are required to select a major. Consequently, it is often seen as a time for career exploration and decision making. The year is also a time for making sense of who one is in the college environment, in contrast to who one was prior to college. Identity development, therefore, is the major question of the year for many students (Wilder, 1993). Margolis (1976) argued that the identity crisis so often seen in the sophomore year is akin to that found in middle age and then again in later life. He suggested that sophomores find that there is no barometer for success, no solid support group, but increased academic and social demands. These things contribute to a student's introspection and, therefore, to an exploration of her or his own psychological self. It is this existential turmoil that engages sophomores (Margolis, 1989).

Theories of college student development provide an important lens through which administrators and faculty can look to understand how best to help second-year students answer these questions and maximize their engagement and learning. This lens has important components, particularly understanding how students view themselves in relationship to self and the world (psychosocial theory), how they view knowledge and make meaning in their lives (intellectual development), and how they perceive moral challenges and make moral choices in their lives (moral development). This chapter will use all these theoretical perspectives to consider the transition into college and adulthood.

Transition theory, as described by Bridges (1980), provides the overarching frame for this examination. He defines transition as the psychological response to life changes but notes that not all changes result in transition. In other words, society allows for development and structures young people's experiences so that they can try on a variety of experiences. When one's identity no longer fits in a new situation (that is, the new college environment), then he or she can seek to retreat or to transition into a new sense of self. Similarly, students who are preparing for graduation from college and find the doors to the world opening to them must shift their view of self in light of this new life situation.

Entering College

Transitions, Bridges (2003) asserts, are different from change. Change is the event in life that brings about a psychological transition. Without transition, going to college is simply a change in venue. With transition, going to college is letting go of the old self and coming to a new definition of self with the new experiences and insights of college taken into account. Transitions, then, begin with an ending. Students may enter college certain about who they are and what they want for their lives. However, in this new setting, with new relationships and new intellectual challenges, students often are no longer able to hold on to their old notions of self. When one's identity is fully functioning in a new setting, he or she is not necessarily aware of that identity. It is in the midst of transition, or when one begins to test out possible new ways of being, that identity becomes an issue (Josselson, 1987). Moratorium, or the testing of possible identities, begins when one recognizes, even subconsciously, that the precollege identity does not work well with the new information and experience associated with college. As students come to terms with this experience and these changes, they make decisions that will either pave the way for personal transitions or maintain their former selves. College can be a developmentally supportive environment in this process of redefining self as an adult, or it can feel like abandonment, resulting in disorientation (Kegan, 1982).

Random Exploration

Students are not able to make decisions about identity or the other important questions of college without first exploring what is available to them. As a result, many college students engage in *random exploration* during their initial move into college (Schaller, 2005). Random exploration is an almost exuberant time when students go about the process of investigating what college has to offer, expressing their freedom and autonomy, and meeting new people. Steve, a sophomore at a liberal arts college, discussed his view of his first-year experience:

> Last year was more a process of trying to figure out what I wanted to be doing. If you're looking at academics, well, what do I want to major in, maybe I should be taking this class just to see. You know, extracurriculars, maybe I'll go to the first meeting of this, see if I like it, you know I tried to find my place, I guess in the school and I guess in each organization.

With these new experiences comes the challenge to build a new set of competencies, to learn to manage one's emotions in the new setting with new relationships, and to develop healthy relationships with new people (Chickering & Reisser, 1993). These are challenges in part because of the ongoing identity development process and the struggles to remain autonomous in our highly connected society.

As students explore the new setting of college, they often do so with a clear view of what is right or true about the world (Baxter Magolda, 1992). Many students enter college viewing truth and knowledge as an absolute. These students may rely on authorities to provide guidance and direction in decision making and in sifting through new information (Baxter Magolda, 1992). However, when faculty members contradict one another or when students build relationships with others who are different and previously judged as unacceptable, students must find ways to integrate these new experiences with their old ways of seeing the world. The dissonance experienced by college students can be significant.

The Transition Between the First and Second Years

Although the experiences of the first year of college are exciting and challenging, students seem to need time to make sense of these experiences. For some students, this "making sense" begins near the end of the first year, and, for others, a summer break provides the time to examine where one is headed. These new experiences can cause a disenchantment, disengagement, disidentification, and disorientation for the student who is unable to transition into a new identity during the first year of college (Bridges, 1980).

Students end the first year with new sources of information and then must integrate that knowledge and understanding of the world into a new sense of self, eventually concluding the *ending* process. The first-year student is no longer saying goodbye to the old self because there is so much new information about the world, self, and others that did not exist previously. This leads to a period of great insight when students integrate the new information into a clear (new) sense of self (Bridges, 1980). Prior to the new definition of self there is a neutral zone

(Bridges), characterized by an emptiness. The old definition no longer exists, but students must construct the new via an exploration of alternatives to their notion of self, values, relationships, career futures, and other issues (Marcia, 1993).

The Sophomore Year

Although not all students have moved through what Loevinger (1976) called the *conformist* stage by the end of the first year (when they conform to a set of external rules), many of the sophomore stories that emerged from the qualitative studies describe the process of gaining control over these external influences as a central function of the sophomore year. Loevinger's title for this is the *conscientious* stage. In this process, individuals become self-evaluative, self-critical, responsible, and differentiated. It seems that the sophomore year is a key starting point for this process. As students move into the neutral zone (Bridges, 1980), they have gathered information about the self and now have the opportunity to evaluate information that exists. Dan, a sociology major, provided a metaphor that illustrates this point:

> [The first year] I think it's more like, if you're going to build a house, like you're just getting everything together . . . so then your sophomore year, you build like a solid foundation, because you really make a lot of decisions your sophomore year of what the rest of your college is going to be like, and what the rest of your years are going to be like. So, the decisions you make now, like where you're gonna live next year, are really gonna impact you. Like picking a major . . . I think you make really strong decisions that way.

Students' epistemology, or the way they view knowledge, may also change from the first year to the second. They may enter college viewing knowledge as absolute, convinced that there are right and wrong answers to all questions, but during the sophomore year, many students move into *transitional knowing* (Baxter Magolda, 1992). In this stage, they begin to recognize that knowledge is sometimes uncertain; however, they still assume that the answers to most questions will one day be found. As students become more critical of self and of information that they have taken in as "truth," they search for direction and begin the process of becoming open to multiple perspectives about the world.

Nina, a psychology major, serves as a good example. She was an excellent student, quite reflective, and seems to be in the neutral zone (Bridges, 1980):

> As a sophomore . . . you still need to get your grounding and be more comfortable with who you are, and also . . . finding yourself, and discovering

who you are as a person. And, it was hard for me this year . . . when I sat back, I'm like, "Wait, who am I?" That's why I think me being so moody, and not really comfortable with how I have been this year, has a lot to do with it because I really, you really need to know!

Focused Exploration

Nina's description of herself in the sophomore year sounds as if she is actively looking to understand who she is rather than simply experiencing college randomly. This shift from a nondirected search to an active search can be thought of as *focused exploration* (Schaller, 2005). Those in focused exploration may actively seek insight into relationships, future, and self (Bridges, 1980).

Relationships. Parks (2000) traced the process that young people move through as they negotiate their own development and their need for community. She pointed out that the American and, perhaps, the Western perspective values independence and autonomy. Therefore, young people recognize the struggle to balance the need for belongingness with the need for autonomy in adulthood. The sophomores whose stories are shared here often had conventional communities as a place to start (Parks, 2000). They had family or community connections that allowed them to feel secure as they came to college. The first-year process allowed them to expand their notion of a community to include increasingly different types of people. Parks called this a "diffuse" community (p. 92). During the first year, students may expand their notion of community to fit nearly everyone. This selection comes under critical review in the second year when students search for a mentoring community, one where individuals connect to a viable network of belonging (Parks, 2000). Thus, many sophomores are actively exploring fit.

Amy, a photography major, was actively seeking insight into her friendships. She thought at the end of the first year that she had made wonderful friends. Their separation was filled with tears. And yet they did not speak over the summer between the two years. Amy said, "It's really weird for me to sit there and like be really close to someone and love 'em to death and say, 'Why am I friends with you?'" Amy was trying to understand how she chose her friends and what she needed from others. Rob, an American studies major, said that he was looking for friends who would "understand" him. He thought that friendships would help him to "get to know myself better." Similarly, Joe, who was struggling between four different major choices, said, "I feel like I've lost almost all my friends." His first-year friends were not focused enough on academics. He thought these relationships were unhealthy, so he left them but had found few new relationships as replacements.

Keith, a finance major, had significant relationship problems during his sophomore year. He missed his friends from high school and struggled to find relationships with others that he could trust. He said that, "[as] an indirect maturation, you start thinking about your family when you're a sophomore." Keith's frustrations with his friendships set forth a new review of his family and historical friendships.

Parks (2000) suggested that the "tested adult" exhibits a confidence in an internally directed self and a self-selected community. The challenge, then, for sophomores is to not move from relationship to relationship without also becoming (a) aware of the impact of others' expectations on one's own life, (b) critical of those relationships based on what is the best fit for one's self, (c) connected to a mentoring community that becomes a place for a new connection and for transformation, and (d) capable of expanding one's relationships to allow for self-selection of communities and relationships.

Future. The sophomore year seems to represent a shift for many students from a focus backward or in the present, to a focus forward and toward the future. The answers to the questions of the future are not easily answered, as students cannot ignore the feeling that the end of childhood or the precollege life is over but its replacement is yet to arrive. Mary, a newly decided education major, was one of those students busy gaining insight into her future. She experienced a shift in the middle of the year when she began to realize that she had to start taking school seriously. She said, "I think the expectations of the real world are hitting us now. Where I'm going to be in 10 years and who I'm going to be friends with at that point is important to me now." Melissa's (an elementary education major) awareness accompanied her turning 20. She said,

> That's the first thing that I think of for this year, is like, it's really stressful, because—not really the classes and such, I mean, that's stressful, but the stress that I'm talking about is more like, what I'm going to be doing for the rest of my life; where am I going and like who I associate with and stuff like that.

Students often talk about the importance of setting up internships; of preparing themselves in their leadership or service activities to "make a mark" on the campus; and of making good choices about classes, professors, and study habits to set themselves up for graduate school. The future seems both close and frightening to many of these students.

Steve, a student who was a leader on a campus with a sophomore-year experience program, commented:

> Sophomore year is the year you are in your place in the college, and that's the year to make things happen, whether it be figuring out what to do with your life or finding ways to make the experience as fruitful as possible.

He was clear that this would be the year that he would make very important choices for his future, both on campus and once he left.

There are a number of competing factors facing sophomore students regarding the future, which complicates their decision making. As students struggle in the sophomore year to face the reality that their future as full-fledged adults is pending, they also struggle to find ways to identify their own dreams in the midst of so many messages sent to them. In his study of sophomore men at Colgate University, Bellani (2007) found that a fear of failure, anxiety over big life choices, and expectations held by others could cause men to avoid thinking about the future.

Self. As most of the student quotes show, figuring out "who I am" seems to be a clear task for the sophomore year. Some of the sophomores found ways to do this, primarily in the social or community setting. Others were finding themselves in circumstances that caused them to judge previous choices or current positions. Sue was one of those sophomores who had selected a major because she thought she could change her career direction after college. She had a group of friends who were very diverse and described herself as "breaking away from parents." She also said, "This year was also kind of finding yourself more. Like last year, you were more the people you hung out with and you were more the people on your hall, whereas this year you become your own person." Ed, an English education major, said:

> A lot of the things I do, actually, have to do with who I am or at least finding out who I am. So, it's still sort of in that sort of process. I'm just kinda discovering things I like. I'm still taking in all this stuff, and trying to sort it out.

What is interesting about the descriptions that sophomores give about their search to understand themselves is not so much that it is occurring, but that they were so articulate about the process. Grotevant (1992) suggested that the work of identity formation is found in the exploration process. If students are able to examine their developing self, assess the influences that others have had upon them, and evaluate their past choices, this is a sign that students are moving on from an externally defined self. The challenge is that this is a long process, requiring tremendous energy and an ability to remain in the search. It may also require a time for mourning, as students come to terms with parts of self that do not fit prior definitions. The process of letting go of the dream of being a doctor, or of fulfilling other lifelong plans, may now need to be laid to rest. Career-decision self-efficacy is positively influenced by the extent to which one has engaged in exploration and commitment to an identity (Nauta & Kahn, 2007). Students who do not engage in complex processing about their interests and direction are more likely to rely on extrinsic motivation and thus have lower levels of academic self-efficacy (Walker, Green & Mansell, 2006). Students who give in or who rely on parents, society, or others to guide them in their decision making about their futures may make tentative choices to please those parties rather than as an expression of self.

Lesbian, gay, or bisexual students who come to terms with their sexual orientation and no longer view a straight lifestyle as a realistic future may also face this difficult challenge in the sophomore year. Students may make a tentative choice to remain closeted or in denial of their sexual orientation if external pressures are overwhelming and internal supports have not yet been developed. In the future, students who face new revelations about self often celebrate their growing awareness, but in the process they can be engulfed in pain and loss as they let go of childhood or parental notions of self.

Spiritual and Character Development. Spiritual development can be defined as the search for ultimate purpose and truth (Dalton, 2001). The careerism and materialism of today's society provide a direct conflict with a search for meaning and purpose. However, because of the developmental questions facing students during the sophomore year, it is a fertile time to begin to ask questions related to life purpose and meaning. College is "a time of great potentiality and vulnerability in development, when concerns about individual purpose, meaning, and commitment interact with the forces of cognitive development, maturation, and social expectations" (Dalton, 2001, p. 18). Students often enter college using conventional moral reasoning, relying on those close to them both in their peer groups and family, or on the larger community, to determine acceptable moral choices. By the time students leave college, they are often using postconventional moral reasoning, relying on universal moral principles to guide decision making (Pascarella & Terenzini, 2005). Sophomore students may experience a retreat in this development, relying more heavily on peers and the people who make up their immediate circle in their moral decision making (Cohen, 1982; Kohlberg & Kramer, 1969).

What students do in college tends to make the greatest difference in character development (Astin & Antonio, 2004). Astin and Antonio identified six important components that shape one's character: (a) civic and social values, (b) cultural awareness, (c) volunteerism, (d) importance of family, (e) religious beliefs and convictions, and (f) understanding of others. Specifically, exposure to interdisciplinary courses, participation in religious services and events, socializing with students from a variety of backgrounds, participation in leadership education and training, performing volunteer work, and having faculty who provide emotional support facilitate the development of character. Sophomore students who have had these experiences also tend to reflect about the impact of service on their lives and their own impact on others.

Tentative Choices

The next stage of sophomore development is tentative choices. Charlie, a business major, exemplifies this stage. He had selected his major, was feeling relatively good about it, but had yet to make a firm commitment to the decision. During his interview, he shared that he had been offered a post-graduation job from his co-op site. However, as he talked, he realized an ongoing dream to be an educator like his father. The tentative choices stage feels like a place of no return, except for the fact that often by the time sophomore or junior students get here, they have experienced multiple brushes with solid decisions. If students are going to make internally directed decisions about the future, then tentative choices need to involve either (a) significant personal exploration and decision making or (b) decision making that allows for later change. This significant personal exploration requires an understanding and valuation of one's personal attributes and characteristics (Jones & McEwen, 2000). Engaging in reflection is vital to a successful transition (Bridges, 1980); however, students are often tempted to make decisions by relying on the expectations of family and society rather than themselves. If one remains in exploration, then a new understanding of self emerges, and this new awareness can become a centering or guiding force in making internally directed choices.

Beyond the Sophomore Year

A genuine new beginning is dependent upon an inner realignment rather than some external shift (Bridges, 1980). Although new beginnings may involve new relationships, new places, or new projects, they also involve new feelings or a new sense of self. The junior and senior years of college are exciting years for college students who have actively selected a major and feel confident in their choice. Courses in the major provide the opportunity for in-depth study of selected topics and greater contact with faculty. Students who are clear about what they want out of the college experience may be more purposeful in the junior and senior years in their involvement in leadership, service, and other cocurricular involvements. For college students to truly make a new beginning, they must make it through the neutral zone having gathered important information about the self, the world, and realistic options. Steve was one of those students who indicated that he was becoming more purposeful:

> Now I think that's pretty much, not that I'm not trying new things, but I think that's pretty much more cemented. Now it's more I'm not trying to find my place, but put my mark on those groups, whatever that might be. For me, that's the biggest difference.

Students must identify what others want for them and still find ways to choose for themselves. Those choices can be made separate from or in connection with others. In any case, they are most lasting when they are made based on a thorough review of the self.

Recommendations

Supporting sophomore students is complicated by the diversity that students experience. Clearly, we are not going to be able to change the academic experience to wait for students to negotiate finding an internal definition of self. Students need to make decisions about their major by the end of the sophomore year or earlier. However, there are ways that we can alter the sophomore-year experience to support them. I provide a number of suggestions here.

Define the Year as Different

Students are best served when they are provided with information about what is coming. Students are prepared for entering college during the year prior to college and over the summer. Sophomore students would benefit from a similar period of preparation. Prior to the sophomore year, students could be told what to expect. Knowing the challenges that are typically faced in the sophomore year could assist students in preparing themselves for the work they need to do. Students should know prior to entering the year that they will need to make many decisions about their future, that they will have many opportunities to engage in conversations and learn from others about the process, and that there will be support for them in the process.

Provide Ongoing Opportunities for Relationships with Adults

Parks (2000) makes an excellent case for the importance of providing a "mentoring community" for young people. Sophomores seek and need opportunities to talk through where they have been and where they might head. Providing opportunities for sophomores to hear stories from alumni who have selected majors and then changed careers or who have found balance in their lives can be one way to signal to sophomores that when the childhood dreams do not work, there are other possible choices available.

Yet the mentoring community also needs to acknowledge the contributions sophomores bring to the table. Baxter Magolda (1992) encouraged us to validate students as knowers, to allow them the opportunity to think for themselves, to share their perspectives, and to provide a real contribution to relationships. In other words, advisors, faculty, student affairs professionals, and work supervisors can develop authentic relationships with sophomores by first treating them as individuals with a voice and then encouraging and validating their perspective.

Challenge Students to Label External Forces

In the middle of the first year, students often begin to label and criticize external forces. They question the expectations held for them by their parents and friends, and they often begin to question what they have been taught by teachers, their religious traditions, and society. While this questioning is uncomfortable for the "other," it is an important step in the students' move toward feeling clearer about who they are. We can support students in this process by providing them with opportunities to acknowledge what it is that society expects of us based on our race, gender, and socioeconomic status. Specifically, we need to provide opportunities for students to ask the questions: How do I feel about this? How does my family feel about this? How do my friends feel about this? How do I cope with any differences that may exist here? If a student has yet to fully explore the self, labeling what others expect may do little more than encourage further exploration. However, if students do not acknowledge that some expectations are from others, they may make tentative choices without fully exploring their own wishes, needs, and preferences.

Encourage Experiential Learning and Real World Connections

Institutional programs that encourage service learning, internships, study abroad, and connection to society have a powerful impact on student's growing sense of responsibility to community. When students are fully engaged in self-reflection, they may become self-involved if institutions do not support a larger world view. Promoting spiritual and character development entails developing a critical moral consciousness with a sense of responsibility to the world (Mustakova-Possardt, 2004). Self-development and moral development are paired processes. Institutions and academic programs should set high expectations for students to engage in exploration of both self and society.

Encourage Self-Reflection

Self-reflection is a central responsibility of moving toward an internally defined self (Marcia, 1993). The sophomore year is a prime time for students to evaluate past choices, examine belief systems, acknowledge personal strengths and weaknesses, and begin to identify values. By examining incongruities in one's life, individuals can examine the underlying value systems that guide their behavior. We may see students who say one thing and do another. This lapse is an opportunity to acknowledge that either what one says is not a truly held belief or what one does is not a personally accepted choice. Educational conversations structured to encourage reflection when students violate policies offer powerful self-reflective opportunities. Academic advising, coaching or mentoring in student leadership and service involvement, preparation for study abroad decisions, and career exploration and counseling each provide timely opportunities for sophomores to reflect. For second-year students preparing for transfer from a two-year to a four-year or between four-year institutions, reflection is simply requisite for success in the decision-making process.

Provide for Expansion of Peer Relationships

As students seek to find an acceptable self, they also search for a changing community. Sophomores describe having a growing sense of self and then needing to find others who share those new values. This requires ongoing opportunities for new connections and peer relationships. In addition, this supports students' expanding view of knowledge. Because sophomores view peers as playing an important role in coming to understand knowledge and the world, increased interaction in the classroom, group work in organizations, and other opportunities to come together with other students will support students' identity development and their intellectual development.

Conclusion

Higher education's structure requires that students be prepared to declare a major or transfer from a two-year to four-year institution by the end of the sophomore year of college. Although the structure of higher education is not going to change, we can and should provide students with the support they need to make these critical choices. Support, however, should take the shape of challenging students to engage in the difficult work of learning about one's interests, abilities, and values and connecting a growing sense of self with major, careers, and other learning opportunities. Programs will not be successful if they merely serve to make sophomores feel good about being in our institutions. Sophomores do need to become fully integrated and engaged in their institutions while they are also exploring what college has to offer and making key choices about what they want out of the college experience. At the same time, sophomores should be encouraged through service-learning, leadership, study abroad, and other experiences to explore their role in the world. The sophomore year is an exciting time for students to make sense of how college will play a role in their future lives and in the future success of our society.

PART TWO

APPROACHES FOR ENGAGING SECOND-YEAR STUDENTS

In Part Two we focus on another one of our guiding questions: What are the academic and programmatic options that promote sophomore student success? Our goal is to encourage educators to provide an integrative, comprehensive approach to the second year; however, in Part Two the authors explore unique approaches to helping second-year students with the primary challenges in the second year. These inherent issues are major selection and developing purpose. The components explored in the following chapters when taken together form a holistic approach to the second year.

To that end, in Chapter Five Virginia N. Gordon focuses on academic advising; in Chapter Six Paul A. Gore, Jr., and Mary Stuart Hunter provide insights into career advising. Both are essential elements to assisting students in the primary challenges in the second college year: declaring a major. In Chapter Seven Scott E. Evenbeck and Sharon J. Hamilton discuss curricular approaches designed to encourage intellectual development in the second year. Laurie A. Schreiner tackles the critical role of faculty and faculty development in Chapter Eight. In Chapter Nine Steven G. Jones and Robert W. Franco discuss important educational benefits through service-learning in the sophomore year. Susan Buck Sutton and Stephanie L. Leslie describe the value of providing study abroad opportunities for second-year students in Chapter Ten. In Chapter Eleven Kathryn J. Wilson and Mary Crowe discuss the power of undergraduate research specifically geared to engaging sophomores. Jimmie Gahagan and Mary Stuart Hunter explore in Chapter Twelve the unique opportunities to engage students through residential life. Jennifer A. Lindholm concludes Part Two with a discussion based on national research of students' perceptions on spirituality, thus shedding light on the other sophomore goal of finding purpose.

CHAPTER FIVE

ACADEMIC ADVISING

Helping Sophomores Succeed

Virginia N. Gordon

Academic advising has long been acknowledged as an integral part of higher education. It has transformed in recent years from a course registration function to a more student-centered approach that focuses on how advising can support and enhance college students' academic progress and success (Creamer, 2000; Grites & Gordon, 2000; Kuhn, 2008). In light of this change, academic advising programs were reorganized to meet the needs of special populations, including first-year students, where they have proved to be extremely effective. Recognition of the importance of continuing this focus on second-year students is now well established. Many researchers and writers have highlighted the unique concerns that students experience in their sophomore year (Gahagan & Hunter, 2006; Graunke & Woosley, 2005; Schaller, 2005).

Kramer (2000) outlines the advising themes that define the sophomore year, including crystallizing academic plans, developing through student experience, integrating with campus life, and reflecting on academic progress. These themes incorporate educational tasks that sophomores need to address, such as determining their academic path and expectations, developing accurate expectations for their selected major, and exploring career opportunities within the major.

As noted in other chapters in this book, the term sophomore refers to students who are enrolled in their second year of college. For advising purposes, it also refers to the number of credit hours a student has completed. Students may have sophomore credit hours (for example, advanced placement, transfer, or placement test credit) but actually may be in their first year of college. Part-time and nontraditional students may be in their fourth or fifth calendar year but still be second-year students in terms of credits earned. Other second-year students may have earned enough credits to be of junior standing. Although community college or technical school "sophomores" are confronting many of the same issues as their four-year counterparts, their advising needs may be different in some unique ways. For example, these students' greater maturity, more varied past academic experiences, and career goals will require different advising knowledge, techniques, and resources. Consequently, each second-year student presents a profile that is special to that individual's background, concerns, and experiences.

Other chapters in this book have provided descriptions of sophomore characteristics and identified some of the important events that take place during the sophomore year. The unique concerns of these students are often expressed in advising contacts. Kramer (2000) emphasizes the personal attention that advising can provide students who are expressing academic, personal, and social concerns that might impede their progress through the sophomore year. This chapter focuses on the three primary areas of concern relevant to the academic advising of sophomores: major choice, academic planning, and readjusting to the campus environment (Gardner, Pattengale, & Schreiner, 2000).

Major: Making the Choice

Choosing an academic direction is one of the most important decisions that students make while in college. Students' choice of major will lead them down a path that incorporates contacts with faculty and peers, exposure to academic content, and the type and depth of academic experiences that might affect later decisions involving the identification of career alternatives or post-college education. The process of choosing a major itself has an impact on students in many ways. The few students who enter college decided about a major and eventually graduate in that major require a different advising approach than those who end up changing their major or those who are undecided. Advising these three groups of sophomores not only requires different advising skills and knowledge but also a sensitivity to the issues and concerns that individual students confront as they engage in academic planning.

Decided Sophomores

Advising sophomores who have selected a major and who are capable of completing a degree in that area of study does not involve just scheduling and registration (as some students think). Decided majors need help formulating an academic plan that takes them to graduation. They may also need assistance with course selection and sequencing, balancing their course schedule, and in some cases considering a minor course of study. An important advisor function is to help sophomores experience a smooth transition into their chosen major by explaining the institution's procedures for making it official and helping them make the transition to their new advisor (when indicated). Advisors need to make contact with their sophomore advisees early so that this transition is not delayed.

Orndorff and Herr (1996) speculate that the reason so many decided students change their majors might be their lack of information about the occupations they have chosen. Therefore, these students need to be engaging in both short- and long-range academic and career planning, as well as identifying and taking action to set up relevant learning experiences (e.g., internships, volunteer work, service-learning, and occupational). Decided sophomores also need information about graduate or professional study and the planning involved in furthering their education.

Major Changers

Some majors force students to be "decided" immediately upon entering college because of the sequencing of courses (such as health areas, or music) or because of a requirement that all students "declare" an interest in at least some broad area of related disciplines. Entering first-year students, especially, may feel institutional, family, or societal pressures to choose a field of study (Berrios-Allison, 2005; Pearson & Dellman-Jenkins, 1997). However, after a few terms of coursework in their initial area of study, they have a better idea of their interests and their abilities to perform in that major. Sometimes this realization occurs during their first year, but they may delay a decision until the beginning of their sophomore year. Theophilides et al. (1984) found that 15 percent of students changed their major in their first year and 15 percent in their sophomore year. Forty-five percent of students, however, changed their major during both their first and second years. This is valuable information for advisors. Helping students trace their history in changing majors might offer insights into how they engage in academic decision making in general.

Sophomores who are in the process of changing majors require many of the academic and career advising approaches that are used with undecided students, such as collecting major and occupational information. They present, however, more complex advising challenges. Many have accumulated credit hours in courses that may or may not fit into other major curricula. Some major changers may have feelings of failure or even be depressed about changing. A lifelong career dream may be shattered or they may feel they have let others down. Some may be anxious about prolonging their college career or consider dropping out of college. These emotional concerns must be acknowledged by a sensitive advisor who can provide the support these students need as they experience their major transition. Some major changers, however, go through the process with minor concerns, many taking advantage of the help that advisors can provide (Steele, Kennedy, & Gordon, 1993).

Undecided Sophomores

Although little research has been performed specifically on "undecided" sopho-mores, this group faces even more complications than those indicated above. Like major changers, they have accumulated course credit that may not fit with other majors' course requirements. If they chose a selective admissions major (such as health areas), they will probably extend their college years. There are advantages in taking time to explore, however, especially for liberal arts majors who have had the opportunity to sample many different fields of study. Undecided sophomores who have not confronted their situation, however, will find scheduling courses increasingly difficult as time passes. It takes special advising expertise to help students see how past academic credit fits into the curricula of the alternative majors they are considering.

The research that has been conducted on undecided students stresses the diversity of this population, including their degrees of indecision, their personal constructs, and their decision-making approaches (Hagstrom, Skovholt, & Rivers, 1997; Kelly & Pulver, 2003; Newman, Gray, & Fuqua, 1999; Wanberg & Muchinsky, 1992). The range of students' indecision includes being "tentatively undecided" to being "completely undecided" (Gordon, 2007; Gordon & Steele, 2003). Other researchers have addressed the concerns of multicultural students and how they make academic and career decisions (Arce, 1996; Berrios-Allison, 2005; Chung & Sedlacek, 1999; Mau, 2000). Advisors need to determine each student's degree of indecision, since this will affect the amount and type of aca-demic and career information the student requires, how decisions have been made in the past, and the personal concerns regarding indecision the student is willing to share. As advisors work with still undecided sophomores, they need to probe into what, how, and when past academic decisions were made. This not only provides a starting place for discussion but also offers both the advisor and the student insights into how this might influence future exploration tasks.

In Chapter Six, Gore and Hunter address the career-related issues that many second-year students face. All students, but especially undecided students, need advising that includes career exploration as well as academic information.

Gordon (2006) describes three aspects of the career advising process: *inquire, inform,* and *integrate*. Undecided students who are in the *inquire* phase have only a vague idea about their future, have not rejected any possible alternatives, and have no plan of action as yet (Tiedeman & O'Hara, 1963). They are in the questioning phase of who they are and have yet to set academic or career goals. In the *inform* phase, they have questions about what career information they need, where they can find it, and how they can use it. They begin to recognize that there are alternatives and start weighing the advantages and disadvantages of each. As they begin to narrow down their choices, they need to *integrate* all the knowledge they have gathered about their strengths, interests, and values and the information they have collected about occupations and academic major relationships. As they eventually make a decision, they realize the importance of future planning. As Tiedeman and O'Hara (1963) point out, these decision-making stages are fluid and flexible and can be recycled at any point. An important advisor responsibility is to help sophomores understand all the ramifications of delaying their decision and the planning that is required to implement it.

Most students return for their second year; however, they do so as more mature individuals than they were only a year earlier, much wiser about the academic process, and are able to make a choice of major before the year has ended. However, sophomores who are not yet willing or able to make a decision present an advising challenge, since time is not on their side. If they are indecisive or have a debilitating decision-making style, they may need to be referred to a counselor for additional assistance.

Academic Planning

Many of the issues that sophomores confront in academic planning have already been discussed. Academic planning can be defined as the process of gathering academic and career information that is incorporated into a graduation plan. The plan must reflect the student's interests, values, beliefs, and goals. The plan must also include the tasks and experiences that students need in order to succeed in college and that prepare them for future work and life. Kuh (2008) defines college success as "academic achievement, engagement in educationally purposeful activities, satisfaction, acquisition of desired knowledge, skills and competencies, persistence and attainment of educational objectives" (p. 68). Advisors need to help students monitor their plan so that changes or additions are based on their academic progress and personal preferences.

The role of advisors in academic planning cannot be overstated. Svanum and Bigatti (2009) found that the level of student engagement in their coursework influences not only academic success but also other indices of college success, such as degree completion. Advisors should emphasize the importance of establishing good academic behavior and habits, especially with how they approach their daily coursework. Some sophomores still haven't acquired study habits that are so critical to becoming a successful student.

Advising second-year students may be viewed as an ongoing process that involves at least three phases: (1) *reviewing,* (2) *immediate planning,* and (3) *long-range planning.*

The *reviewing* phase of the advising process involves helping students reflect on their previous year's experiences: What have they learned about themselves; how satisfied are they with the decisions they made; what have they learned from their past academic, social, and career exploration experiences; and how can they use this knowledge in the future?

The agenda for the *immediate planning* phase will depend on students' decided-ness about a major, since it involves short-term course selection and developing a curricular plan for the remainder of the sophomore year. In addition to planning course schedules, the plan should include the types of on- and off-campus learning experiences that are involved in academic and career exploration. The *long-range planning* phase is difficult for some students because they must begin to project goals for their remaining college years and for life after graduation.

Reviewing

Although the *reviewing* phase can take place any time, it is most critical at the beginning of the sophomore year as students begin to reflect on their first-year experiences. Offering a sophomore orientation program, as some institutions do, provides a special opportunity to help students review and reflect on their previous year's experiences as they begin to develop a plan for their second year. This period of student reflection may engender questions such as

- What did I accomplish academically, personally, and socially during my first year of college?
- What academic goals do I want to set for my second year of college?
- What do I need to do to reach these goals?
- What type of career exploration tasks do I need to engage in this year?

The answers to these questions will depend on where students are in the major choice process and how they can build on the academic, career, and personal goals they have already accomplished.

Decided Sophomores. As advisors and decided students begin the review task, they should carefully examine the student's transcript to identify academic strengths and areas where improvement is needed. Reflecting on past experiences in the classroom can help students think about future course selection, areas of emphasis within the major, and, when applicable, consideration of an academic minor. This process is important for community college students who intend to pursue a baccalaureate degree, as well as students already attending four-year institutions. Advisors should help students reflect on the value of past on- and off-campus experiences, what they learned from those experiences, and what new learning opportunities need to be considered.

Major Changers. Advisors who work with sophomores who wish to change their academic direction need to help them reflect about past decisions. What are their reasons for changing? What majors are they considering? If they have chosen a new major, what attracted them to this new choice? On what information have they based this decision? What processes did they follow to arrive at this decision? Helping students reflect on how they made choices in the past might help them understand how they might make future decisions more effectively. Examining their transcript will help reveal past academic interests and successes that should be considered as they identify major alternatives. An honest appraisal of how they went about choosing a major their first year can help them reflect on where they are in the process and what tasks they still need to complete.

Undecided Sophomores. Helping undecided students reflect on their inability to select a major might reveal feelings of anxiety and frustration. Sophomore students, in particular, often feel increased pressure to choose a major, and this may lead to unrealistic choices. Helping students think about their past efforts to gather information (such as about self, majors, career fields) can lead to discussions about the kind of information they still need to acquire. Helping them analyze how they approach the decision-making process itself might reveal areas where they need assistance. The review process with undecided sophomores is especially important, since it can help to identify the exploration steps already taken and what steps the student still needs to consider in order to make a decision.

Immediate Planning

When advisors and sophomores meet at the beginning of the second year to formulate plans, what transpires will depend on where the student is in the major choice process.

Decided Sophomores. Advisors who work with students who are following a prescribed curriculum will need to check the student's progress in the major and help them map out the rest of the year's courses. Many sophomores begin their year without engaging in "reviewing" where they are in terms of academic progress, and even those following a structured program will benefit from discussing and updating their plans and goals. Those who are not performing up to the curriculum's standards will need to acknowledge their deficits and discuss specific ways to improve. Students who are in a competitive academic area and who are not performing well may need to reevaluate their choice. This is not always a pleasant topic for advisors to initiate, but an honest discussion of students' understanding of their situation needs to take place. It is important for students to feel supported as they evaluate their academic status and make new plans. In some cases, examining alternative majors might reenergize a student, especially if those majors are in areas that encompass a student's general interests and goals. Planning that takes place at the beginning of the sophomore year can guide decided students' academic and campus experiences and might help eliminate future problems.

Major Changers. The timing for immediate planning for sophomores who are in the process of changing majors is critical. Students and parents are always concerned about prolonging the years it takes to complete a degree. Students who have accumulated many credit hours need to engage in the exploration process immediately so that realistic alternatives can be identified. Advisors need to be especially proactive with students who have not acknowledged their need to change and who are drifting without a direction. Academic planning for these students must not only include specific action steps for exploration but also a timeline for completing those actions. Some students may need assistance with reworking plans that are no longer viable. Contact with these students at the beginning of the year is essential before more undirected coursework takes place.

Undecided Sophomores. Undecided sophomores are also under pressure to make a major choice. Like major changers, immediate planning will include exploration activities. Sophomores are more likely to have narrowed down their major options and may have already engaged in activities that have led them to a tentative decision. Discussing the academic requirements for this major and how their completed coursework fits into its curriculum might help them confirm or reject their choice. For students who have made a decision, this often means referring students to a new academic department so that a new advisor may be assigned and targeted academic planning can immediately the take place.

The first order of business for students who are considering two alternatives and cannot decide between them is to help them assess the pros and cons of each choice. This may lead to initiating a new round of information gathering. The advisor's role as a sounding board while providing the support students need at this stage is important.

Totally undecided sophomores present the greatest challenge since they may not have seriously engaged in the exploration process. It is sometimes too easy for procrastinating students to drift through their second year without making the effort to engage in the exploratory tasks that are so critical at this time. Advisors need to identify these students early and help them understand the urgency of their situation. Some students need help reflecting on the information and experiences they have already accumulated and simply need advisor support in committing to a decision.

When students cannot make a decision, advisors need to help them reflect on their decision-making style and analyze how they made academic decisions in the past (such as did they rely on other people, were they motivated, did they have the right kind of information?). Advisors need to be alert for the "indecisive" student who is unable to make a decision about any aspect of life. Although these students are rare, they need to be identified early (Gordon, 2007) and referred to the campus counseling center.

Long-Range Planning

Long-range planning involves setting goals that take students through their senior year and beyond. It is sometimes difficult for students to contemplate the future because it seems so abstract and far away. Setting long-term goals, however, will identify many of the actions that need to be taken during the sophomore year. Students who plan to enter the workforce after graduation need to establish a long-range plan that helps them identify the experiences and skills necessary to prepare them for a changing work world.

It has long been acknowledged that first-year students need to develop a résumé so important accomplishments and experiences can be recorded as they happen. Students might also consider developing an e-portfolio because it can also provide evidence of achievement or take advantage of a cocurricular transcript option if offered at their institution. A résumé can be changed and added to as sophomores continue to acquire the knowledge, skills, and competencies they will need to attract future employers. Through careful planning, sophomores also have the time to fill the academic and experience gaps. Campus career planning services and the Internet have a wealth of material that can help students with many of the tasks associated with workplace preparation. Advisors might want to create a handout or an online list of Web site addresses listing these resources.

If students aspire to attend graduate or professional school, the sophomore year is the time to start gathering information about the entrance examinations required (such as the GRE, LSAT), graduate programs that specialize in their academic area of interest, criteria for entrance, and other pertinent information. Advisors should impress upon students the need to make themselves known to faculty members who would be willing to write letters of recommendation for this purpose. Students should be encouraged to start a graduate school file where they can store and organize information as they collect it.

Advisors also should encourage sophomores to participate in cocurricular activities in which they can strengthen their knowledge and leadership skills. Study abroad opportunities can expand their cultural and language expertise. Many employers today stress the need for actual work experience that may be acquired through internships, service learning, and volunteer activities. Research indicates that courses that incorporate "engaged learning" engender student satisfaction and retention (Pascarella & Terenzini, 2005). Establishing long-term goals that include academic and career aspirations and designing action steps to accomplish them can make the difference between being an average or outstanding student or job candidate. Advisors should not only encourage students to incorporate such experiences in their academic plan but should also help them with their implementation.

Return to the Campus Community

Students returning to college after their first year will have many different perspectives on their past college experiences. Most students return more mature, more comfortable in the campus environment (both physically and socially), more comfortable with faculty, more familiar with campus resources, and more capable in the classroom. Some sophomores, however, may need to readjust to different living arrangements, new roommates, or new friendships, or in the case of commuter students, new time schedules and perhaps family and employment demands. Other sophomores may need to establish contact with a new academic department and a new academic advisor.

Research has shown that positive integration of students into the campus community takes place when they are involved with faculty members and campus activities (Pascarella & Terenzini, 2005; Tinto, 2006). Other studies, however, have found that some second-year students may feel ignored, lost, less competent, or less engaged as they struggle through a period of readjustment

(Schaller, 2005; Schreiner & Pattengale, 2000). Academic advisors' early and frequent contact with second-year students who are feeling disconnected from the campus environment may prevent problems that could lead to academic failure or withdrawal. Establishing contact periods (such as by e-mail, text-messaging, cell phone, in person) with sophomores should be built into advising routines.

Tetley, Tobolowsky, and Chan write about the importance of creating special programs for sophomores in Chapter Fourteen. These programs require the cooperation and support of many institutional service providers and key campus stakeholders. Torres (2003) indicates that the most influential aspect of academic integration of minority students is the role of faculty members, the campus climate, and the "creation of cognitive maps that help students navigate the college experience" (p. 340). Kuh, English, and Hinkle (2003) conclude that "changing circumstances on and off campus make highly collaborative, responsive, student-centered academic services essential" (p. 407). Academic advising plays a critical role in helping to make this student-centered environment a reality.

Related Sophomore Issues

This chapter has stressed academically related issues that affect students in their sophomore year. Other factors that have an impact on student satisfaction and success require additional and more specialized advising knowledge and techniques.

Sophomore Transfer Issues

Transfer students are a significant part of college enrollment. Community colleges contribute the largest number of transfer students to postsecondary education (National Survey of Student Engagement [NSSE], 2006). The background of students who transfer as sophomores is varied. They can be moving from a two- or four-year institution and may have articulation issues involving course credit as well as concerns about adjusting to a new environment. Or they may be moving from four-year to two-year campuses to improve basic skills, realize cost savings, improve their grade point averages, and for other legitimate reasons. Although they require the same advising information as students already enrolled, advisors must be aware of the special issues they bring to academic planning.

King (2002) enumerates the issues related to transfers that are unique to community colleges. She suggests that in addition to focusing on program requirements at the community college, attention needs to be paid to requirements at the four-year institution so that the maximum number of credits can be transferred. There is also a need to help students identify transfer institutions quickly so their program can be designed to take advantage of existing articulation agreements. King emphasizes that academic advisors have a responsibility to identify early in the process those qualified students who have yet to view transfer as an option and to provide them with the support, encouragement, and skills needed to explore such opportunities successfully. These are important considerations when helping community college students create their academic plan.

Family Issues

Advising sophomores will involve many types of students from very different cultural, economic, and social backgrounds. Much has been written about parents' involvement in their millennial children's college life, especially in the first year, but this involvement often continues into the sophomore year. Family members need to be aware of the special needs of their sophomore students and the resources on- and off-campus to assist them. Like advisors, parents can act as referral agents to their students when they are aware of the resources that exist and how to access them.

Advisors should welcome any contact that family members might make, keeping in mind the provisions of the Privacy Act. Cultural influences may play a part in students' choice of major and other academic decisions (Clark & Kalionzes, 2008; Coll, 2008–2009). Advisors should be knowledgeable about different cultures and the role that family plays in students' academic and career decision making. First-generation sophomores are especially at high risk for attrition, so advisor contact with family members might be particularly important (Smith & Gordon, 2008). Advisors must be aware of how family responsibilities influence adult students' academic progress and when they need assistance in finding resources that might help alleviate a problem. Students whose academic and career choices were based on negative family influences may need to reevaluate their prior decisions during the sophomore year. Advisors should be especially sensitive to students who are struggling with family issues such as finances, time pressures, and academic decisions based on family dictates.

Academic Resources

In addition to special attention to individual sophomores' advising needs, advisors also should be involved in any campuswide programs designed to assist second-year students. They can be instrumental in encouraging the establishment of a sophomore orientation program or a sophomore seminar that includes academic planning. One of the most useful resources is a credit course designed to help undecided and major-changing sophomores systematically make academic and career decisions (Gordon & Sears, 2009). These courses are especially timely for sophomores, and students may be more inclined to become involved when structure is provided. Special sophomore Web sites can be useful because they can offer important information about academic planning resources and department-related campus activities. Sophomore residence hall programs should include an academic advising component that involves departmental and faculty advisors in helping students with academic information and planning. Academic advisors can work with campus career centers for joint programming that assists sophomores with major and career exploration workshops, and advisors can offer their assistance in helping to teach career courses. Campuswide major fairs or those sponsored by departments might offer special sessions that are directed specifically to sophomore curricular planning and personal needs. Academic advising components can enhance any sophomore initiative.

One of the most important competencies that advisors need to refine is the referral function. In a study to determine the differences in how faculty and students perceived the importance of advising functions, students and faculty disagreed on the importance of the referral function (Allen & Smith, 2008). Faculty considered referring students to campus resources significantly more important than did the students in the study. Students may not feel the need to be referred to other services and therefore do not recognize this as important in their advising contacts. Faculty, however, are familiar with the consequences of ignoring problems that can interfere with academic learning and progress and are more likely to have experienced the value of their referrals. When referring, advisors should stress the reason for and importance of the referral. Resources to which advisors commonly refer include Internet sources, campus resources such as tutoring or study skills help, career exploration activities, cocurricular activities, financial aid, or counseling. It might be instructive to discuss with sophomores to which campus resources they were referred in the past, whether they followed through with the referral, and what they learned from the experience. When referring a student, advisors should request feedback immediately so a follow-up can determine its usefulness.

Transition to the Junior Year

Another important advising task is to help second-year students make the transition to their junior year. Careful academic planning throughout the sophomore year will help make this transition a smooth one. As sophomores move into their third year of college, they should be able to integrate their academic plans with their career plans. When advisors help sophomores become more adept at making plans for the future, the process will evolve more smoothly as they continue to graduation. Advisors can also help students contemplate their interest in graduate or professional school and refer them to the resources on campus that can assist them.

Advisor Development

Most of this chapter has focused on the advising needs of sophomores and some advising techniques that can make working with this special group more effective. Just as advising first-year students requires special advisor knowledge and competencies, advisors who work with students at other levels (such as sophomores, juniors, seniors, graduate students) need to develop the special expertise that advising each groups requires. Understanding the special academic and career needs of students in each class can not only help focus on the issues they present but can also enhance the advisor-advisee relationship. Advisor training and development programs are the best vehicles for helping advisors learn and refine the special knowledge and skills required to advise sophomores effectively. Training programs can be tailored to advisors who are predominantly working with sophomores or those who would benefit the most from the information. This includes faculty and professional advisors and residence hall and other student life personnel.

Sophomore advisor training programs can be offered in many formats using a variety of methods. The first important step is to set program objectives: What should advisors know, and what competencies do they need to be effective in advising sophomores? Although the most common advisor training method is to offer workshops, small group discussions or presentation of information by printed or technological means, such as Webinars, are also effective.

The topics included in a training program for advising sophomores should be determined by the needs of the participants. Surveying advisors and others who work with sophomores in many campus environments (for example, departmental faculty advisors, career services counselors, residence hall directors, and peer advisors) can reveal their interests and the topics they think are important.

Some examples are a discussion of sophomore characteristics (how are they different from first-year students); theory presentations that help advisors learn where sophomores are developmentally (for instance, traditional-age, adult students) in maturity and in their quest for identity and purpose; special sophomore advising concerns; career advising and resources; and other relevant information about sophomores at the institution. Training topics might be presented through case studies, simulations, role playing, Webinars, or other online sources. Advisor training efforts should reflect the unique needs of the institution, what advisors want to learn, and the needs of the sophomores who are being advised.

Recommendations

In closing, here is a list of specific recommendations for advisors who work with sophomore students.

- Advisors should encourage their advisees at the beginning of the sophomore year to reflect on their previous year's academic experiences and help them review the goals they want to accomplish their second year.
- The sophomore year is a critical time to review with students their academic plan for graduation and revise it to reflect any changes or additions.
- Advisors should discuss with their sophomore advisees early in the year their past study habits, time management, writing, and other academic skills, identify any areas that need to be improved, and refer them to appropriate campus resources.
- Advisors should identify at the beginning of the sophomore year students who are in competitive majors and who are not performing well. A frank discussion of their academic standing may motivate them to take steps toward improvement, or if change is indicated, the decisions made might save the student disappointment and time.
- Special attention should be paid to the reasons sophomores give for changing majors. They often have different concerns than first-year major changers, and they have a year or more of course credit that might influence their identification of new majors to consider.
- Advisors working with students who are still undecided in their sophomore year need to question the students' approaches to decision making and the amount and type of major and career information they have collected.
- The sophomore year is an important time to help students identify and consider special academic and career-related opportunities. Advisors need to help students begin to prepare for their areas of special interest, such as graduate education, study abroad, or internships.
- Advisors are in an excellent position to encourage sophomores to participate (or continue to participate) in cocurricular activities. Advisors can help students understand the importance of using cocurricular or volunteer experiences to develop academic and career-related skills.

- Advisors need to be especially sensitive to special groups of sophomores, such as transfer students, and their needs. The second year may bring new challenges to students who are still adapting to the campus environment.
- Special advisor training programs should focus on the needs, problems, and concerns that are unique to sophomore students.

The role of the academic advisor remains a critical one in the second year of college, whether a student is at a two-year or four-year campus. Advisors provide invaluable assistance for students in the second year regarding their choice of major, academic planning, and readjustment to campus.

CHAPTER SIX

PROMOTING CAREER SUCCESS IN THE SECOND YEAR OF COLLEGE

Paul A. Gore, Jr., Mary Stuart Hunter

There has been a gradual but unmistakable trend during the past 40 years in college regarding students' reasons for deciding to go to college. Today, many students say they attend college to get a better job or to get training for a specific career (Pryor, Hurtado, Saenz, Santos, Korn, 2007). This observation is punctuated by data reported by Astin (1998) that documents a surge in students' endorsement of "being well off financially" as a prominent personal value. Today's college graduate will face a workplace very different from that of her or his parents. Students can no longer assume that a college diploma will be a ticket to lucrative and stable employment. Employers want employees who can communicate, work in teams, are self-determined, conscientious, and flexible, and have a strong work ethic (O'Toole & Lawler, 2006). Fortunately, these are the same general characteristics that promote student academic success. Students today must identify how their educational experience (both curricular and cocurricular) is preparing them for tomorrow's workforce. The second year of college is a time when many students make critical educational and career decisions. It is also a time during which higher education professionals can positively influence students' lives by helping them become active managers of their career development.

Our intent in writing this chapter is to assist higher education professionals in considering ways of improving programs and services directed at second-year students. We first offer a general overview of career-related issues faced by many second-year students. We then review recent changes in the workforce that have implications for the career planning of college sophomores. We highlight recent empirical evidence pointing to key characteristics of student and workplace success. In doing so, we emphasize the parallel between the types of attitudes, skills, and behaviors that promote student success and those that promote positive outcomes in the workplace. We then briefly review current theories of career development with specific attention to how they inform career advising with students during the second year of college. Finally, we highlight several institutions' curricular and cocurricular models of promoting career success. Our hope is that readers will assess how their current programs are informed by existing career research and theory and how those programs are preparing students for the new workplace.

The Second Year of College

Increased attention is being focused on the issues faced by students during their second year in college (Schreiner & Pattengale, 2000; Tobolowsky & Cox, 2007a). Pattengale and Schreiner (2000) argue that the sophomore year may be a time in which students tend to disengage from their academic life. Alternatively, several authors have described the second year as a time of moratorium in which students are struggling to crystallize their career decisions and life goals (Anderson & Schreiner, 2000; Boivin, Fountain, & Baylis, 2000). There is growing evidence supporting the challenges faced by sophomores with respect to their career and life planning (e.g., Foubert, Nixon, Sisson, & Barnes, 2005; Gardner, 2000; Poe, 1991).

Although post-secondary risk is most often associated with first-year students, the second year of college is also a risky time for many students, especially those who have not yet decided or are having second thoughts on their academic major. Because institutional efforts to promote student success and persistence have historically concentrated on the first year of college, sophomores who have not yet established an academic home may receive less academic guidance and support compared to their first year and may be at risk for attrition. Ironically, the lack of support experienced by many second-year students may further complicate the choice of a major and prolong the time a student spends outside the confines of an academic home.

Academic integration and engagement are important concepts championed by a number of student development theorists (e.g., Astin, 1999; Kuh, Kinzie, Schuh, & Whitt, 2005; Tinto, 1993). Academically integrated students have more meaningful interaction with faculty members, feel more connected to their college major, and begin to incorporate the values and norms of their academic discipline. Tinto argues that academic integration promotes the development of, and commitment to, academic and career goals. Career development theorists such as Donald Super (1992) also highlight the benefits of academic integration. Super's work suggests that academic integration helps students learn the values and culture associated with a career path and develop a sense of purpose.

Gardner (2000) suggests that deciding on a college major may be the most significant personal decision faced by second-year students. Yet some second-year students may experience anxiety when facing the prospects of declaring an academic major. This anxiety may stem from the often-misguided belief that choosing a major excludes certain future career options. Hawkins, Bradley, and White's (1977) results suggest that major choice anxiety can significantly delay the process of declaring a major and may be associated with lower levels of major certainty once a major is declared. Significant affect may also be experienced by those who later decide to change their major. These individuals may face regret over having chosen poorly or having delayed their eventual graduation and entry into the workforce.

Recent research sheds new light on the importance of early career development efforts, especially those designed to help students find an academic home within the institution. Graunke and Woosley (2005), for example, reported that interactions with faculty and commitment to college major were both significant predictors of second-year students' academic performance. Reporting on results from a longitudinal study of college students, Tracey and Robbins (2006) found that the fit between students' interests and their chosen college major was an important predictor of second-year academic performance. The relationship between major choice and outcomes is not always simple. These authors also found that interest-major fit was predictive of second-year college persistence as well, but only for students with low levels of overall interest. More recently, Robbins and his colleagues (2009) documented the significant relationship between participation in academic and career advising and first to second-year student retention. Choosing a major and a career can be a daunting and anxiety-provoking process for students. Moreover, even students with a declared major admit various levels of uncertainty or indecisiveness. Peterson, Sampson, Reardon, and Lenz (1996) provided a framework for understanding differences in decision-making status. They categorized individuals as decided, undecided, or indecisive. Individuals in the decided category have made some type of commitment to an occupation or major. However, these authors suggested that decided students may still need guidance. For example, a student may need to confirm a tentative decision or clarify the appropriateness of their choice by comparing and contrasting it with other possibilities. Alternatively, a decided student may need help implementing a career choice. Finally, a decided student may have committed to a career path prematurely to reduce stress or avoid conflict with significant others.

Peterson et al. (1996) categorize students who have not made a career decision because they lack specific knowledge as undecided and further subdivide this dimension to include (a) the undecided–deferred, (b) undecided–developmental, and (c) undecided–multipotential student. For some students, it may be appropriate to be undecided–deferred. An example is a first-year college student taking general education classes and exploring career interests. A student who is undecided–developmental is unable to commit to an occupational or major choice due to a lack of self-information, occupational information, or career decision-making skills. These students may need help clarifying their interests, values, skills, and personality, or may need additional career or educational information. Alternatively, these students might need help analyzing and synthesizing information they have gathered. Finally, the undecided–multi-potential category is used to describe students who feel overwhelmed by too many interests, skills, and opportunities (Fredrickson, 1972; Pask-McCartney & Salomone, 1988). In addition to helping these students narrow potential occupational choices, it may be important to help them identify possible barriers to making their decision.

The final category of decision making is the indecisive student. The indecisive student is similar to the undecided student but has a dysfunctional level of anxiety and a maladaptive approach to problem solving (Chartrand et al., 1994; Peterson et al., 1996; Savickas, 1989). This student may be an appropriate candidate for a more formal, comprehensive, and supportive program of career development such as a structured career development workshop. These students may also need personal counseling to learn how to manage their anxiety, which may partially explain their inability to make a decision. Together, these findings point to the importance of developing more comprehensive programs and services to meet the needs of the second-year student.

Changing Nature of Work and Career

Work is a social and economic phenomenon shaped by current contextual forces. Just as the nature and location of work changed as we moved from an agrarian and rural society to one dominated by urban living and manufacturing, so too the nature and location of work today is changing as we move away from an industrial and then post-industrial economy to an information-based and global economy. Today fewer employers offer the potential for lifetime employment (O'Toole & Lawler, 2006; Savickas, 2000). Hierarchical/bureaucratic organizations are diminishing, and flatter organizations are evolving that are more responsive to change. Organizations take advantage of contingent workers and arrange and rearrange noncontingent workers into teams as needed. The competitive edge once held by the United States has been dulled as the result of rapidly expanding economic and workforce trends abroad. Friedman (2005) notes additional forces driving current workforce changes such as open sourcing (global networking/collaborating on a single work project), outsourcing, and off-shoring (transferring work or manufacturing to a foreign location). Savickas (2000) suggests that workers should consider themselves "self-employed" and their employers as "customers" (p. 57). This, he argues, will create a mindset that promotes career self-management, lifelong learning, and a sense of determination and goal striving. Such a mindset will need to be cultivated in today's college students. The sophomore year is a perfect time to begin this mindset development in that it parallels the self-management skills we hope to instill in undergraduate students through their academic and cocurricular experiences.

Not surprisingly, these changes are being reflected in employers' expressed needs. Results from a survey conducted by the National Association of Colleges and Employers (NACE, 2006), for example, suggests that employers want staff who have a strong work ethic; are motivated and show initiative; have highly developed interpersonal skills; and who are adaptable, self-confident, and conscientious. A report from the Secretary's Commission on Achieving Necessary Skills (SCANS, 1991) echoes these findings. In addition to having fundamental communication skills, this report suggests that successful workers will need to have interpersonal skills; be efficient working with data and information; have an understanding of, and skills for working with, organizational and technological systems; and have personal qualities such as responsibility, self-esteem, integrity, and self-management.

Just as educational systems responded to the shift from a pre-industrial to an industrial workforce by formalizing curriculum, separating students by ability and age, decontextualizing content, and standardizing the school day, today's educational systems must respond to the changes that are occurring in our workforce if they are to be successful in preparing students for future work and careers. Many institutions have already made great strides in adapting their educational and student support systems to meet these new challenges.

Student Success Factors

The alarming rates of postsecondary attrition (ACT, 1999, Tinto, 1993) and the profound personal and societal ramifications of this phenomenon (Baum & Payea, 2004; Pascarella & Terenzini, 2005) continue to fuel efforts by educational and psychological researchers to understand and predict postsecondary success and persistence (Astin, 1999; Daugherty & Lane, 1999; Gardner, Keller, & Piotrowski, 1996; McGrath & Braunstein, 1997). Current models of attrition emphasize motivation (Covington, 2000; Eccles & Wigfield, 2002); combine motivation and skill constructs (e.g., Pintrich, 2000; Schunk & Zimmerman, 2003); or focus on the roles of personal context, social support, and student engagement (e.g., Bean, 1985; Tinto, 1993) to account for student success and persistence.

In an effort to integrate extant findings on student success, Robbins and his colleagues' (2004) conducted a meta-analysis of the relationships between psychosocial and study skills constructs and two important college outcomes: academic persistence and college grade-point average. These authors identified nine broad constructs that were predictive of college success: (a) academic motivation, (b) academic goals, (c) institutional commitment, (d) perceived social support, (e) social involvement, (f) academic self-efficacy, (g) general self-concept, (h) academic-related skills, and (i) contextual influences. After controlling for the effects of traditional predictors (e.g., high school GPA and standardized achievement test scores), three psychosocial constructs demonstrated incremental validity in predicting academic performance (academic self-efficacy, achievement motivation, and academic goals), and six constructs were found to be predictive of college persistence (academic goals, academic self-efficacy, institutional commitment, academic-related skills, social support, and social involvement). Subsequent research studies have supported the utility of these constructs in understanding the long-range persistence and performance of two- and four-year college students (Gore, 2006; Gore, Leuwerke, & Turley, 2006; Robbins, Allen, Casillas, Peterson, & Le, 2006).

There exists substantial conceptual overlap between factors that promote student academic success and characteristics employers seek in their employees (Gore & Keller, 2007; see Table 1). For example, students who are conscientious about their student role might also evidence a strong work ethic on the job. The student success factors listed in Table 6.1 were proposed by Robbins and his colleagues (2004) and dovetail nicely with workplace success characteristics described by the National Association of Colleges and Employers. By promoting the development and use of attitudes, skills, and behaviors that promote student success, higher education professionals are simultaneously preparing their students for future workplace success. This observation has not eluded authors and directors of academic and student support services. For example, many leading student success textbooks (e.g., *From Master Student to Master Employee, Your College Experience,* and *Step by Step to College and Career Success*) explicitly acknowledge the relations between academic and workplace success factors.

TABLE 6.1. A COMPARISON OF ACADEMIC AND WORKFORCE SUCCESS FACTORS

Academic Success Factors	Workforce Success Factors
Academic discipline	Work ethic
Goal striving	Motivation/initiative
Commitment to change	Organizational commitment
Social activity	Interpersonal skills
Social connection	Adaptability
Academic self-efficacy	Self-confidence
General determination	Integrity/dependability
Study skills	Job-related skills
Communication skills	Communication skills
Emotional control	Well mannered/polite

Source: NACE *Job Outlook,* 2006.

Theories of Career Development

There are many models of career choice and development (Swanson & Gore, 2000). Most current models share the idea that career development is a process that unfolds over time and that responds positively to intervention efforts. Because development occurs within an environmental context, most theorists also concede that critical junctures in career and academic choice and implementation are, in part, established by our educational and career systems. For example, sophomores at four-year colleges and universities may feel pressure to declare an academic major, whereas sophomores at two-year colleges may face important decisions involving continuing their education by transferring to another institution or transitioning into the workforce. In this section, we briefly review how the dominant theories of career development help guide advisors and other college personnel professionals as they work with second-year students.

John Holland's (1997) person-environment typology and theory of career choice is the most widely studied and applied career theory. Holland suggests that (a) persons and environments can be categorized according to six types (realistic, investigative, artistic, social, enterprising, and conventional; RIASEC), (b) persons tend to seek environments that will allow them to implement the characteristics of their work personality, and (c) behavior is a product of the interaction between personality types and environments. Congruence, or the degree of fit between person and environment, is hypothesized to predict individuals' level of career satisfaction. Although this theory is often criticized for its simplicity, research clearly supports the utility of constructs such as interest and college major fit and Holland's hypothesized structure of academic and career interests.

Second-year students are often in the process of choosing an academic major or confirming a choice they have already made. Holland's typology provides a structure for introducing students to the college major and career exploration process. Formal or informal assessment of career interests may be followed by the use of materials such as the College Majors Finder or Occupations Finder in an effort to help second-year students make more informed academic and career decisions based, in part, on their career interests. Further, the structure of interests and occupations outlined by Holland's theory provides an excellent organizational platform for discussing other factors important in making career decisions such as skills, self-estimates of ability, and work values.

Super (1992) offered a life-span theory of career development, suggesting that individuals adopt many life roles (such as child, spouse, parent, and worker) and that education and work are embedded within those roles. He proposed a series of stages beginning with *growth* in early childhood and moving through *exploration, establishment,* and *maintenance* of a career and into *disengagement* in later life. As with many developmental models, Super's model includes critical developmental challenges that must be overcome before an individual can progress to a subsequent stage. College sophomores may be in the exploration or establishment stages of the model. The primary challenge for a student in the exploration stage is to differentiate and articulate an educational and career self-concept. Sophomores who are already embedded within an academic or career discipline (such as nursing or a skilled trade in a two-year institution) may have one foot in the establishment stage as well, so that their challenge is to become socialized into the discipline and to learn what is required and expected of them in their work.

Super's theory suggests college student programs and services should target specific developmental stages. In particular, programs and services should focus on helping second-year students develop a more comprehensive understanding of their personal interests, attitudes, skills, and values, and become more accomplished at articulating those characteristics to others. Programs should also be developed to facilitate the transition from exploration of college majors to integration into academic colleges and departments.

Lent, Brown, & Hackett (1994) proposed a social-cognitive career theory that describes academic and career-related interest development, choice, and performance. According to this theory, individuals are exposed to academic and career-related experiences based on environmental and personal factors (for example, socioeconomic status, genetics, and personality variables). As a result of their experiences, individuals develop self-efficacy beliefs and outcome expectations for these activities that, in turn, lead to the development of academic and career-related interests. In short, people will develop interests in activities for which they have strong positive self-efficacy beliefs and for which they perceive desirable and highly probable outcomes. In the absence of environmental barriers, and in the presence of environmental support, interests will be translated into academic or career goals and, ultimately, academic or career-related behaviors (such as course enrollment, occupational information-seeking activities, job search behaviors).

This theory highlights the importance of experience, goals, and the role that self-perceptions (self-efficacy beliefs and outcome expectations) have in the career decision-making and implementation process. In our experience, many students, especially those early in the career exploration process, have poorly informed or inaccurate information about the nature of occupations to which they aspire, and many have not spent time reflecting on their short and long-range academic and career goals. Programs should be designed to help students explore their short- and long-term goals and to translate them into a set of realistic actions. Further, programs should promote the development of realistic career and academic expectations and career decision-making and college self-efficacy.

Critical Ingredients in Career Choice Interventions

Fortunately, higher education professionals have some guidance when developing specific interventions to promote the career planning of second-year students. Brown and his colleagues (Brown & Krane, 2000; Brown et al., 2003) found that, of the many strategies used to help students make effective career choices, five specific activities were routinely associated with the most beneficial outcomes. These "critical ingredients" include (a) the use of written exercises, (b) individualized one-on-one attention, (c) use of information about the world of work, (d) modeling, and (e) attention to building supports. For example, second-year students might be encouraged to write summaries of interviews with upper-class students pursuing desirable college majors or to create summary sheets of occupational alternatives and how each of those alternatives fits with their measured interests or work values. Written exercises can also be used to help students list which transferrable or career success skills they currently possess, which they would like to further develop, and how they plan to develop those skills. Brown and his colleagues (2003) noticed that career guidance efforts were more effective if they included an opportunity for students to meet with an individual counselor or advisor. This is not to discount the effectiveness of group or classroom-based career advising but rather to emphasize how those efforts should include mechanisms for students to meet with advisors personally at some point to discuss their academic and career plans.

In addition to written exercises and individualized attention, students should have access to reliable and current sources of academic and occupational information. There are a growing number of reliable public and private sources for occupational information—many of them available via the Internet. Based on results from his 2003 study, Brown suggests that introducing students to educational and occupational information may be the most important of the five key ingredients. It is critical that advisors or counselors take the time to ensure students develop confidence in their ability to use the information system. (For more information about sources of occupational information, readers are referred to Gore & Hitch, 2005.

Modeling refers to the process of exposing students to individuals who can share their experiences for the purpose of advancing the career development of the student. There are many opportunities to include models in the career guidance domain. For example, many advising offices have developed peer advising programs to capitalize on the benefits of using age-related peers to help students identify potential educational and career directions. Alternatively, students involved in service-learning opportunities, internships, externships, and academic clubs and societies are likely to increase the number of relevant adult models to which they are exposed.

Finally, helping students build their support network will go a long way to prepare them for a successful transition into their major and the world of work. A support network might include such resources as the O*NET (for occupational information), an alumni association, friends, family, advisors, and professors. Getting involved with curricular and cocurricular activities on campus, seeking campus employment or other part-time work opportunities, and taking advantage of career services functions such as on-campus interviewing, employer presentations, or internships are also excellent ways of strengthening a support network.

Institutional Models That Promote Academic and Career Success

Second-year students are at a critical juncture in their academic and career development. Sophomores have "survived" the first year thanks in part to commendable levels of new student support services and programs. The focus of academic and career planning in the second year should not be to survive, but rather to thrive. With the changing nature of work, the workforce demands that students today be prepared with more than content knowledge. Fortunately, the skills, attitudes, and behaviors that students need to develop for a successful workforce transition are the same skills, attitudes, and behaviors that promote success in college. Programs designed to support the academic and career development of second-year students should continue to support students as they solidify their transition into the institution and simultaneously prepare them for their next transitions into an academic major and eventually to a career.

In this section, we review specific college and university curricular and cocurricular models used to promote the career success of second-year students. We emphasize, when possible, the connections with existing career theory, highlight the use of critical ingredients in career choice counseling, and point out which student and workplace success skills are being promoted. On two-year campuses, career development initiatives tend to be developed for all students, whereas at four-year colleges and universities career development initiatives are much more frequently geared toward students at various points in the undergraduate experience.

Northeast Community College

At Northeast Community College in Nebraska, a career-planning course is designed to guide students through a process of career development. Open to all current and prospective students, this one-credit course engages students in career research, educational exploration software, and meetings with advisors. Students focus on their interests, abilities, and values throughout the course through using a variety of print and multi-media resources (Northeast Community College Web site).

Beloit College

Beloit College has a well-developed sophomore program, the Sophomore Year Initiative. A few of the key goals of the program include efforts to provide opportunities for sophomores to cultivate self-knowledge, make informed and thoughtful decisions about their future, and become aware of and use resources for academic and personal planning and growth (Beloit College Web site). As such, this program relies heavily on the theoretical foundations offered by Holland, Super, and Lent, Brown, and Hackett and promotes the development of characteristics for students' academic and workplace success.

Beloit College holds an annual Major Exploration and Declaration Fair in the spring just before the advising period for the upcoming fall semester. The event is collaboration between the first-year and the sophomore-year initiative programs. Among the fun, interactive, and educational activities at the fair, students can learn about opportunities and possibilities related to on-campus and off-campus internships, field experiences, scholarships, and domestic and study abroad. Campus-sanctioned internships, externships, and cooperative programs are excellent ways to promote student socialization into specific disciplines and are most effective with students transitioning from an exploration stage of career development to a choice and implementation stage. These practical experiences promote familiarization with workplace expectations, provide students with an opportunity to develop new transferable skills, and can help students further narrow their career alternatives.

Rensselaer Polytechnic Institute

Rensselaer Polytechnic Institute is a small private four-year university. Its career development center boasts a Sophomore Career Experience that is co-sponsored by multinational companies such as BAE Systems, Exxon Mobil, GE, and IBM. Over the course of a single academic year, the center offers programs such as a résumé workshop, interview preparation, and career exploration and job search workshops. These experiences are restricted to sophomore students who register with the Sophomore Career Experience (SCE). To further promote registration and attendance, the career center has instituted an SCE Rewards Program similar to frequent flyer programs. Students who register with the rewards program and have validated attendance are eligible for multiple giveaways and drawings (Rensselaer Polytechnic Institute Web site).

The SCE program was recently recognized by the National Association of Colleges and Employers (NACE) as one of four institutional recipients of the NACE Excellence Award for College Educational Programming. The SCE program is noteworthy in that it provides an opportunity for career center professional staff to establish an early and ongoing relationship with their second-year students. By focusing students' attention on career exploration and job search strategies in the second year of college, the SCE is, in essence, taking students at the end of one transition (into college) and preparing them for their next transition (to work).

University of Cincinnati

The primary goal of the University of Cincinnati's Sophomore Initiative (CSI) is to retain sophomore students at the university by providing intentional academic and career resources to prevent the "sophomore slump." Funded and supported by the university's alumni association, the program communicates to students that even though their transition from high school to the university is complete, their growth and development continues. Second-year students are encouraged to develop personal connections with alumni and consider internships, co-op, leadership, and research opportunities. It also encourages students to write résumés, engage in mock employment interviews, and learn dining etiquette (University of Cincinnati Web site).

University of South Carolina

The University of South Carolina's The Sophomore Initiative (TSI) includes a number of activities and initiatives. A Web site for sophomores includes information on advising and scheduling, career planning, majors and degrees, planning for graduate school, and enrichment activities. The TSI task force developed and now mails to rising sophomores every summer a brochure outlining important information and "top tips" for second-year students. Information is included about changing majors, academic advising, the Career Center, the Student Success Center, Academic Centers for Excellence, and other resources of special interest to second-year students (USC Web site).

The Career Center at the University of South Carolina hosts a robust Web site with resources for second-year students, including a four-year student plan (http://www.sc.edu/career/studentplan.html). Suggestions for the second year include exploring career interests through information interviewing, job shadowing, part-time jobs, or volunteer work; discovering career options in the career library or through Web resources; remaining involved in student organizations; identifying volunteer opportunities to increase skills and gain experience; maintaining positive relationships with professors and advisors; exploring undergraduate research opportunities; updating résumés; making contact with potential employers at job fairs; and obtaining a career-related summer job.

As interest in second-year student success increases at institutions of all types and the resulting institutional initiatives expand, new approaches will develop. We encourage educators to share their approaches through programmatic Web sites, conference presentations, newsletter articles, research journal articles, and other avenues. Sharing promising practices with the greater higher education community will continue to help second-year students succeed.

Recommendations

Evidence abounds throughout this volume that academic and career issues are of importance to second-year students. Students' personal development and the curricular challenges they face especially affect career development in the second year. The following recommendations are offered to educators desiring to enhance the career development of second-year students.

Connect Efforts to Institutional Priorities

When planning initiatives for sophomores, link goals and objectives to institutional mission, strategic directions, and priorities. Doing so communicates to the entire campus community that the second year and the initiatives designed to strengthen the student experience are related to and extend the institutional mission.

Understand Students

Understanding second-year students is a critical basis for program development. Learn about the experiences of second-year students by establishing a collaborative relationship with the campus institutional research officer. Understanding sophomore student development theory and connecting that knowledge to institutional data can provide a more complete understanding of student needs and characteristics.

Become Aware of the Changing Nature of the World of Work

Follow the futurist writers as they provide information about the ever-changing economic and social factors influencing the world of work. Use that knowledge to shape efforts for second-year students. Develop initiatives based on what work settings will be like when students graduate, not what they have been in recent years.

Become Familiar with Student Success Factors

Study and follow trends and issues related to student persistence and success. Use that knowledge in concert with knowledge about students and the world of work as a basis for evidence-based institutional efforts to promote student academic and career success.

Understand Career Development Theory

Become familiar with theories of career development, and incorporate the best elements from multiple models into institutional programmatic efforts. Program development based on frameworks of empirical research will strengthen program components and will help program administrators continue to grow and development themselves.

Engage Students in Planning Efforts

Make sure that planning efforts include student input. Consider focus groups, surveys, and student representation on committees or task forces. Not only will students help program developers design programs that will appeal to students, but engaging students in program design will be an educational and engaging experience for them as well.

Assess Efforts

Plan for the assessment of new initiatives from the start and build assessment into ongoing efforts. Develop learning outcomes, plan assessment strategies, conduct assessment, and then use results for continuous program improvement. Making data-driven decisions will help prove that programs work and will also provide suggestions for improving them.

Conclusion

Any attempt to develop institutional initiatives designed to enhance the success and development of second-year students must include attention to career and academic development. It is during the second year when students begin to look more seriously at their academic and personal life goals. We have attempted to make a case for increased attention to the developmental nature of second-year students and to provide a theoretical rationale for career-related attention to the second college year. We have also offered examples of institutionally based career-development initiatives for the sophomore year that can be used as ideas to generate additional ideas for program development on other campuses. The second college year is a pivotal time in the lives of students as they progress toward a career and a life after college. Attending to their developmental and career concerns at this point will assist students in becoming productive members of their campus community and, eventually, contributing members of society at large.

CHAPTER SEVEN

CURRICULAR APPROACHES FOR THE INTELLECTUAL DEVELOPMENT OF SECOND-YEAR STUDENTS

Scott E. Evenbeck, Sharon J. Hamilton

The sophomore year is important, but through benign neglect we have done little to attend to the explicit intellectual demands and potential of the second year in undergraduate education. Fundamental to an intentional focus on intellectual development is the recognition that students do not experience this type of development simply as a result of being on campus and completing courses. The first year of college has been the focus of educators' efforts because of the many well-known challenges associated with that transition. As is suggested elsewhere in this book, the sophomore year is also a time of transition, with its own unique set of challenges. Many sophomores are beginning a new path as having declared majors; others are in the process of determining their majors; while still others are weighing their programmatic options. In the second year, students may be increasingly confronted by degree programs fully "packed" with required courses. A range of curricular and cocurricular supports in the sophomore year designed to foster intellectual development will improve students' ability to make choices about majors and individual courses and, one hopes, accelerate degree attainment. In this chapter, we discuss the importance of intentionality in fostering students' intellectual development, review some key programs common to the first year that can be continued into the second year, and offer additional recommendations for second-year programming that will enhance success and improve persistence.

Intellectual Development

A common assumption exists that students develop intellectually as they move through academic programs despite the tremendous variation among under-graduate programs at institutions across the nation. This assumption has been questioned in the literature (Feldman & Newcomb, 1994; Pascarella & Terenzini, 2005) for a host of reasons. A summation of theories of intellectual development leads to one concept that Baxter Magolda (1992) has identified as context. It is the context for learning that we in higher education have the most control over, yet even that control is only partial. As Feldman and Newcomb (1994) and Pascarella and Terenzini (2005) point out, we cannot control the socioeconomic backgrounds of our students, their preparation and predispositions for learning, or their motivations for coming to college. What we can control, once they arrive on campus, are the contexts for learning both in and around the classrooms, the curricular and cocurricular programming we provide, and the supports for moving through the curriculum as successfully as possible.

It is essential that we understand how best to control these contexts for learning because both internal and external stakeholders in higher education are beginning to question the fundamental assumption that intellectual development is an inevitable consequence of a college degree. The work of the Spellings Commission (U.S. Department of Education, 2006), for example, is an influential document demanding greater accountability for teaching and learning at our colleges and universities. Yet demands to demonstrate intellectual development among other important college outcomes come not only from the federal and state levels but also from the corporate level. Employers demand evidence that our students are not just degreed but are also truly educated in those ways of knowing that we associate with intellectual development: critical and creative thinking; communicative competence; ability to integrate and apply knowledge; ability to collaborate to solve problems effectively in a multicultural, global environment; and the ability to engage in society with integrity (Casner-Lotto, 2006).

As a National Center for Education Statistics report indicated (Jones & Hoffman, 1995), very few institutions of higher learning can demonstrate the intellectual growth of their students. Transcripts record courses passed but do not provide evidence of what students actually know and can do. Exit interviews provide some self-reporting on what students think they have learned, but this information is rarely tied to evidence. Employer interviews indicate that although most graduates are knowledgeable about the facts and concepts of their majors, many of them are less qualified than they—and we—think they are in the essential intellectual skills of critical thinking and communicative competence.

As documented in a series of interviews conducted by Floyd and Gordon 1998, it is evident that employers' concerns about graduates suggest that content knowledge is insufficient and that, as Jones (2005) points out, we need to be more intentional in our creation of contexts for learning that will enhance and document intellectual development throughout the undergraduate curriculum, and for sophomores in particular.

Examples of intentional approaches at institutions across the country include gateways to the major, the use of engaging pedagogies, critical inquiry, service learning, study abroad, internships, undergraduate research, common readings, cocurricular leadership opportunities, and curricular-linked on-campus employment. Some of the approaches are continuations of programs that may have begun during the first year; others are designed to address the unique transition issues of sophomores. For example, the Honors College at the University of Vermont uses the second year to have sophomores narrow their field of study and focus on an area of interest. They work with other honors students and faculty in small seminars. The university also requires students to take sophomore seminar courses, which cover a variety of topics, including civil liberties, the environment, and human health. The sophomores are encouraged to pursue cocurricular opportunities such as undergraduate research, internships, and study abroad. All these strategies engage faculty in conversations to intentionally determine how the intellectual demands of the sophomore curriculum will advance students along a continuum of intellectual development, in whatever way the faculty in a particular school, department, or discipline agree to define that concept.

Integration of Experiences That Support Student Learning in the Second Year

Students encounter different approaches to the curriculum when they begin postsecondary study. Many campuses have developmental and remedial classes; most campuses have general education courses; some campuses have core curricula; and, finally, a growing number of campuses have developed core competencies or principles of learning to guide the undergraduate curriculum. As there is increasing attention to a seamless P–16 system as espoused in the Liberal Education and America's Promise (LEAP) project of the Association of American Colleges and Universities (2007), the sophomore year—particularly the curriculum in the sophomore year—is critical in moving students toward the baccalaureate degree. Students in their sophomore year continue in their general education courses and are making the transition to the major. It is a particularly important year to support their intellectual development and provide cohesion within the classroom and with other experiences.

That said, how do we maintain the momentum begun in the first year and support our students as they move into the demands of the second year? The remainder of this section addresses specific strategies for doing just that through the curriculum, pedagogical approaches, integration of experiences, and the cocurriculum.

Develop Curriculum That Spurs Critical Thinking

Ensuring that the curriculum is based on the continuing growth of intellectual demands is critical. We should be expecting "more" of our students in their sophomore year, but we should be able to define what that comprises. For example, if critical thinking is an important intellectual skill, then how do critical thinking abilities differ between the first year and the sophomore year? If integration and application of knowledge are key intellectual skills, how would the intellectual expectations for first-year students differ from those for sophomores? If knowledge of key concepts is important, then how do we differentiate between the kind of conceptual knowledge we expect from first-year students and the kind of conceptual knowledge we expect from sophomore-level students? If we cannot answer those questions, how can we explain to sophomores the kind of intellectual development that we—and they—are aiming for? On an intellectual journey, we are much more likely to reach the desired goal if we can identify what that goal is.

Use Engaging Pedagogical Approaches

First-year improvement initiatives generally introduce a wide range of active pedagogies, such as collaborative learning and interactive learning, which engage students in their academic pursuits. During the first year, these forms of intellectual inquiry entail, of necessity, a general introduction to the academic community. Taking these interactive forms of learning to the next level involves introducing students to the special forms of intellectual inquiry relevant to particular disciplines. Each discipline has its own tacit tradition of how knowledge is discovered and how information is presented, as well as governing paradigms for modes of inquiry and further exploration of discipline-specific concepts. Being introduced to these concepts and processes in very general terms may occur during the first year, but attention to these disciplinary ways of knowing is a natural cognitive transition from the first year to the sophomore year. Ideally, instructors pay explicit attention during the sophomore year to helping students figure out how specialists in the discipline organize and communicate the knowledge of the discipline.

One method of introducing students to discipline-specific forms of intellectual inquiry is the "critical inquiry" course. The critical inquiry program at Brooklyn College (New York) started with a FIPSE grant to provide developmental instruction to students to help them succeed in core and general education courses. The program is designed to help students increase their reading, research, writing, and study skills. At Indiana University-Purdue University Indianapolis (IUPUI), critical inquiry is a one-credit course taught in conjunction with an advanced first-year or sophomore-level course that is challenging for many students. It is intended for students who feel they would benefit from an intentional focus on how concepts are presented and discussed in disciplinary areas that are new to them or that may have presented difficulties in earlier years. Faculty members show students how textbooks, articles, and other documents in the discipline are organized and how knowledge is presented in the discipline. Beyond that, faculty help students understand the kinds of questions that are asked and explored by experts in that discipline and the intellectual tools they bring to bear in trying to answer these questions. By highlighting the salient intellectual forms, processes, and ways of knowing in a particular discipline, critical inquiry courses help students become more successful while concurrently enhancing their intellectual development.

Provide Opportunities for the Integration of Experiences

The Association of American Colleges and Universities (2007) has emphasized the importance of focusing on learning outcomes, including integrative learning, in their LEAP report. They have also articulated Principles of Excellence, which include connecting knowledge with choices and actions. A wide range of experiences provide opportunities for sophomore-level students to connect their learning to real-world experiences.

Service-Learning. Courses that include service-learning enable undergraduates to connect ideas they are learning in sociology, political science, English, and other courses with real people in real situations in their local communities. Since the signing of the National and Community Service Act of 1990, which established a new and independent federal agency to support higher education service programs, funding has been available to develop and document the impact of service-learning programs. As a result, programs have been developed in colleges and universities around the nation. IUPUI staff are in the early stages of implementing a means to document the impact of these programs on student engagement, retention, and performance. The goal is to promote integrated learning through active participation in service experiences; provide structured time for students to reflect by thinking, discussing, and writing about their service experiences; provide opportunities for students to use their skills and knowledge in real-life situations; extend learning beyond the classroom and into the community; and foster a sense of caring for others. (See Chapter Nine for more information on service learning.)

Study Abroad. On the other hand, study abroad enables students to integrate through experience what they know and understand of their own culture with the social, political, economic, and relational customs of other cultures. Clayton Hubbs (2006), the founding editor of *Transitions Abroad*, writes of the important learning integration that occurs:

> I saw that my students who returned from an overseas sojourn—after having worked, volunteered, studied, or simply lived for a period of time in a community—were more open to learning after having encountered cultural values and ways of life different from those they had hitherto taken for granted.

(See Chapter Ten for more information on study abroad programs.)

On-Campus Employment. Educators recognize that internships enable undergraduates to integrate and apply what they are learning in class with the expectations in a corporate culture. However, students can also gain a lot from on-campus employment. For decades, campuses have employed students in clerical positions, food services, and student support services. Until recently, however, students have viewed that kind of work as primarily a way to earn money unconnected to their studies or even, in most cases, to their future employment. As working on campus becomes increasingly identified as having a positive impact on student retention and persistence, institutions are scrutinizing the intellectual and academic benefits of campus-based employment (Pascarella & Terenzini, 2005). For example, IUPUI has introduced a program in which supervisors engage student employees in conversations and even written exercises during which students identify the intellectual demands of their work and relate them both to the IUPUI Principles of Undergraduate Learning and to the career center's inventory of employment skills. In this way, students see that even a job answering the telephone or giving directions engages them in communication skills, integration and application of knowledge, and understanding the needs and interests of diverse cultures. Thus the work experience reinforces classroom learning. Again, the sophomore year is an ideal time to recruit students for campus-based work opportunities so that they can develop these intellectual connections throughout their undergraduate careers.

Undergraduate Research. Recently, undergraduate research has also been acknowledged as a key component of the college learning experience and one that should begin as early as possible in our students' academic careers. Certainly by the sophomore year, students should have widely available opportunities to collaborate meaningfully in research with their professors. The Council on Undergraduate Research stresses the importance of these faculty-student collaborations as a major means of introducing students to and engaging them in the academic enterprise leading to intellectual development. Undergraduate research enables students to apply the scientific and social concepts they are learning within an academic, experimental context so they become not just receivers of knowledge but participants in the discovery of new knowledge. (See Chapter Eleven for more information on undergraduate research.)

Connect Students to the Cocurriculum

At many institutions, the cocurriculum is now partnering with the curriculum much more intentionally, particularly in institutions with common learning outcomes and common learning experiences, or with learning communities that explicitly include cocurricular participation. Confronted with a dizzying array of cocurricular and extracurricular opportunities competing with work or domestic responsibilities, students may opt out of cocurricular learning opportunities unless their connection to curricular learning is made explicit. And yet strategic participation in cocurricular activities, in addition to connecting students more meaningfully to the institution and to their fellow students, can enhance students' understanding of what they are learning in their courses and can add to their potential for graduate school or employment.

The sophomore year is an ideal time in the undergraduate program to develop strategic cocurricular collaborations. For example, student life personnel might collaborate with business faculty to develop leadership opportunities that become part of sophomore-level business classes. At IUPUI, faculty in the School of Liberal Arts collaborate with Division of Student Life personnel and the staff in the Office of Student Affairs to develop opportunities for multicultural fairs, discussions, programs, concerts, exhibits, and poster sessions, with plans for participation to become part of the sophomore-level curriculum. In addition, faculty in political science encourage their sophomores to become engaged in student governance and in the Democracy Plaza, a place where students can meet for candid discussions of social issues. By targeting second-year students for disciplinary clubs and other cocurricular opportunities, this collaboration encourages students to make explicit connections between curricular and cocurricular learning and allows for their assumption of leadership positions during their ensuing undergraduate years.

There are additional ways to be innovative when integrating experiences that support student learning in the curriculum. The key for maximizing the effectiveness of these integrative learning strategies is for students to connect their many undergraduate experiences into a coherent, meaningful story of their learning. Having students collect and organize the artifacts of their learning experiences, and then reflect upon these artifacts in relation to their career goals and life objectives, helps students consider larger contexts for their learning and discover how everything they have done fits into these larger contexts. Since 2006, IUPUI has offered a one-credit course for exploratory sophomores called Career Connections. It was developed to help sophomores integrate self-reflection with major and career exploration. The course emphasizes experiential learning to encourage students to connect with people, activities, and resources that serve as reality checks for their tentative major and career choices. This experiential learning and exploration occurs through information interviewing, networking with alumni mentors, job shadowing, and attending career information events. The pedagogy of the Career Connections class supports the developmental model for sophomores proposed in Schaller's (2005) research. Based on her four-stage theory, Schaller sees the optimal learning environment for college sophomores as one that moves them from lack of engagement to ownership of their learning experiences. To create that environment, Schaller suggests that faculty and staff should encourage students' self-reflection, including exploration outside the classroom, examination of all options, and personal responsibility for their own education.

Technology plays a role in integrating learning strategies into the second year. The capacity of technology to support, document, assess, and enhance all the above initiatives is manifesting itself in the dynamic development of electronic student portfolios. A wide range of commercial, homegrown, and open-source portfolio software is being developed to meet the diverse expectations and needs of campuses across the nation (Jafari & Kaufman, 2006). While many portfolios focus on the first year or the capstone, such as the student portfolios at Portland State University (Oregon), others, such as the electronic portfolios at Bowling Green State University (Ohio), Alverno College (Wisconsin), and LaGuardia Community College (New York) are constructed on the assumption that each student's learning story has important plot elements every year. Explicit attention to designing opportunities for students to include and reflect upon key learning experiences during their sophomore year can help students make those important connections that are essential for their intellectual journey. The electronic portfolio becomes the compass for students to make these connections along the way (see Hamilton & Kahn, 2009).

Lessons from the First Year

Sophomores do not have a separate and distinct curriculum. Second-year students continue to take general education courses, which may have been the whole of their first-year curriculum, while they begin to take more major courses, which will form most of the curriculum of their remaining undergraduate years. Yet it is clear that the second-year curriculum must be connected not only with the past and future years of study, but also take into account intellectual development and connections with intentional programming that wraps around the curriculum. Both the curricular initiatives and other academic supports that follow should aid in helping students make those necessary connections. A number of first-year initiatives might be extended into the second year for this purpose.

First-Year Seminars

Most campuses offer first-year seminars in various forms to help students make the transition to successful postsecondary study. These programs range from extended orientation courses to intentional introductions to the major to topically based seminars of interest to students. The seminars have had a powerful impact on student success and learning.

Adapting the seminar for second-year students may play an equally significant role for these advancing students. Seminars for students in their second year, particularly for students who continue to explore majors and careers, are critical interventions for sophomore students.

Learning Communities

Many campuses offer a set of courses, with interdisciplinary linkages across courses to cohorts of students, providing them with an integrated curriculum in their first years of study. Both the format of the learning communities (for example, interdisciplinary learning or the incorporation of service learning) and the cohort itself have a positive impact on students.

Some majors, for which students are taking largely the same set of classes, often as a cohort, are natural contexts for using the lessons learned from learning communities in the first year for enriching the educational experiences of sophomore students. Johnson C. Smith University, an Historically Black College in Charlotte, North Carolina, offers a sophomore learning community, which builds on the Freshman Academy. In this program, students participate in interdisciplinary research and writing, career development, and civic engagement and make plans for a professional career or to continue their education at a graduate school. Improving retention to the third year and academic progress are also some of the goals of the program.

After having taken general education courses in their first year, sophomores at Stonehill College, a selective, religiously affiliated college near Boston, enroll in two disciplinary courses and a third course as the integrative seminar focused on an issue or question. These learning communities, part of the Cornerstone Program of General Education for the college, include experiential education linked to the learning communities. After taking courses in literature, history, philosophy, and religious studies (grounding in the disciplines) in the first year, Stonehill faculty believed that students would be better equipped for interdisciplinary work as sophomores. Travel programs embedded in the curriculum (domestic and international), related to the themes of the learning communities, have resulted in student reports of increases in self-efficacy (Favazza & Talentino, 2008).

Such an approach for sophomores is ideal. Linking cohorts of students across at least two classes, which is typically the structure of learning communities, infuses interdisciplinary approaches for second-year students. The required curriculum for sophomores at one urban campus included interdisciplinary courses for sophomores, but the approach was abandoned because of logistical concerns with faculty load and teaching loads in general. The common work approach can be successful, as documented at the Washington Center, without the cohort approach of linking courses. In their learning communities research for the Washington Center for Improving the Quality of Undergraduate Education, Lardner and Malnarich (2008) found that learning communities can be successful in integrating learning, but the challenge is in "balancing the importance of disciplinary or field-specific grounding with the power of integrating ideas and approaches to address a substantive issue." Lardner and Malnarich found this approach to designing and assessing successful integrative learning to be "transformative."

Orientation and Advising

Most campuses offer a formal orientation program, giving entering students an introduction to expectations and connecting them with campus. When they attend orientation, students often see their academic advisors and register for classes. Many orientation programs also invite parents and family members to attend to encourage their ongoing support of their students. In addition, many orientation programs now include a common reading for all incoming students.

Sophomores' needs are clearly different from first-year students, but there are several lessons to be learned from this program. A campus could have a mandatory convocation for returning second-year students with an academic focus, perhaps continuing with a common reading included in classes or extending the common reading programming to first-year and sophomore students. At the University of North Carolina at Chapel Hill, the campus has instituted sophomore orientation. The program is clearly designed to meet the unique needs of second-year students, such as helping students narrow their academic interests and giving workshops on summer internships. The program, known as sophomore "reorientation," is "meant to help second-year students sift through the sometimes daunting options for their academic careers. Students . . . receive so much information in their first year that it's sometimes lost by the time they really need it as sophomores" ("Sophomores get chance to reorient," 2007).

Summer Programs

Many campuses now offer bridge programs prior to the beginning of fall classes for first-year students. This is an opportunity for students to engage in learning that is more formal; become familiar with academic expectations; explore majors; develop contacts with faculty, advisors, staff, and other students; and learn to use campus resources. Some bridge programs offer cocurricular programming designed to help students begin their academic careers more effectively. National data show a strong correlation between taking summer classes and educational attainment, so sophomore bridge programs should include formal course work requirements (Adelman, 2006). Other aspects of the program might include campus employment or cocurricular experiences designed for sophomores.

Mentoring Programs

Many campuses offer mentoring services to incoming students. The mentors may be students, faculty, community members, or staff. Persons in mentoring roles support students in academic and personal areas to make the transition to successful postsecondary study. Supplemental instruction, developed at the University of Missouri–Kansas City, is probably the primary program around the world for enhancing student learning where students act as mentors for other students in mastering their courses. As Arendale (1997) points out, the Supplemental Instruction program "became one of the few postsecondary programs to be designated by the U.S. Department of Education as an exemplary educational program." This program can easily be adapted to serve the needs of sophomores. Students, particularly low-income and first-generation students, will be well served by having mentors and peer advisors as the students move to their second years of study.

Another powerful mentoring program is peer-led team learning (PLTL), which "preserves the lecture and introduces a new structure, a weekly two-hour workshop, where six to eight students work as a team to solve carefully structured problems under the guidance of a peer leader" (Varma-Nelson, 2006, p. 19). There are many positive outcomes of the PLTL model, including increased retention, improved GPAs, and greater students' satisfaction with their educational experience. In addition, many students who serve as peer leaders in this capacity report that it is a "transforming experience" (Varma-Nelson, 2006).

Recommendations

Campuses should consider many factors in designing the curriculum of the sophomore year, including the following ideas.

Focus on Student Learning

The articulation and assessment of learning outcomes is central to enhancing undergraduate education. Students in their second year are moving into their majors or continuing their quests to identify majors and careers. It is important in the second-year curriculum, after students have made their start in college but are still in the first half of their academic careers, to stress the expected learning outcomes.

Broaden the Definition of Learning Outcomes

Learning outcomes for students are not only what a student knows but also what the student is able to do. Too often students experience higher education as a place of memorization and passing the hurdles of tests. When students leave a campus, what they know will be important, but what they do will perhaps be more important.

Build on What Students Already Know and Are Able to Do

Much energy of policymakers and educators is now focused on reducing gaps in the educational pipeline. It is critical that the curriculum in the second year of college build on the first year. Faculty do have the opportunity to consider what students know and are able to do as a function of the first year of college. What can those experiences, knowledge, and behaviors bring to a strengthened curriculum in the second year?

Examine and Strengthen Prerequisite Requirements

Campuses have long established prerequisites in certain areas—introductory psychology before abnormal psychology or physical chemistry before advanced geology classes. If there are prerequisite skills and knowledge in first-year classes needed for second-year classes, then articulate and enforce the prerequisites.

Consider Thresholds for Certain Classes

Students too often assemble their classes as a function of work or other schedules with little regard for the overall experience of the curriculum. Students may, for example, choose to delay a speech, math, or writing class—defined by faculty as essential for success in college learning—to a time very late in their undergraduate experience. Consider mandating certain classes for completion by certain levels (for example, speech by the end of the third semester of study) and ensure that there are an adequate number of seats to meet the demand.

Provide More Flexibility in the Curriculum

Despite the emphasis of many professional accrediting bodies for defining the undergraduate experience as a broad and rich experience, not overly focused on the major, the curricula for too many of our students are highly structured with little flexibility in course choice. Changing a major in the second year becomes a near impossibility if the student wants to finish with 120 or so credit hours. The rules of the NCAA now complicate the situation for student athletes who are mandated to be at a certain threshold of total credits for a degree at certain points in the undergraduate years (National Collegiate Athletic Association, 2006). These rules and those defining satisfactory academic progress for financial aid purposes—all motivated by the desire to see students graduate—in fact lead to students abandoning athletic careers to pursue desired majors, being locked into majors in which they have no interest, or moving to generalized majors (admittedly very good programs for many students) instead of pursuing their first-choice major. Although there is no single solution for curricular flexibility, there is a definite need to explore alternatives that will maintain programmatic integrity while concurrently meeting the needs of today's sophomores.

Link the Classroom to the Student Experience Outside the Classroom

Edgerton and others have drawn attention to the powerful pedagogies, such as learning communities, study abroad, internships, service learning, and undergraduate research (Edgerton, 1997; Edgerton, & Schroeder, 2003). The second year is the optimal time to involve students in these strong learning experiences linking classroom learning with powerful contexts for learning outside the classroom.

Put Students in Leadership Contexts

Students in their first year of collegiate study are often helped by other students in peer support roles (such as orientation leaders, supplemental instruction leaders, and peer advisors). Students in their second year of study are close to the experiences and understanding of entering students—with appropriate selection and training they are excellent campus resources for serving entering students. The impact on the students in these roles is very powerful.

Provide Mentors

Although second-year students are ideal mentors for entering students, they also benefit from being mentored. They are well served by upper-division students or alumni whose majors and careers give students connections with their interests and who help them navigate the second year.

Focus on Careers

First-year students are often exploring majors and career interests as they take introductory courses and participate in curricular and cocurricular contexts designed to give them information and experiences to help them make good choices. Sometimes students take career exploration inventories or use Web resources designed to help them make choices. Some campuses offer externships, mini-internships, or job experiences in which students can have a better understanding of careers. Yet often students in their first year are primarily focused on taking general education courses and making the transition to postsecondary study. The second year, when they may begin to experience anxiety or parental pressure on making a career choice, is the ideal time to structure curricular experiences to help students make such decisions. These may take the form of separate courses, modules included in other classes, or cocurricular services available at set times or by appointment for students to explore their career interests.

Use Technology

There is some evidence that students' use of technology has a positive impact on their learning (Junco & Mastrodicasa, 2007). Campuses, working alone and with one another and sometimes with vendors, can provide electronic resources, contextualized in courses or in career centers, to help students explore their interests.

Help Students Consider Alternate Degree Programs

Many students are unable to enter their preferred major due to capped enrollments or highly competitive admissions protocols. Nursing provides a case in point, wherein there are far more students meeting the published qualifications to enter the program than most nursing schools can accommodate. Developing and advising students of related alternative career paths can result in fewer students who are not admitted to their first choice dropping out of college. Externships and other field experiences coupled with courses and career services will help students identify appropriate alternative degree programs.

Conclusion

Most important, for sophomores and for all students, is to build on what students know and are able to do while considering their intrinsic interests and values as we help them develop pathways to graduation. In accreditation self-studies and in program evaluations, campuses are increasingly focused on the success of entering students. Hence there is substantial and increased attention to student learning and the retention of students who move from the first to second year of postsecondary study. The assumption that they move seamlessly to success in their majors after a year of interventions is false. Attention to the curriculum and academic supports in the second year is fundamental for enhancing student learning and achievement for all students in postsecondary education. Recognition of the sophomore year—and the curriculum and cocurriculum in that year—is critical to enhancing student academic achievement and persistence.

CHAPTER EIGHT

THE CRITICAL ROLE OF FACULTY AND FACULTY DEVELOPMENT IN SOPHOMORE SUCCESS

Laurie A. Schreiner

Students return for their second year of college with a sense of positive antic-ipation. Although many find their expectations are fulfilled, those whose expectations are not met often find themselves in a "slump"—experiencing reduced motivation, lower academic performance, and even leaving the insti-tution as a result. According to the *Sophomore Experiences Survey* (described in Chapter Three), about 14 percent of sophomores report that their second year is "worse or much worse" than their first year of college. These are the students who are "slumping" in their motivation and performance and may be poised to leave the institution. Motivation and engagement in learning are key issues for the sophomore year, yet little attention is paid to them in the training and development of most faculty. This chapter highlights aspects of the sophomore experience that mitigate against engaged learning and the principles of motiva-tion that foster greater levels of student engagement. It applies these principles specifically to the issues that are most salient for the sophomore year and outlines recommendations for faculty development emerging from research on sophomores.

Although engagement is not a uniquely sophomore issue, certain aspects of the sophomore experience can become obstacles to engaged learning. The following scenario highlights many of these features:

Katie is a sophomore psychology major who is eager to be back on campus. She feels a sense of accomplishment as she considers how well she did in her first-year classes, and she is looking forward to getting into classes in her major. She is eager to reconnect to her friends, get to know more of the faculty in the psychology department, and become involved in internships or research related to her interests.

As she arrives on campus, she compares her fall class schedule to those of the friends she made last year—and her heart sinks. None of her friends are in any of her classes, and the courses she really wanted to take were all full by the time she registered. She has a large lecture section of U.S. history, when she had hoped to take world cultures. She hates chemistry, so she put it off until this year so that she would have a good first year of college. Some of her courses look promising, but then there's statistics, that "killer" course required of all psych majors in the sophomore year.

As Katie heads to her first history class, she is already feeling discouraged. There's nothing to look forward to this year, she thinks. She hopes there's a seat in the back of the room, so that when the lecture gets too boring she can text her friends without being noticed. She walks into the cavernous lecture hall that seats 500 and watches the professor load his PowerPoint presentation and dim the lights. She realizes she could spend the next hour doing almost anything she wants without being noticed. . . .

Some of the curricular experiences sophomores may encounter are large lecture-style courses, survey courses that cover a vast array of introductory material in a discipline that students will never study again, and "killer" courses that are designed to weed out students in the early stages of a particular major. Students may also be enrolled in courses they simply do not want to take—courses they put off during the first year and ones that were chosen because they were the only ones available at the time of registration. Such experiences can have a dramatic impact on sophomores' levels of motivation about their learning experiences. In a recent study of sophomores' experiences at 26 public and private four-year colleges and universities (see Chapter Three) one student expressed his concern as follows:

> I feel as if many of my classes are pointless. I know I am attending a liberal arts college so I can become a "well-rounded" person, but most of those core classes remind me of being in high school again. The professors know that students are only in the class to fill up their core, so they don't seem to care as much.

Lower-division courses aimed toward students in their second year can be among the most challenging to teach. Particularly in the type of survey courses that typically exist at larger institutions with distributive general education requirements, students may enter the course with little intrinsic interest in the topics, the lecture-style class sections make it difficult to engage students in active learning, and the size of the classes often prevents faculty from connecting personally to students. Even in smaller institutions or in institutions that attend carefully to class size, the array of lower-division courses that compose a sophomore's course schedule are among the most challenging to teach, as a mix of class levels, abilities, and student interests are often represented in the classroom. As Evenbeck and Hamilton noted in Chapter Seven, additional challenges are posed by the variety of career decision-making stages in which sophomores may find themselves. Some sophomores are clearly decided on their major and anxious to be fully involved in major courses. For them, many of the sophomore-level courses are hurdles toward the courses in which they are most interested. For other students, the major they had planned to pursue has not materialized. Due to highly competitive admissions processes and caps on enrollment in their preferred major, or due to their poor academic performance in their first year, these students face different challenges with engaging in courses during the sophomore year. Their intrinsic interest lies elsewhere, and they may feel lost as to how to proceed to choose another major. And finally, some second-year students are continuing with the exploration begun in their first year and are taking courses in an attempt to find something that captures their interest. As a result, engaging sophomores in the learning experience can be particularly challenging, because all three types of students may be sitting in the same classroom but with different expectations and levels of interest in the course.

The paradox is that many times the faculty who teach lower-division courses in which sophomores are likely to be enrolled are those who are least equipped for the challenge. Adjunct or part-time faculty who leave campus after teaching the class, junior faculty with little teaching experience, those who have been newly hired and have not yet obtained the seniority to teach the upper-division courses in the major are often the faculty who are assigned to teach courses at the sophomore level. And in all but the rarest of cases, they are faculty who have had little or no training in pedagogy and may not receive adequate support in the form of faculty development to help them engage students in the learning process in these classes.

Is it any wonder that some of the comments we hear from sophomores reflect high levels of disengagement in the classroom? In the *Sophomore Experiences Survey* (Schreiner, Chapter Three), we heard such comments as, "I actually dread going to my classes most of the time," and "it seems like a lot of busy work, not much learning or new ideas relating to my major." Students reported "too many classes taught by TA's" or "adjunct professors who are rarely on campus and aren't available to answer my questions," and expressed that many of the classes they were taking were ones that "no one would take unless they were required."

The Sophomore Experience

Engaging students in their own learning is the primary challenge all educators face, whether teaching sophomores or not. Yet there are aspects of the sophomore experience that might be helpful for faculty to understand more clearly as they prepare to teach courses at this level.

As already noted, second-year students are frequently enrolled in courses that do not hold a great deal of intrinsic interest for them (Slavin Miller, Schreiner, & Pullins, 2008). If they are taking courses that they deliberately postponed because of fear of failure, their lack of academic preparation for the course may be compounded by emotional barriers to their success. Their concerns about their competence may lead to anxiety and fear (Perry, Hall, & Ruthig, 2005).

The second aspect of the sophomore experience that may be helpful for faculty to understand is that many of these students are in a stage of what Schaller (2005) calls "focused exploration" (p. 21; also see Chapter Four in this volume). One of the major developmental tasks that tends to occur in the second year of college is exploration that leads to choices about a major and provides a sense of direction about the future. In talking to sophomores, it is not uncommon to hear phrases such as, "I can't justify this amount of tuition when I don't know what I'm doing with my life," or "I need to find out who I am before I put my life into a box." There is considerable anxiety around deciding on a major and discovering whether that major is a good fit. Some sophomores have chosen a major but have done so because of the external pressure and the need to graduate on time, and as a result they may feel stuck with a choice they are discovering was the *wrong* choice. Their focused exploration in the second year may have a sense of urgency about it that may translate to frustration with courses that appear unrelated to their interests or to a potential major. Practical applications and relevance to their lives and futures are paramount among their expectations for a class. They need to see the connections between what they are learning in class and what they will need in order to be successful in the future.

The third aspect of the sophomore experience that may provide helpful insights to faculty is that relationships develop a new dimension for students in their second year. Although many sophomores begin to solidify their friendships, those who find themselves having to establish all new relationships are more at risk during this year, as satisfaction with peers contributes most to their overall satisfaction with the college experience (see research in Chapter Three). Several sophomores in the *Sophomore Experience Survey* noted that they were lonelier than in their first year, and many commuter students were disappointed that the friends they had made in their first-year classes were no longer in any of their sophomore courses. Courses that engage students with each other, as well as with the course material, provide a key opportunity to address the relational challenges of the second year.

Finally, sophomores report becoming more intentional and selective about their involvement on and off campus as they learn they cannot continue to juggle work, cocurricular activities, and friendships and family relationships in the same way now that their academic demands are increasing. Their relationships with faculty become more important as they are seeking direction about their "possible future." As discovered in the *Sophomore Experience Survey*, student-faculty interaction and satisfaction with that interaction were significant predictors of every sophomore success outcome studied. Classes that capitalize on relational dimensions are likely to engage students—and the more engaged students are, the more likely they will be to seek out faculty for further dialogue outside of class.

Engaged Learning

Shift the scene to a sophomore class as it could be—engaging the student in what John Tagg (2004) calls "deep learning," the kind of learning that lasts well beyond the final exam:

As Katie walks into her statistics class—the one she heard was a "killer" course to weed out students from the psychology major—she notices that the seats are arranged around tables of four. The professor introduces herself as Katie looks for a spot and explains that helping nervous psych majors master the art of "sadistics" is one of her favorite things to do. As students get settled, the professor asks everyone to complete an index card with their contact information but then also asks that they include "anything I need to know about you to help you learn more effectively."

The professor tells the students that learning statistics is like learning a new language or using a new tool. It may feel unfamiliar and awkward at first—and some may feel they don't have what it takes because their family or culture told them they don't have a math brain. But then she tells them there's no such thing as a "math brain"—that anyone can learn statistics if they invest the time and energy. She explains that there are strategies for learning statistics and that it's her job to teach students those strategies. She further explains that they will work in learning teams on real-life problems throughout the semester. She tells the students a little about her background and training, but focuses mostly on how she became interested in statistics despite being "not that great at math" when she was younger. She tells them that her goal for the semester is for them to be able to see how statistics is used in psychology as well as in their daily lives. She reminds them that they are entering a profession whose language is statistics, and that by the end of the semester they will not only be able to read and understand research that uses this language, but they will also be able to design it themselves. She tells the students that the course will challenge and stretch them, but not beyond what they are capable of. "You'll be surprised at what you can do by the end of the semester," she assures them.

As Katie leaves class the first day, she is excited about taking the first step toward becoming a professional psychologist. She thinks about her initial fear of this class and realizes that fear has been replaced by a new emotion she hasn't experienced very often in her academic career so far: genuine interest.

What are the hallmarks of the scene described above? They all contribute to *engaged learning*, defined as "a positive energy invested in one's own learning, evidenced by meaningful processing, attention to what is happening in the moment, and involvement in specific learning activities" (Schreiner & Louis, 2006, p. 9). There is a positive energy in a classroom where students are engaged. Their interest and attention is captured, connections are made that enable them to meaningfully process the information so that it sticks with them, and there is an active participation in the learning process.

Tagg (2004) refers to many of these elements as features of a "hot cognitive economy" (p. 14) in the classroom. They are intended to capture students' interest and generate "authentic motivation" (Ryan & Deci, 2000, p. 69) to engage in the learning process. The following sections expand on each of these elements and connect them to particular aspects of the sophomore experience that are most salient.

A Sense of Community in the Classroom

Although a sense of community is a powerful predictor of retention and graduation for all levels of students (Schreiner, 2007a), it becomes particularly important for sophomores who may be feeling "invisible" as the institution shifts its collective attention to the next incoming class. In a study of sophomore retention in 31 faith-based liberal arts colleges (Juillerat, 2000), one of the key features that distinguished sophomores who left their institutions from those who remained enrolled was their significantly lower levels of a sense of community.

Particularly for sophomores who commute and for students attending two-year colleges, the classroom is the primary location where a sense of community can be developed on campus. A sense of community comprises four key elements:

(a) *membership*, or a sense of belonging; (b) *ownership*, or a sense of voice and contribution; (c) *relationship*, or emotional connections with others in the community; and (d) *partnership*, or an interdependence in working toward mutual goals (Schreiner, 1998).

The first day of class sets the tone for the development of a sense of community. As the instructor emphasizes relationships between student and professor, as well as among the students as fellow learners, students begin to see themselves as members of a group that will develop into a community. Sophomores whose friends from the first year are no longer in any of their courses can begin to establish a new network of friendships and can feel confident that this network will contribute to their learning, as it is woven into the course itself. As a result, a sense of membership that leads to feelings of belonging begins to develop. Learning teams enable students to form emotional connections, and as a group, students can accomplish more than they could individually. Encouraging feedback from students fosters the sense of ownership by communicating to students that they have a voice and that their contribution to the class matters. Two ways of encouraging this type of feedback include the use of classroom response systems—also known as "clicker technology" (Bruff, 2009)—in which student input is gathered via handheld clickers and is immediately evident by their survey responses on a screen in front of the classroom, and the use of the "one-minute paper" (Cross, 1998) at the end of a class session, which asks students to write down one thing they learned in class that day and one question they have about the material.

Knowledge About Students and How They Learn

In a study of 20 colleges and universities participating in the Documenting Effective Educational Practice (DEEP) project (Kuh et al., 2005), one characteristic held in common by these institutions was a strong commitment to knowing their students, "where they came from, their preferred learning styles, their talents, and when and where they need help" (p. 301). These 20 institutions were ones where levels of student engagement in behaviors empirically linked to learning were higher than predicted, given their institutional features. Particularly in the sophomore year, as issues of identity development may not have been resolved, this knowledge can not only be useful to the instructor but can also provide opportunities for reflection and dialogue that will facilitate students' identity development.

Collecting information from students about their interests, previous experiences, and what facilitates their learning can be helpful, as can institutional information about the types of students who enroll. But even more individualized information about students can connect them in powerful ways that can foster their engagement in class. Intentionally asking sophomores about where they are in the career decision-making process, or discovering how sure they are of their major and how they feel about taking the course, can provide instructors with information that may help them motivate students more effectively. Some instructors administer a short inventory of students' learning styles and ask students to write a paragraph about how their learning style might affect their experience in the class. Others use a more involved process of identifying their students' strengths and possible contributions to the class. They assign students to take an inventory outside of class and journal about their results, then to come prepared to discuss with their learning team in class the strengths that each person on the team contributes to their mutual learning. Examples of such inventories for identifying students' strengths include the *Clifton StrengthsFinder* (The Gallup Organization, 1999) and the *VIA Classification of Strengths* (Peterson & Seligman, 2002). Through such exercises and opportunities for written reflection and group discussion, instructors can connect to students in sophomore-level classes and find personal ways of engaging them in the course.

In *What the Best College Teachers Do*, Bain (2004) notes that the best instructors look for what each student brings to the learning environment and communicate both appreciation and respect for those individual talents. These faculty have great faith in students' ability to achieve and appear to subscribe to what Kuh and his associates (2005) term a *talent development approach*, "the notion that every student can learn under the right conditions" (p. 77). By actively collecting information in sophomore-level classes about each student and what he or she brings to the class, instructors have a powerful means of connecting to the diverse students in their classrooms and communicating that each student is an important contributor to the learning process.

Growth Mindset and Academic Control

Students' beliefs about themselves and their abilities can have a pronounced effect on the way they approach the learning experience. Students who perceive their intelligence and other attributes to be relatively innate and unchangeable have a fixed mindset, according to Dweck (2006). In contrast, students with a *growth mindset* see their attributes as malleable with effort. What difference does this make in the classroom? As it turns out, these self-theories create meaning systems that affect students' goals, investment of effort, responses to failure and setbacks, and even the strategies they use to learn (Dweck & Molden, 2005).

Students who are taught to approach the learning process with a growth mindset place a higher priority on their own learning and growth as a result.

Rather than focusing on grades or exam performance, they focus on learning for its own sake, for what difference it makes in their lives. This focus on learning leads them to invest more effort in the learning process, for they perceive effort as a natural part of learning. For them, effort is what leads to greater learning—a conclusion that Robbins and his colleagues (2006) have verified across large samples of college students. This perception of effort is in sharp contrast to those with a fixed mindset who perceive effort as an indication that a person is not naturally bright or competent.

Students' mindset also affects how they interpret feedback and respond to failure. Those with a fixed mindset view failure as a threat to their self-esteem; thus, feedback is perceived as criticism and tends to be avoided or ignored. Students with a growth mindset tend to view failure as a temporary setback; for them, feedback is helpful information on how to change their strategies in order to be more successful. As a result, the strategies employed by students with a growth mindset are quite different from those used by students with a fixed mindset. A growth mindset appears to promote active strategies to master course content: deep-level study strategies, time management, and the self-regulated learning that leads to mastery. In contrast, a fixed mindset appears to foster defensive or avoidant strategies that mitigate against learning: procrastination, not asking for help, taking a surface approach to memorizing material for a test, and giving up when tasks become difficult (Dweck & Molden, 2005).

As sophomores enter their second year of classes, they may have a fixed mindset that has been reinforced by their successes as well as their failures in their first year. They may have become adroit at avoiding courses that require the level of effort that they perceive may highlight their lack of competence. Their experiences of failure may have led them to conclude that they have little control over their academic future and that any further effort is pointless. Because sophomore-level courses are often considerably more challenging to students than first-year courses, the instructor becomes even more important in conveying to students the role that effort and effective learning strategies play in their success.

Instructors in sophomore-level classes can encourage a growth mindset the very first day of class. As highlighted in the scenario earlier in this chapter when the statistics professor emphasized that there is "no such thing as a math brain," dispelling myths and giving students information about how the brain changes as a result of the learning process can foster a growth mindset. When the instructor stressed that statistics could be mastered by investing the time and energy to learn the strategies that she would teach them, she demonstrated that student learning was under their control and that there were specific strategies for success. Throughout the course, feedback to students that acknowledges the *actions* they took to be successful, rather than praising how smart they are or how "good at stats" they are, will continue to cultivate a growth mindset.

Encouraging a growth mindset in sophomores can have multiple positive effects. Because a growth mindset focuses on learning as the goal, it fosters the acquisition of effective strategies for learning. The focus also provides students with a greater sense of academic control, and students who are in transition are in particular need of feeling in control. As sophomores transition into more difficult courses where there is less support, they may experience uncertainty about their ability to be successful. By teaching sophomores a growth mindset, professors can affect students' feelings of control, which in turn increases their motivation to learn, their level of effort invested, and their persistence in the face of setbacks (Perry, Hall, & Ruthig, 2005).

A growth mindset can also protect students from the debilitating effects of stereotype threat. Stereotype threat occurs when capable students are negatively affected by reminders of cultural stereotypes regarding their ability (Steele, 1997). Students who are taught a growth mindset demonstrate a significant increase in their valuation of academic work and in their enjoyment of it, and they appear to be inoculated against the impact of negative stereotypes that may affect the academic performance of African American students, in particular (Aronson, Fried, & Good, 2002).

Connections for Learning

Parker Palmer (1998) writes that "good teachers possess a capacity for connectedness. They are able to weave a complex web of connections among themselves, their subjects, and their students so that students can learn to weave a world for themselves" (p. 11). Learning is all about making connections. These connections may be to what the learner already knows or feels, to other experiences that the learner has had, to what the learner naturally finds interesting, or to meaningful goals. Learning is an active process of making meaning through these connections (Tagg, 2003).

In student comments from the *Sophomore Experience Survey*, it was clear that sophomores were most engaged when their courses connected to their current interests or to what they envisioned themselves doing in the future. When that did not happen in the classroom, students reported feeling bored, as noted in the comment, "most of my classes are a waste of my time. I am not learning anything foundational for my life as an adult."

For sophomores who are struggling to find a sense of direction and make decisions about a major and career goal, the learning experience in the classroom can seem disconnected from this process. They may not be able to see clearly the connections between what they are learning and what they want to do in life, and they sometimes expect the connections to be immediate and concrete. Thus, part of an instructor's role may be to help sophomores create meaning for themselves, rather than making meaning for them. As a number of theorists emphasize, knowledge is actively constructed rather than passively received (Baxter Magolda, 1999; Bransford, Brown, & Cocking, 1999; Vygotsky, 1978). The role of the professor is to light the fire of motivation that leads students to construct such learning for themselves. We do this by crafting a learning environment that facilitates student engagement, supports the autonomy necessary for authentic motivation to flourish, and provides meaningful opportunities to connect the course content to important issues in their present or future lives.

Lee Shulman (1999) has asserted that the first influence on new learning is not what instructors do pedagogically but what is already inside the learner. Thus, it becomes important to ascertain what the learner already knows. This process might include a survey given the first day of class so the instructor has a grasp of where each student is beginning in the course content. Even for large classes, calculating the average score and the range of scores on a "pretest" for what will be taught in the semester can help the instructor target the class to build on what students already know.

Connecting to students' current knowledge and experiences can also occur through asking students to journal outside of class about their learning process, or to write a paper describing what they already know or experiences they have already had with the course content. Class discussions can focus on the worldviews and assumptions that students bring to the class from their families of origin or the subcultures and environments in which they live. Instructors can ask students to identify their goals for the class or can gather information about students' majors, career plans, or life goals. This information provides instructors with ways of connecting to students and helping students connect to the course content.

Active Learning

Classroom learning experiences that actively engage students with the content and with each other lead to greater learning (Chickering & Gamson, 1987). Sophomores are often in the process of solidifying relationships that began in their first year, but many are trying to form new peer networks that are more supportive and connected to their major interests. The classroom can provide a context for the development of these relationships.

In the *Sophomore Experience Survey*, one sophomore wrote at length about how her relationships had changed in her sophomore year and the important role that the classroom played in that process. She pointed out that connecting with other students who had her same interests resulted in greater enjoyment of the learning process. Compared to relationships in her first year that were more "social and fun-oriented," she described a more close-knit group of friends in her major and reported that "I think about practical applications and talk about the topics in my classes now." Such comments reflect the importance that emotional connections and relationships play in the learning process.

While the classroom can provide a context for these relationships, many students also develop complex social networks online. Instructors who design their courses to capitalize on technology and the social networks created on the Internet can leverage the relationships that students naturally form both in and out of the classroom. Particularly for students who do not feel comfortable actively participating in class discussions, Internet chats and blogs can provide a means by which they can connect their learning to the learning of others.

Active involvement in learning not only encompasses involvement with other learners, but also involvement with the course content. In *The Courage to Teach*, Palmer (1998) refers to *subject-centered teaching* that puts "a great thing at the center of the pedagogical circle" (p. 116) to introduce students to a world larger than themselves. An intentional focus on student interaction with the subject matter enables them to experience first-hand the passion and energy that exists in the discipline. It also sends an empowering message to students. It communicates that they are learners who are capable of discovering, analyzing, and constructing knowledge together, with the expert guidance or coaching of the instructor to support them in that process. As sophomores engage in the preliminary courses in their major, it is important to convey what it means to be a professional in that discipline.

Creating learning teams in the classroom can be a powerful way of connecting learners and course content. Such teams can capitalize on the strengths each individual contributes to the group process and can foster interdependence and multiple perspectives, while also holding individual learners accountable. Learning teams are most effective when the task they are assigned to complete requires higher-order thinking skills and group synergy that goes beyond what the students have learned individually (Nilson, 2003). Specific, structured tasks that are harder to complete than an individual could do alone tend to produce the greatest amount of learning (Michaelsen, Knight, & Fink, 2002). Even in the large survey courses that may be an unavoidable feature of the sophomore experience, such learning teams can create a psychologically smaller class size and can solidify the concepts from the texts and the lectures.

The Importance of Feedback and Choice

One of the ingredients necessary for learning to occur is feedback. Frequent, specific, and informative feedback targets actions the student can take to move to higher levels of excellence. When such feedback is constructive rather than critical, it also motivates students to do their best (Kuh et al., 2005). Students care deeply about how their instructors evaluate their work, and many faculty agonize over the evaluation process, yet "evaluation done well is one of the most significant spurs to learning" (Brookfield, 2006, p. 174). Frequent feedback to students on their progress toward meeting the learning goals they have set for themselves demonstrates that instructors are responsive and care about their learning.

The most helpful feedback to students is (a) timely, (b) clear and specific, (c) regular, and (d) individually educative (Brookfield, 2006; Chickering & Gamson, 1987; Kuh et al., 2005). Timely feedback allows students the opportunity to make the changes necessary for future success on assignments in the class. Clear and specific feedback communicates the criteria used to assess the student, gives examples of where the student met the criteria or not, and outlines actions the student can take to improve, all in language the student can understand. Regular feedback creates a communication loop between the student and the professor that signals the expectation that the student should be continually progressing toward his or her learning goals. When that feedback is also individually educative, it provides the student with a clear path for reaching those goals. The focus is on what the student has done to be successful and on what can be learned from the feedback that provides direction for future success (Brookfield, 2006).

It is even more challenging providing this kind of feedback in large lecture courses that are common in the sophomore year, particularly in larger institutions. Instructors may be tempted to rely on multiple-choice exams and computerized test forms for ease of grading. Yet in the sophomore year, instructive feedback that is customized to the student can be of enormous help beyond success in just that class. Such feedback can form the foundation for the sophomore exploration and help refine the decision making about choices of major and career. In the *Sophomore Experience Survey* students reported that the encouragement and feedback they received, often in an unexpected area, led them to reconsider aspects of themselves and their future.

Providing choice in assignments is also an important aspect of engaging students in the learning process. As Ryan and Deci (2000) note, authentic motivation occurs when students' needs for competence, relatedness, and autonomy are met. When students are given choices in assignments, within the context of mastering the course content, this process meets important needs for autonomy that fuel their motivation to learn. Choosing an assignment that connects to other interests, their strengths or abilities, their learning style, or to their own learning goals enhances not only their interest in the assignment but also ultimately their performance.

For sophomores who may be struggling with required courses or who find themselves enrolled in courses in which they have little interest, these elements of feedback and choice can be vital to their engagement and success. The feedback from faculty can provide clear pathways to future success on assignments in the course. Having a choice of exam questions or projects can give students a greater sense of control that can be foundational to their success and can enhance the autonomy that leads to greater interest and motivation within the course.

Recommendations for Faculty Development

The challenges to engaged learning in the sophomore year call for strategies that may not be addressed in the opportunities that many colleges and universities offer for faculty development. Encouraging faculty involvement in such opportunities may also be a challenge, as time constraints and heavy workloads prevent greater investment. The best faculty development programs are structured around the recognition that good teaching is not as much about the practices as it is about the person. As Bain (2004) notes:

> The key to understanding the best teaching can be found not in particular practices or rules but in the attitudes of the teachers, in their faith in their students' abilities to achieve, in their willingness to take their students seriously and to let them assume control of their own education, and in their commitment to let all policies and practices flow from central learning objectives and from a mutual respect and agreement between students and teachers. (p. 78–79)

Palmer (1998) echoes this emphasis in his assertion that "we teach who we are" (p. 1). Good teaching flows from a person who is passionate about students, passionate about his or her discipline, and passionate about the learning process. Such teachers do whatever helps students learn, and the way they do that is by constant attention to how students experience their learning and perceive what the instructor is doing (Brookfield, 2006).

Until faculty are encouraged to focus on student learning and to see it as their responsibility to facilitate that process, even the most effective instructional techniques are not likely to have an impact on the students who need it most. Perry, Hall, and Ruthig's (2005) research has demonstrated that students who are most at risk for failure are those with a low sense of academic control; these are also the very students who are least likely to benefit from effective instructional techniques. Yet these same researchers have documented that attending to those students' beliefs about themselves and communicating that there are strategies they can learn in order to succeed in the course can dramatically improve their motivation and academic performance.

Findings such as these underscore the need to address how faculty perceive students and how they understand the learning process. Helping faculty reframe student apathy or underpreparedness and refocus their energies on student engagement can lead to higher levels of learning in their classrooms. Ensuring that they understand the challenges in the sophomore year that affect student learning can assist in this process as well. But how does one create opportunities for faculty to learn how to effectively engage sophomores specifically?

There are three key recommendations for faculty development opportunities that will have a positive impact on sophomore success.

Emphasize Connections and Authenticity

The first is to emphasize faculty connecting authentically to students and becoming what Brookfield (1995) calls a "critically reflective teacher." This process is enhanced when faculty become part of a community of learners with other faculty members and can talk openly about their teaching (Palmer, 1998). Teaching is typically a very private practice that colleagues rarely observe; talking about teaching provides a glimpse into this private world and allows faculty to reflect on who they are when they teach. From these conversations often emerges the realization that effective faculty are not all alike. They approach the teaching process in their own unique style, capitalizing on their own set of gifts and strengths to facilitate the learning process. This recognition can bolster the confidence of instructors and can encourage them to focus on how their own strengths can be leveraged to enhance student learning.

When faculty know themselves and are encouraged to teach from their own strengths, they are likely to be more authentic with students. This authenticity is one of the hallmarks of effective teachers. Authentic teachers are viewed as "allies in learning" (Brookfield, 2006, p. 67) who have students' best interests at heart. They are persons of integrity whose actions match their words and who can be counted on to do what they say they will do. As a result, they can be trusted. They explicitly communicate their expectations, reveal the criteria by which they will evaluate students' work, respond to students' needs in ways that foster learning, and are transparent about how they interpret, think about, and struggle with the big questions of the discipline and the course. They use personal examples and stories that connect to students in ways that enhance learning and foster a sense of community in the classroom. They constantly attend to how their actions affect students' learning and actively seek student feedback about the learning process.

One of the strategies that some institutions use to encourage faculty to dialogue about their teaching is to develop faculty learning communities. Although their format varies, these communities typically involve 8 to 12 faculty in a collaborative year-long process of focusing on engaged teaching and learning. The emphasis is on community building, the scholarship of teaching and learning, and activities that provide opportunity for dialogue and reflection about learning experiences (Cox, 2004). Specifically, creating an opportunity for small groups of faculty who teach sophomore-level courses to meet regularly to focus on the needs of sophomores and how to engage them in the learning process could allow for a deeper understanding of the challenges of these courses and could provide support for these faculty, many of whom are among the least experienced in the institution.

Focus on Engagement

The second recommendation for faculty development programs to foster sophomore success is to keep the focus clearly on the engagement process. For example, faculty may respond more positively to professional development opportunities that target "engaging today's students in learning" than to opportunities labeled as workshops to "improve teaching skills." In Sorcinelli's (2007) survey of faculty developers, the most important need identified was for learner-centered teaching seminars. A focus on student learning and engagement enables faculty to explore the role that motivation plays in learning; as a result, they are likely to examine what they do in the classroom through a different lens. When they become acquainted with the array of students' learning styles, background experiences, and social capital that exists within their institution, they are likely to perceive their students through a different lens as well. Faculty who are exposed to the issues that are most salient to sophomores can begin to tailor their approaches in the classroom to sophomore needs. The end result is that instructors critically reflect on the learning process and create ways of fostering learning more effectively in their own classroom.

Include Faculty Engagement Initiatives

The third recommendation for a faculty development program that would enhance sophomore success is to structure such a program around the key principles that foster faculty engagement. Just as students' learning styles, strengths, cultural capital, previous experiences, and needs for competence, relatedness, and autonomy all affect the extent to which students engage in the learning process, these same elements are critical ingredients for engaging faculty in their own learning process about student engagement. As a result, structuring a variety of learning opportunities for faculty is likely to lead to greater investment in the process. The three human needs that must be met for authentic motivation are competence, relatedness, and autonomy (Ryan & Deci, 2000). Addressing these three needs through a variety of programming can lead to faculty being authentically motivated to focus on student learning. Workshops that focus on specific ways of engaging students may address faculty needs for competence. Small group discussions, book groups, faculty learning communities, mentoring networks, and conversations about teaching can meet needs for relatedness. Perceiving the variety and having a choice about which programs to attend will meet instructors' need for autonomy. Institutions that offer a variety of options for faculty to understand how students learn and what their particular needs are in the second year of college provide a means for faculty to gain competence while meeting their needs for autonomy. By also providing opportunities to relate to other faculty who are dealing with the same type of issues, institutions are likely to have the greatest faculty involvement in such programs (Sorcinelli, 2007).

Conclusion

Throughout this chapter the focus has been on student engagement in the midst of the challenges of the sophomore year. Although there are many experiences in the second year of college that mitigate against engaged learning, there are also ways in which faculty can positively affect the student learning process despite those challenges. Focusing intentionally on faculty as persons who can have a dramatic impact on the learning process for sophomores, providing opportunities for faculty to learn about student engagement and the challenges of the sophomore year, and structuring those opportunities in ways that engage faculty can lead to a more positive sophomore year experience—not only for the students but also for the faculty who teach them.

CHAPTER NINE

SERVICE-LEARNING IN THE SOPHOMORE YEAR

Steven G. Jones, Robert W. Franco

This chapter explores the role of service-learning in contributing to sophomore success, particularly when integrated into formal second-year programming. For the purposes of this chapter, we define service-learning as the integration of community service into learning activities that have identified and articulated learning objectives and in which structured reflection is required. Ideally, service-learning is integrated into for-credit coursework, but we found that many second-year programs are not eligible for academic credit because they are based in residential or student affairs programs. However, all of the programs featured in this chapter do have articulated learning objectives and required, structured reflection. These are the components that distinguish them from cocurricular community service and volunteerism. In other words, when a group of college students participates in a park clean-up activity as part of a volunteer project that has no learning objectives or structured reflection integrated into that project, then by our definition, such an activity is not service-learning. On the other hand, the same type of activity would be service-learning if it was organized around specific, explicit learning objectives and if structured reflection linked to those objectives was also required.

Although our emphasis in this chapter is service-learning in organized second-year programs, we also address the contributions of service-learning to sophomore learning and success where formal programs do not exist. To date, there are relatively few colleges and universities with organized second-year programs and fewer still into which service-learning is integrated into sophomore programs. Consequently, we argue that service-learning can be a useful strategy for sophomore success, even in the absence of formal programs.

As we discuss below, there are significant differences between students in their second year at two-year colleges and those at four-year colleges and universities, which may affect how service-learning contributes to a student's academic success. For this reason, we explore service-learning in sophomore programs in both two-year and four-year institutions.

Models of Student Development in the Sophomore Year

Like many of the chapters in this volume, we take as our point of departure Schaller's (2005) theory that addresses issues linked to the second college year. Schaller identifies four stages of sophomore development related to the students' personal and interpersonal development and their academic and career emphases: (a) random exploration, (b) focused exploration, (c) tentative choices, and (d) commitment. Students in the random exploration stage make relatively unfocused decisions about their own lives, their interpersonal relationships, and their academic and career development, with little thought given to the long-term consequences of their decisions. In the focused exploration stage, students begin to make more focused decisions based on their personal goals. During the tentative choices stage, students take greater responsibility for their decisions and begin to recognize the potential consequences of their choices. Students in the final stage make commitments to personal and interpersonal behavior and commit to a field of study or career choice. (For more on Schaller's theory, see Chapter Four.)

Schaller's approach is similar to other developmental theories that focus on college students. Her focused exploration, tentative choices, and commitment stages are similar to Perry's (1970) "contextual relativism" and "commitment to relativism" positions. In these positions, students begin to critically examine competing moral and knowledge claims and, after making tentative decisions, develop deeper commitments to their choices.

Likewise, Schaller's model recalls four of the seven "vectors" of college student psychosocial development postulated by Chickering and Reisser (1993). The vectors to which Schaller's stages bear the greatest resemblance are "moving through autonomy toward interdependence," "developing mature interpersonal relationships," "establishing identity," and "developing purpose" (Chickering & Reisser, 1993). As students move through the vectors, they become more self-aware, develop deeper personal and interpersonal commitments, increase their greater capacity for tolerance and acceptance of difference, and clarify personal and career goals and plans (McEwen, 1996). The primary difference between Chickering and Reisser's vectors and Schaller's stages is that the former occur throughout the college career, not solely within the sophomore year.

One of the benefits of applying Schaller's model to evaluating the impact of curricular and cocurricular programming on sophomore student development is that it explicitly addresses the particular struggles of second-year college students. In addition, Schaller's model provides a more integrated perspective on the complex decisions sophomore students make related to personal, social, and academic development and their own emerging awareness of the interdependence among their decisions. Consequently, her approach provides a rationale for the argument that sophomore student success will be enhanced though programming intentionally designed with sophomores' unique needs in mind.

There are a number of ways in which college programming can respond to the needs related to self-, interpersonal, and academic development. For example, students can explore the intersection of self- and social development through student clubs and organizations, campus-organized social functions, and Greek Life. They can explore the intersection of personal and academic-career development opportunities through their coursework, career development workshops, and academic advising. They can explore the intersection of social development with academic and career options through collaborative learning activities in the curriculum, internship and externship opportunities, and study abroad.

Such activities are typical of most colleges and universities and are available to all students. It is when these programs are coordinated and targeted specifically for second-year students that their full contribution to student success is most likely to occur. Service-learning is one of the few learning experiences that allows students to explore self, relationships, and academics simultaneously. In addition, service-learning encourages students to develop social networks in the wider community, reflect upon their current and future civic commitments, and apply their academic learning to real-world problem solving. Indeed, as Schaller emphasized repeatedly throughout her article (Schaller, 2005), in order to move sophomore students from random exploration to focused exploration and commitment and to allow them to fully comprehend the interdependence of their personal, interpersonal, and academic choices, they will need structured, critical reflection. Although service-learning is not the only pedagogy that integrates structured reflection, research has demonstrated that is the *sine qua non* by which learning and personal development best occur through service-learning (Eyler & Giles, 1999).

Of course, the degree to which service-learning actually allows for these multiple explorations will depend on the nature of the service-learning experience, as well as on how reflection activities are structured. Later in this chapter, we make some suggestions on how to capture the full potential of service-learning toward these ends.

In addition to suggesting that students be given opportunities for exploration of self, relationships, and academic choices, Schaller, citing Baxter Magolda (1992), also discusses the importance of helping second-year students make the transition from "absolute knowing" to "transitional knowing," or moving from passive acceptance of information to active questioning of new information and personal preconceptions (p. 21). She also cites Baxter Magolda's emphasis of helping students achieve "self-authorship," that is, the ability to make decisions based not on external expectations but on the self-knowledge that emerges as a result of self-exploration and reflection (p. 21). In raising the developmental objectives, Schaller makes the distinction between "random exploration," in which students are given responsibility to make choices across a range of alternatives without external direction, and "focused exploration," in which students begin to question their prior personal and academic choices as well as their plans for the future.

For students in the random exploration stage, Schaller (2005) recommends experiences that "give students responsibility for learning," "require reflection," and create opportunities for "new relationship building" (pp. 21–22). As a pedagogy, service-learning contributes to all of these objectives. One of the characteristics of service-learning, especially when it is integrated into coursework, is that it removes the faculty member as one of several sources of knowledge and learning and makes students more responsible for their own learning. This characteristic is most likely to emerge when reflection activities are structured in such a way as to require students to consider multiple perspectives and alternatives to a particular problem. Furthermore, service-learning, by definition, requires reflection. However, as noted by Schaller, reflection should be structured in such a way as to avoid accepting superficial responses from students. Finally, service-learning can contribute to the emergence of greater tolerance of difference in the creation of new relationships, particularly when students perform their service in communities or with individuals from social groups different from their own (Ward & Wolf-Wendel, 2000).

Schaller (2005) recommends "providing opportunities for exploration," "structuring reflection," and "providing support" (pp. 23–24) to assist students with the process of focused exploration. She specifically mentions service-learning as a strategy for exploration, particularly in that it provides an opportunity for students to explore the world beyond campus. Service-learning provides opportunities for exploration at other levels as well. It allows students to explore the implications of disciplinary knowledge through its application and integration to issues that emerge through the service experience. It can allow students opportunities for self-exploration, particularly around ethical issues and the students' roles and responsibilities as members of a larger society and community (Wallace, 2000). It can also provide opportunities for career exploration (Fisher, 1996).

Structured reflection, with instructor feedback, is a critical element in service-learning. As mentioned above, when reflection prompts become more targeted and outcome-specific, students are more likely to engage in deep reflection and move beyond superficial description of activities and lessons learned.

Service-learning instructors can support students in focused exploration through providing "authentic" service-learning opportunities, by structuring reflection around personal as well as academic learning, and by providing constructive and critical feedback to students' reflections. By authentic service-learning, we mean service opportunities that are not only clearly aligned with learning objectives but that also allow students to address important and complex social issues.

Though useful, Schaller's (2005) perspectives on sophomores are limited, because the students she studied are traditional-aged, residential students. Given that the average age of community college students is 29 (American Association of Community Colleges [AACC], 2007) and that few community college students live on campus, Schaller's developmental perspectives may not apply to second-year community college students. For example, because the second year may be the terminal year in community colleges, the community college students following this trajectory have already made academic and career decisions; they are past the exploratory stages that Schaller emphasizes. In addition, for many community college students, there is not a "second year" at all; instead, these students may take years to progress through the equivalent of second-year status in terms of credit hours earned, or they may have transferred to a four-year campus before completing the second year. Furthermore, given their older average age, community college students, in general, tend to be further along in their cognitive and emotional development than the 19- and 20-year-olds that Schaller describes. Thus, although second-year community college students are likely to have needs different from those of traditional students, service-learning can still contribute to the satisfaction of those needs.

Recognizing the role of service-learning in sophomore programs in general terms, we now turn our attention to specific cases of the use of service-learning in the sophomore year—first in four-year colleges, then in two-year colleges. In addition to our home institutions, we highlight other institutions where service-learning is implemented as part of a formal second-year program.

Service-Learning in Four-Year Institutions

The National Resource Center for The First-Year Experience and Students in Transition (n.d.) lists 40 four-year colleges and universities with formal sophomore-year programs. Although this list is not exhaustive, a review of those programs' Web sites by one of the authors showed that of those colleges and universities, nine integrate service-learning as a component of the sophomore-year experience: Beloit College (Wisconsin), Bridgewater State College (Massachusetts), Colgate University (New York), Colorado College (Colorado), Emory University (Georgia), Fairfield University (Connecticut), McPherson College (Kansas), Southern Illinois University, and William Jewell College (Missouri). In only three of these institutions is there a required sophomore-year experience; in others, the sophomore-year program is an option. In some sophomore-year programs, the service-learning experience is required, and in others it is optional. In some programs, service-learning is located in the cocurriculum and in others in the curriculum. However, in all nine cases, service-learning is linked to identifiable sophomore-year learning objectives.

Given this variation, we can identify several sophomore-year program types that include service-learning. A brief description of each type and the similarities and differences within each type follows.

Model One: Sophomore Experience Required/Service-Learning Required

At William Jewell College, the second-year program is based in residential life, and all sophomore residential students are required to participate in at least some second-year activities, including a mandatory all-class service-learning project (William Jewell College, 2007). The other two institutions that require all sophomore students to participate in sophomore programming, McPherson College and Bridgewater State, do so through required sophomore seminars, which fulfill core curriculum requirements. Service-learning is an integral component of these sophomore seminars. McPherson's sophomore seminar is a single course required of all students that focuses on leadership, career planning, and service. Bridgewater State offers students a variety of courses that are either speaking- or writing-intensive and include a service-learning component.

Model Two: Sophomore Experience Optional/Service-Learning Required

In many of the college programs described here, participation in the sophomore experience itself is optional. In the two cases in this model, Southern Illinois University and Colorado College, the second-year program is based in residential life and the curricular, cocurricular, and social programs are integrated as part of a sophomore living-learning community. Although the sophomore-year programs at Southern Illinois University-Edwardsville and Colorado College are based in residential life, the service-learning requirement is curricular. As at McPherson College and Bridgewater State College, the service-learning requirement is fulfilled through a required sophomore seminar. At Southern Illinois, students choose from a variety of seminar topics, and at Colorado College, all students take a common course.

Model Three: Sophomore Experience Optional/Service-Learning Optional

With the exception of Beloit College, all of the institutions in this category implement sophomore-experience programming through residential living-learning communities. In addition, students must apply for these communities; participation is not guaranteed. Furthermore, service-learning is just one of many sophomore learning experiences available to students. At Colgate University, the sophomore living-learning communities emphasize leadership and civic engagement, but service-learning is optional. The elective service-learning opportunities are connected to the theme or focus of their respective residential community, and many students choose to participate.

Emory University's residential community, Second Year Emory, also emphasizes leadership and service as an institutional value. Consequently, the program directors and student advisors work closely with the campus Office for University-Community Partnerships to identify service-learning opportunities for interested students and to support students in their service.

Fairfield University's sophomore living-learning community is grounded in the institution's faith-based mission and emphasizes the importance of self-discovery and meaning-making through the lens of Franciscan principles. In addition to support services and community-building activities, students also fulfill specially designated courses. However, the courses from which students select may or may not have a service-learning component.

Beloit College offers a wide range of services and programs to its sophomore students; service is one of many options that students can select. One of the innovative programs open to sophomores at Beloit is the Venture Grants, which provide students with funding to engage in "entrepreneurial, self-testing, or intellectually challenging activities in which the winner(s) attempt something (academic or nonacademic) that benefits others, either directly or through an organization. Projects may be of a personal, service, or commercial character" (Beloit College, 2007). Several recipients have completed service-learning projects as part of their Venture Grant activities. For example, one recent recipient traveled to Thailand, where she completed an AIDS orientation course and subsequently provided AIDS-related community service (Beloit College, 2007a). Another student developed an art-based community empowerment project to raise community awareness about sexual assault and to raise funds for a local assault recovery center (Beloit College, 2007b).

How and why service-learning is integrated into these programs also varies. In some cases, for example, Emory University and William Jewell College, service is seen as a value in itself. In other cases it is one of many types of activities that allow sophomore students to develop a sense of community. Other institutions (such as Bridgewater State College, Colorado College, McPherson College, and Southern Illinois University) recognize the value of service-learning as a pedagogy through which students can more deeply examine academic and career choices and their personal values and civic responsibilities. Those institutions in which service-learning is an option (such as Beloit College, Colgate University, Emory University, Fairfield University) incorporate it as a choice among many that sophomore students are encouraged to explore. As Kim Taylor, dean of the Sophomore Experience at Colgate University, explains:

> All components of our SYE [Second-Year Experience] are optional. We focus on helping students develop the skills of active citizenship and finding their passions. We believe the rest will be done by them. [However], our learning community . . . often lead[s] to service either in the local community or in the students' home town. This is intentional and we connect students with various organizations and resources through Colgate and our alumni base. In particular, we connect students with the Center for Outreach, Volunteerism and Education. (Personal communication, 2007)

Service-Learning in Colleges and Universities Without Sophomore-Year Programs

Although relatively few colleges and universities have organized, structured, sophomore-year programs, many of them have formal service-learning programs. In some instances, colleges may not have organized service-learning programs, but service-learning courses are available (Campus Compact, 2007). Consequently, even colleges that do not have formal sophomore programs can address the needs of sophomore students through service-learning. For example, at Indiana University-Purdue University Indianapolis (IUPUI) many departments and schools intentionally offer service-learning courses in the sophomore year, primarily to engage students more deeply in their chosen majors or careers.

Most sophomores in these majors were already introduced to service-learning in their first-year Gateway courses (introductions to the major) or first-year learning communities. For example, every section of the Introduction to Sociology course incorporates a service-learning option. Students who go on to major in sociology will find a variety of 200- and 300-level courses with service-learning components. Likewise, most sections of the Introduction to Social Work and Foundations of Education incorporate a service-learning component, not only to introduce students to the major, but also to prepare them for the community-based course work that they will encounter in the major.

Applying service-learning as a means to help sophomores explore career and academic choices is just one way that service-learning can address the issues identified by Schaller (2005). When provided opportunities for deep, structured reflection, students can also explore the degree to which academic and career choices align with their personal values. They also allow students the opportunity to explore themselves as members as a larger, more diverse community than they may have otherwise.

The Community College Context

Since 1904, the "junior" and then "community" college has represented equal higher education opportunity for all Americans pursuing a two- or four-year degree or employment and career training. In literature, community colleges are lauded as "America's democracy colleges" (Brint & Karabel, 1989; for fuller discussion of this institutional identity, see Franco, 2002a, 2002b). Further, the community college is a uniquely American institution that is being successfully exported to and implemented in developed and developing countries around the world.

For decades, research on two-year institutions has focused on the opportunities, challenges, and perils confronting community colleges and the students they serve. The community colleges are the fastest growing sector of nonprofit American higher education, with recent enrollment increases three times larger than those at public four-year colleges (Boswell & Wilson, 2004). Community colleges enroll 11.5 million credit and non-credit-taking students, or 46 percent of all undergraduates, and the majority of first- and second-year students (American Association of Community Colleges [AACC], 2007; Boswell & Wilson, 2004; Franco et al., 2007). Community colleges serve the most low-income students, including the majority of college students from the lowest economic quintile (Adelman, 2005), as well as high proportions of underserved populations and first-generation college students. According to data from the AACC, two-year colleges currently enroll 57 percent of all Native American, 47 percent of all African American, and 55 percent of all Hispanic college students.

But challenges and perils lie ahead. Increases in access and opportunity for all these demographic groups is impressive; however, as recent findings (Engle & Obrien, 2007) indicate:

> There are substantial gaps in educational opportunity and attainment by race and ethnicity, by gender, and most starkly by socioeconomic status: only 12 percent of students whose families fall in the bottom income quartile earn a bachelor's degree by age 24, compared with 22 percent in the middle quartiles and 73 percent form the top quartile. (p. 11)

A recent Campus Compact Research Brief (2008) entitled "How Can Engaged Campuses Improve Student Success in College?" emphasizes that "expanding college access and success is vital to the well-being of our increasingly diverse democracy" (p. 1). Recent findings from the Community College Survey of Student Engagement (CCSSE) (McClenney & O'Brien, 2006) reported:

> One of the most consistent predictors of persistence, self-reported learning gains, and GPA is "active and collaborative learning," which includes "participated in a community-based project as part of a regular course" and other activities commonly part of high-quality service-learning such as "raised questions in class or contributed to class discussions."

Many community colleges have embraced service-learning as a pedagogical tool to increase persistence (that is, retention across terms or re-enrollment), academic success, and degree completion in their diverse student populations, and some of these are featured in the snapshots presented below.

The Sophomore Year in America's Community Colleges

Many community colleges consider students to be sophomores if they have completed 24 credits, as this is the number of credits needed (with a GPA of 2.0 or higher) to successfully transfer to a baccalaureate campus. Community colleges that use CCSSE track the quality of students' experiences by credits completed (0–29 and 30 plus). Thirty credits completed is half-way to most associate's degrees and is an important boundary crossed on the way to the sophomore year. For other community colleges, students who have completed 36 credits are viewed as sophomores as they are within reach of completing the additional 24 credits necessary to achieve the associate's degree.

The Schaller (2005) framework can be applied to community college students but needs to expand the range of explorations, choices, and commitments in the more complicated and distracted lives of college students who are typically of lower income background, ethnically and experientially diverse, the first in their families to go college, and embedded in the familial, social, economic, and civic fabric of the communities in which they learn and serve. The framework also needs to contract both temporally and spatially as the explorations, choices, and commitments of community college students are both much more temporally immediate and locally rooted than those of sophomore students in four-year universities, especially if these students have left their home communities to attend the four-year institution. In terms of past experience and academic and career goals, sophomores at community colleges are a very diverse group. Four major categorizations capture most of this diversity:

1. *Self-identified associate's degree completers:* These sophomores are enrolled in self-identified two-year Associate in Arts or Associate in Science degree programs that they perceive as either terminal or foundational to university transfer or 21st century careers.
2. *Unclassified explorers:* These sophomores are enrolled as unclassified students exploring courses as they relate to possible majors that are accessible without associate's degree completion, employment and career skills development, or self-enrichment.
3. *Wanderers and wonderers:* These sophomores are wandering in and out of college and wondering about self, relationships, community, majors, and careers.
4. *Returning adult learners:* These sophomores, aged 25–49, may have completed 24–30 credits within the last 10 years but have been out of college for years during which they have been shaped by positive and negative life experiences in the wider community and labor market.

These four types of students are moving through stages of random and focused exploration, tentative decision making, and firmer commitment making. They are exploring and making choices and commitments about a broader range of issues, not just personal development and academic and career considerations but also decisions within a complex matrix of issues involving family, work, health care, and economic survival.

By completing an associate's degree, many community college sophomores have already made tentative choices and completed commitments as they move into jobs and careers. They may decide later that they need to reenter the community college to upgrade skills that make them more competitive in the workforce or to move into new careers and communities as local labor markets decline and transform.

Service-Learning and the Community College Sophomore Year

Since 1995, with funding from the Corporation for National and Community Service, the American Association of Community Colleges' (AACC) Horizons Program has supported high-quality integration of service-learning and civic responsibility at more than 80 community colleges nationally. Their goals are

> to build on established foundations to integrate service-learning into the institutional climate of community colleges and to increase the number, quality, and sustainability of service-learning programs through an information clearinghouse, data collection and analysis, model programs, training and technical assistance, publications, and referrals. (AACC Web site)

According to AACC's Service-Learning Clearinghouse, approximately 60 percent of America's 1,200 community colleges have developed service-learning courses and programs that address the needs of both first-year and sophomore students. The Community College National Center for Community Engagement at Mesa Community College (Arizona) is a leader in "advancing programs and innovations that stimulate active participation of institutions in community engagement for the attainment of a vital citizenry" (www.mc.maricopa.edu/other/engagement).

The following characterization of service-learning in the community college sophomore year is based on nearly 15 years of (a) collaboration and development with these two national community college-serving organizations; (b) ethnographic research, training, and technical assistance supported by Campus Compact in 35 states with 150 community colleges; and (c) coordinating a service-learning program that has been rooted in intercultural and intergenerational education at Kapiolani Community College, a campus that champions diversity in Hawaii's richly textured indigenous, multicultural, and international community.

At most community colleges, service-learning initiatives are integrated into general education courses as faculty discover that service-learning is an important pedagogy for achieving general education learning outcomes in writing and critical thinking, oral communication, ethical reasoning, quantitative reasoning, technology literacy, multicultural understanding, civic responsibility, and global citizenship. Nearly all the AACC Horizons colleges support "civic responsibility" as an important learning outcome derived from service-learning pedagogies. AACC defines civic responsibility as, "Active participation in the public life of a community in an informed, committed, and constructive manner, with a focus on the common good" (Gottlieb & Robinson, 2006, p. 16).

Community college faculty members integrate service-learning as an attractive optional assignment across developmental (pre-college), first-year, and second-year courses without strong programmatic linkages across these years. In response to the diversity of their students, service-learning initiatives in the two-year colleges provide maximal choice and flexibility. This vast array of options has resulted in thousands of exciting and valuable projects but few coherent, sustainable, and assessable service-learning programs across the undergraduate curriculum.

For the four groups of community college sophomores identified above, service-learning courses impact their development and academic and career choices in different ways:

1. *Self-identified associate's degree completers:* For these students, service-learning courses support focused exploration and tentative decision-making regarding self, majors, careers, and civic commitments as those completing terminal degrees are contemplating their soon-to-be lives as employees and citizens.
2. *Unclassified explorers:* For these students, service-learning courses provide a constructive real world context for random and more focused exploration of majors, careers, self, and community.
3. *Wanderers and wonderers:* For these sophomores, service-learning courses provide constructive real world learning experiences that give greater relevance and meaning to their educational experience as they randomly explore and make tentative commitments to engaging with and persisting in college.
4. *Returning adult learners:* For these students, service-learning courses provide alternative and constructive real world contexts that engage them in focused exploration and tentative decision-making regarding the relevance of college within a more complex matrix of family and work considerations.

Examples of Service-Learning Courses for Sophomores in Community Colleges

Service-learning courses provide constructive real-world learning contexts for sophomores who are both in and of the communities in which they serve. These sophomores are exploring and making choices and commitments about a diverse set of personal development, academic, and career considerations in relation to a community of which they are a part, a community that will continue to shape them and be shaped by them. For many community colleges, service-learning is a central component of a larger institutional commitment to civic life, and sophomores are viewed as a valuable human resource ready to make a long-term contribution to the social, civic, and economic development of their community.

At Brevard Community College (Florida), sophomores benefit from well-designed courses where service-learning assignments are integrated into pre-transfer liberal arts courses and vocational and technical courses as well as stand-alone service-learning courses that prepare them for careers in social work in their local community. Because of the comprehensiveness and quality of the Brevard program, their service-learning students, in comparison with their non-service-learners, had substantially higher degree completion rates over the 1999–2005 period.

Grand Rapids Community College (Michigan) has implemented strong service-learning for its dental hygiene students so that their students upon completion of the associate's degree are prepared to work with diverse low-income communities and in community-based health settings. Similarly, dental hygiene students at Miami Dade College (Florida) participate in service-learning activities throughout their two-year program. They teach dental health education in elementary schools and participate in dental screenings in day-care centers and elementary schools to assess unmet dental needs. During their sophomore year, groups of students select different community agencies where they conduct dental health education projects. Students are encouraged to select a site where clients have minimal access to dental care and dental health education. Students gain an appreciation for the health disparities within the Miami-Dade County community and nationally. As evidenced in their "photo reflection journals," students demonstrate an understanding of health inequities among minorities and the physically disabled. Through this effort, students demonstrate comprehension and application of needs assessment methodology, design a dental health education program to address identified needs, and implement and evaluate their program.

At Yakima Valley Community College (Washington), service-learning courses were initially developed to enhance English language learning for new immigrants supporting the agricultural economy in eastern Washington. After recognizing the need for improved early child care for their female students of Mexican-American ancestry, the college invested in the development of an early childhood education degree program and in the construction of a child-care facility immediately adjacent to the campus. In this facility, the early childhood program integrates service-learning courses across its first and second year (for more, see Zlotkowski et al., 2004).

At Broome Community College (New York), strong student interest in sophomore service-learning courses in environmental literature and in English has resulted in the redesigning of alternative spring breaks so that students can more deeply explore environmental issues, degrees, and possible careers.

In 2004, Johnson County Community College (JCCC) (Kansas), a leading Horizons College, introduced its Civic Honors Program, which "provides a framework of courses, training, reflection, and experience which is designed to increase a student's capacity for, self-confidence in, and commitment to effective community engagement and participation." Students who plan to graduate from JCCC and who have at least two semesters remaining at the college are welcome to join the Civic Honors Programs. Since 2005, 18 students, from programs as diverse as nursing, social work, legal paraprofessional, and interior design, have completed associate's degrees through the program.

In 2007–2008, 10 sophomore students in Northampton Area Community College's (Pennsylvania) leadership course integrated service-learning into their curriculum. Through funding from the State Farm Youth Advisory Board, students designed projects that focused on flood and disaster awareness and preparedness. Projects included the creation of a film "Floodman and the Floodkateers," museum exhibits focusing on flood impacts, and a rain garden on campus to absorb runoff and development of a curriculum for middle schoolers to educate them about problem solving and use of best practices to manage stormwater.

At Kapiolani Community College (Hawaii), service-learning students participate in environmental, educational, health, and cultural diversity "pathways" with students from Chaminade University and the University of Hawaii at Manoa (Franco et al., 2007). These students can then transfer more confidently to majors in English, ethnic studies, education, social science, social work, public health, and science. The three campuses also share similar reflection practices and events, as well as assessment techniques. At Kapiolani, 70 service-learning courses, across the developmental, first, and sophomore years, connect students with activities that reduce the severity of social issues in Honolulu's urban environment. One issue, ecological deterioration in Honolulu's fragile watershed and coastal and environments, has resulted in strong student commitment to service-learning and is driving the college's development of a new environmental science baccalaureate transfer pathway.

Service-learning students in sophomore-level liberal arts and health science courses explore long-term care issues in Honolulu's diverse elderly population. Growing student interest in both the social and economic dimensions of long-term care contributed to the college's development of a formal long-term care program.

Sophomores at Kapiolani become paid service-learning pathway leaders after demonstrating success in the earlier pathway courses. These leaders, as evidenced by their written reflections, focus group discussions, and presentations at national conferences, have moved from random and focused exploration as service-learning students to making tentative choices and commitments as service-learning pathway leaders and have more clearly identified degree and career goals.

Since 2004, 150 Kapiolani sophomores, with funding support from the Freeman Foundation, have studied either the Japanese, Korean, or Chinese language intensively for one semester and then studied and completed service-learning experiences in Japan, Korea, and China for a second semester. These students, through capstone reflections, consistently remark on having discovered their majors, degrees, and, most important, their place as citizens of Hawaii and the world. A student who took advantage of an international service-learning opportunity in the Philippines reflected:

> Along this journey my values, confidence, and self-respect were challenged. Thanks to [a] young local boy I met there, I overcame these challenges and along with other experiences in the Philippines understand that providing world service is more dear to me than owning my own business. It has solidified my emotions about this world, and how powerful a single person can be.

At the national level, community colleges do not generally develop sophomore-year programs; however, they are acutely aware that they are preparing graduates who will have immediate impact on their local communities no matter what path they take to degree completion. Leading community colleges are developing their service-learning programs so that all students will have multiple opportunities to serve into and across their sophomore years. Community college students will take advantage of these expanded opportunities to focus and explore and make choices and commitments that will influence them as individuals and as members of families, workplaces, communities, and environments that continue to shape them and that they will shape in turn.

Conclusion

Service-learning as a pedagogy or as a set of cocurricular experiences grounded in student development theory and accompanied with opportunities for structured, critical reflection can contribute to sophomore student success. For example, service-learning allows students to explore career options and develop interpersonal relationships with individuals or groups that may differ from them. When coupled with structured reflection, service-learning provides opportunities for self-authorship and meaning-making as defined by Baxter Magolda (1992, as cited in Schaller, 2005). For these reasons, we believe that service-learning should be a central component of the sophomore year, particularly at colleges and universities without a structured second-year program.

Faculty, administrators, advisors, and student development professionals who are committed to sophomore student success and retention would do well to consider either adopting a formal sophomore-year program or integrating more service-learning opportunities during the sophomore year. Service-learning instructors in particular can support students in focused exploration through providing "authentic" service-learning opportunities by structuring reflection around personal as well as academic learning and by providing constructive and critical feedback to students' reflections. By authentic service-learning, we mean service opportunities that are not only aligned with curricular learning objectives but that also allow students to address important and complex social issues. Expanding the opportunities for student reflection beyond curricular concepts provides opportunities for student development and growth consistent with students' moving through the stages of focused exploration and tentative choices to commitment (Schaller, 2005).

CHAPTER TEN

THE POTENTIAL OF STUDY ABROAD IN THE SOPHOMORE YEAR

Susan Buck Sutton, Stephanie L. Leslie

Although study abroad has been a feature of most U.S. colleges and universities since the late 19th century, the way it has been conceived historically has limited its impact to only a handful of students (Biddle, 2002; Gore, 2005; Vande Berg, 2004, 2007; Wilkinson, 1998). This chapter argues that study abroad is a powerful pedagogy that reaches too few students in too few disciplines. Although the situation is in flux, only 1.2 percent of U.S. students studied overseas in 2005–06, and the largest segment of these were junior liberal arts majors (Bhandari & Chow, 2007). A growing body of research over the last 25 years has shown, however, that the cognitive and psychosocial benefits of study abroad are wide-ranging and significant, and that they can apply to types of students far beyond those who have historically participated. What was once simply referred to as Junior Year Abroad should not just be for juniors any more.

Our increasing understanding of the developmental impact of study abroad upon students makes clear that study abroad encourages the kinds of exploration, reflection, and engagement that many now feel are particularly critical to sophomore success (Schaller 2005, 2007; Schreiner & Pattengale, 2000; Tobolowsky & Cox, 2007a). Indeed study abroad provides a context in which sophomores might grow to understand their goals and identity in the broadest social and cultural context possible. There is a clear intersection between the evolving foci of study abroad and those of sophomore-year initiatives. In this chapter we discuss study abroad as it connects with the recent work on sophomore development. We write from the perspective of study abroad educators, but we hope this chapter initiates conversation across these two fields. We believe carefully structured study abroad experiences can be a productive part of a multifaceted sophomore program.

To place study abroad into the evolving discussion of the sophomore year, we begin this chapter by reviewing the history, nature, and developmental outcomes of study abroad. We then explore the ways in which such outcomes connect to the issues that animate sophomore success initiatives. Finally, we conclude with a set of recommendations for productively integrating study abroad into the sophomore experience.

The History and Shape of Study Abroad

In the United States, study abroad (also sometimes known as overseas study or education abroad) is widely defined by the guidelines set by the Institute of International Education in compiling national statistics, parameters that count all U.S. students (both citizens and permanent residents) enrolled for a degree at an American campus who received academic credit toward their degree for work done outside the United States (Bhandari & Chow, 2007). In this sense, it is distinct from traveling abroad for non-academic purposes (see Gmelch, 1997) or seeking a degree outside one's own country. Study abroad is a momentary period of study outside the United States while still enrolled in a degree program at an American educational institution.

In this sense, U.S. study abroad differs from the massive movements of non-U.S. students who now circle the globe, seeking degrees outside their home nations. These degree-seekers are often more focused on the quality of the academic programs in which they enroll than the developmental aspects of what they are doing—not that they do not grow developmentally as well. The purpose and the structures that logically follow the U.S. form of study abroad, however, have always been both academic and developmental.

This form of study abroad owes much of its heritage, for better and for worse, to the Grand Tour that was once a common feature of the maturation process of the Western European and American elite (Hoffa, 2007; Vande Berg 2004, 2007). In the 18th and 19th centuries, wealthy young men (and sometimes women) traveled through the storied cities of Europe to develop their aesthetic sensibilities, broaden their perspectives, encounter the touchstones of Western civilization, and become part of an elite, transcontinental class that produced both businessmen and artists (e.g., Eisner, 1991; Leontis, 1995). When some U.S. colleges and universities began offering organized tours through Europe (e.g., Indiana University's summer "tramps" through Europe in the 1880s), the

Grand Tour was taken into an academic environment, where it became more controlled, structured, and even credit-bearing (History of Overseas Study, n.d.; Hoffa, 2007).

By the 1930s, this academic version of a European tour had evolved into what was known as Junior Year Abroad (JYA), an experience in which students focused on foreign language acquisition, with additional courses on the art and history of the host nation. JYA enabled many students to experience European travel, but it had a down side as well (Gore, 2005). Study abroad became associated more with women than men, more with the liberal arts than the sciences and professions. Male students tended to travel independently, outside an academic context, and study abroad was often viewed as an add-on, something tangential to one's core education, something that serious students (except those in a few specialized disciplines) generally avoided. Study abroad also remained an activity of the upper-middle class and those prepared for advanced language study (Dwyer, 2004a).

This legacy is still evident. The Open Doors Report figures compiled by the Institute for International Education for 2006–2007 show that 65% of the students studying abroad were female and 41.8% were majoring in the liberal arts (Bhandari & Chow, 2008). They also reveal that only 1.2 percent of U.S. students studied overseas in 2005–2006 (Bhandari & Chow, 2007). (We have calculated the participation rate using the number of students abroad in 2005–2006 and the IPEDS [Integrated Postsecondary Education Data System] record for the number of enrolled students in fall 2005.)

The tide, however, may be turning (Vande Berg, 2004, 2007). The recent embrace of international education across the curriculum is opening study abroad to new audiences, locations, and topics (Obst, Bhandari, & Witherell, 2007). Globalization, immigration, a flattening world of information technology, environmental and health concerns, international conflicts, and postcolonial sensitivities have brought new faces to the table and led many colleges and universities to embed global learning into their undergraduate curriculum (Educating for Global Competency, 1997; Global Competence & National Needs, 2005). Community colleges are also rethinking their definition of *community* to include the world beyond their local boundaries (Raby & Valeau, 2007; Zeszotarski, 2001). In this process, the goals and shape of study abroad are shifting, and its developmental impact for students—across a variety of dimensions and beyond language acquisition—is increasingly recognized.

At our institution, Indiana University-Purdue University Indianapolis (IUPUI), for example, students do service-learning in Africa, develop business plans for Chinese communities, examine ecological issues in Costa Rica, and visit "green" factories in Germany. Furthermore juniors are not the only ones pursuing these experiences. The University of Dallas operates a sophomore study abroad program in Rome (Young, 2004). Roughly 100 students participate each year with beneficial results. In fact, 79 percent of the students who study in Rome during their second year graduate within four years, compared to 51 percent for those who do not (Young, 2004). Community colleges are also embracing study abroad (Hess, 1983), as demonstrated by a 2000 study conducted by the American Association of Community Colleges that shows that over 60 percent of community colleges offer study abroad programs (Blair, Phinney, & Phillippe, 2001). Nationwide, more than half of U.S. study abroad participants now go on short-term programs (Bhandari & Chow, 2007, 2008; Hulstrand, 2006; Obst, Bhandari, & Witherell, 2007), do not pursue language study as their primary goal, and visit a wider range of destinations than ever before (Bhandari & Chow, 2007, 2008). The number of U.S. students studying abroad has grown from under 50,000 in 1985–1986 to 241,791 in 2006–2007 (Bhandari & Chow, 2008). Business majors now constitute 19.1 percent of the total (Bhandari & Chow, 2008). Of particular importance to this volume, 3.3 percent of all study abroad students are in their first year and 12.9 percent are sophomores (Bhandari & Chow, 2008).

The Impact of Study Abroad on Students

As study abroad participation has grown so has our understanding of what it does, how it works, and how it might be reshaped for greater impact. Although different target populations, methodologies, and foci make comparing research on study abroad programs difficult, the following attempts to synthesize what is known.

U.S. study abroad has always been seen as more than what happens in the classroom. For the first 75 years of its existence, study abroad was designed for both academic goals (e.g., language acquisition) and cultural enrichment (through contact with the museums, monuments, and the local population). In the post–World War II environment, some began to understand the enrichment part of study abroad more deeply. As Coelho (1962, p. 55) phrased it, overseas education was increasingly connected to the development of "the whole person." (See Nash 1976 for an interesting analysis on where the forms prominent at that time fit with U.S. economic and cultural structures.) In another early statement, Carsello and Creaser (1976) viewed study abroad as expanding what they called the "humanitarian interests" of the student, under which term they included aesthetics, an expansive outlook, and interest in relating to others (p. 278).

Few analyses before 1980, however, attempted to identify or measure the actual outcomes of study abroad, declaring them to be profound, but leaving the nature of this profundity unspecified and unverified. Those rare exceptions (for example, Carsello & Creaser, 1976; Coelho, 1962) presented evidence that students return from study abroad more proficient in another language; more interested in travel, the arts, and history; and with a stronger sense of self, less prejudiced toward other countries, and with greater "worldmindedness" (a key word of the 1950s, which denotes viewing events from a global perspective and has recently resurfaced; see Douglas & Jones-Rikkers, 2001) than when they left.

In the 1980s, a number of researchers, generally in education and psychology, moved toward greater specificity about the developmental impact of study abroad. Several used psychological inventories, generating categories of learning and developmental outcomes from student statements and assessing how much students grew in terms of these categories, especially when compared to students who did not study abroad. Later a consortium of European and American researchers undertook a multiyear assessment that not only pulled much of this work together, but also identified the greater emphasis on "cultural enrichment" on the part of U.S. institutions than was true of European universities (Carlson, Burn, Useem, &Yachimowicz, 1990; Teichler & Steube, 1991). By the end of the 1980s, these studies had identified a number of significant changes in thinking and orientation engendered by study abroad, although a few also made clear that not all students underwent these (Nash, 1976), and one questioned how long the changes lasted (Hansel & Grove, 1986). These studies confirmed that study abroad students did, in fact, learn much about their host countries and develop their language skills. They also demonstrated that returnees exhibited higher educational attainment in the years following their study abroad experience (Carlson et al., 1990).

Of even greater importance, the studies of the 1980s began articulating the conceptual and psychosocial ways in which students grew from study abroad. Collectively, this research presented measures of students' developing a more cosmopolitan, less conventional, less materialistic outlook; greater tolerance of human differences; and greater awareness of their own values and cultural background (Carlson et al., 1990; Hansel & Grove, 1986; Marion, 1980; Sell, 1983; Sharma & Mulka, 1993). The studies also assembled evidence of personal growth. Study abroad students scored higher than those who had not gone abroad in terms of maturity, independence, adaptability in the face of ambiguity or frustration, self-confidence, self-efficacy, self-reliance, and career definition (Juhasz & Walker, 1988; Stitsworth, 1988). They were also better able to communicate, think critically, and reflect (Kuh & Kauffman, 1985).

Several researchers explored why such growth occurred, reaching the conclusion that study abroad presents students with cultural learning and personal challenges on a daily basis (Hansel & Grove, 1986). Students must constantly make decisions in new situations that are framed by national and cultural differences. Their success in doing this, even in their nonacademic activities such as weekend travel (Gmelch, 1997), heightens their self-esteem and their powers of self-realization at the same time that the contrast between home and host country provides food for thought (Hopkins, 1999). The experiential side of study abroad also provides students the opportunity to practice what they have been learning in the classroom (Chisholm, 2005; Montrose, 2002).

The last 15 years have seen even greater precision in articulating and assessing the outcomes of study abroad (Ingraham & Peterson, 2004; King & Young, 1994; Montrose, 2002; Sutton & Rubin, 2004; Vande Berg et al., 2004). Some of this work has been folded into the emerging field of intercultural competence, following the work of Bennett (1993) in detailing the conceptual shifts of the move from ethnocentrism to ethnorelativism. Under this model, a host of instruments for assessing intercultural skills and sensitivity have been developed (Bolen, 2007; Deardorff, 2006; Durrant & Dorius, 2007; Williams, 2005). Nevertheless, some of these instruments have been criticized for their simplistic view of culture and inattention to other aspects of international learning (Dolby, 2007; Jenkins & Skelly, 2006). Several recent studies have moved to address these omissions, demonstrating that study abroad also leads students to examine the nature of nationalism (Dolby, 2007; Drews, Meyer, & Peregrine, 1996); the role and impact of the U.S. in the world; race, ethnicity, and other forms of diversity at home; and issues of globalization, inequity, and the environment (Farrell & Suvedi, 2003; Gray, Murdock & Stebbins, 2002; Jenkins & Skelly, 2006). Study abroad has also been shown to influence students' engagement in their local and international communities (Paige, Stallman, & Josic, 2008).

Still other studies have provided additional documentation that returned students do better in their studies and have greater persistence toward graduation than students who never study abroad, even when prior GPAs are factored in (Dwyer, 2004b: 157; Young, 2004). They are also more open to working abroad and interacting with people from other countries in the future (Dwyer, 2004a; Farrell & Suvedi, 2003). Certain factors—such as the self-selection patterns of study abroad students and their often high socioeconomic status—may complicate such conclusions and deserve further scrutiny. Recent research has also shown that well-structured, short-term programs have much the same impact as longer ones (Chieffo & Griffiths, 2004; Fry, Jon, Josic, LaBrack, & Stallman, 2009; Hansel & Grove, 1986; Hulstrand, 2006; Kuh, 2007; Lewis & Niesenbaum, 2005; Medina-Lopez-Portillo, 2004). Finally, discipline-specific studies in business and nursing have clarified study abroad's practical and conceptual benefits to professional, as well as liberal arts, students (Douglas & Jones-Rikkers, 2001; Hannigan, 2001; Koskinen & Tossavainen, 2004; Lindsey, 2005; Orahood, Kruze, & Pearson, 2004). The 2007 National Survey of Student Engagement (NSSE) identified study abroad as one of the high-impact experiences (along with service-learning and conducting research with faculty) that increase deep learning and enhance personal development (Kuh, 2007).

Meyer-Lee and Evans (2007) provide a good framework for pulling together most of these outcomes. As research moves forward, it is time to examine which study abroad activities are most successful at promoting such learning and development, and to consider whether such outcomes have been conceived through a distinctly U.S. lens (Jenkins & Skelly, 2007). Deardorff (2006), for example, points out that outside the United States intercultural competence is sometimes understood more in terms of group relationships than personal growth. There is much work yet to be done on the outcomes of study abroad, but it is nevertheless clear that its impact goes far beyond language acquisition and cultural enrichment.

The Intersection of Study Abroad and Sophomore Development

Much of what has been learned about the outcomes of study abroad resonates with the issues animating sophomore-year programs. Unfortunately—perhaps because of the legacy of the Junior Year Abroad paradigm—this resonance has been largely overlooked. A few hints and suggestions have recently surfaced. Schaller (2005), for example, lists study abroad as one of five sample strategies for "focused exploration" by sophomores (p. 23). Several case studies featured in Tobolowsky and Cox (2007c) mention sophomore study abroad. In their concluding chapter, Tobolowsky and Cox (2007b, p. 98) also list study abroad as one of six "educationally purposeful activities" that might be pursued by sophomore programs, mentioning evidence that sophomores who study abroad have greater persistence toward graduation than other students.

In considering why persistence to graduation (and other beneficial outcomes) occurs, we believe it is the strong parallel that exists between the issues with which many sophomores wrestle and the opportunities provided by study abroad. In 2000, Gardner, Pattengale, and Schreiner assessed the need that many sophomores feel for greater meaning and purpose as they make decisions about selecting a major and pursuing a career. The pressure to make life-changing decisions replaces the "random exploration" of their first-year experience (Schaller, 2005, p. 18). In this atmosphere, as sophomores struggle for meaning and purpose, they confront issues of identity-formation and the self-realization about who they are and where they fit in the world (Schaller, 2005, 2007; Tobolowsky & Cox, 2007c). Sometimes such internal debates are framed by a growing sense of isolation and disconnection from other students and faculty, as well as doubts about their own competence as the intensity of their studies increases.

Certain aspects of study abroad respond to each of these issues. As the above-cited literature demonstrates, study abroad gives students a broad frame-work in which to place their lives, a framework that throws cultural and personal assumptions into bold relief, provides comparison and perspective on seemingly insurmountable obstacles, and opens thinking to ideas and activities barely imag-ined before. Exposure to significantly different ways of life inevitably causes reflection on one's own background while it expands one's system of meanings for understanding the world and one's place within it. As Taylor and Bellani (2007) note, Colgate University's sophomore programs revolve around giving students a diverse set of experiences precisely because such exposure is fertile ground for transitioning from absolutist to more relativistic thinking, as the integrity and logic of other ways of doing things become manifest. For many, this leads to greater adaptability in the face of ambiguity or frustration than they had before studying abroad (Juhasz & Walker, 1988; Stitsworth, 1988).

The expansion of systems of meaning that often occurs through study abroad can also lead to clarification of goals, values, and purpose. As mentioned above, students return from study abroad with a greater sense of their own values, including career definition (Juhasz & Walker, 1988; Stitsworth, 1988). A recent article in the *Harvard Crimson* ties this point specifically to sophomores (Howland, 2008). The two sophomores profiled in the article characterize their time abroad as a chance to "find direction in [their] academic career[s]" (Howland, 2008, p. 2). One student joined a medical project in Botswana after questioning whether his declared major in molecular and cellular biology was right for him and now directs his interests in such matters toward public health. The other decided not to major in business after taking classes in Brazil and becoming interested in social and cultural concerns and policies. As discussed above, returning students are better able to communicate, think critically, and reflect than their peers, while also exhibiting greater maturity, independence, self-confidence, and self-reliance (Juhasz & Walker, 1988; Kuh & Kauffman, 1985; Stitsworth, 1988). Many study abroad students take great pride in their ability to navigate another country and are empowered by the experience (Hopkins, 1999).

Study abroad can also give sophomores the dedicated time necessary for what Schaller (2005, p. 20) calls "focused exploration." Too often sophomores feel pressured to make major decisions quickly and end up falling back on received opinions with which they are ultimately dissatisfied. Focused exploration requires time, concentration, and opportunities for reflection. A period of study abroad can provide precisely that. As Flanagan (2007) points out, the stages of growth during study abroad provide an apt analogy for other transitions through which students may be going. The intensive interaction between students and faculty and also between students and other students that often occurs through study abroad can also ameliorate the feelings of isolation and alienation (resulting from less intentional support than in the first year or in the major department) that sophomores often feel (Schaller, 2005; Tobolowsky & Cox, 2007c). Finally, there are some purely logistical reasons that study abroad is just as appropriate (in some cases, more so) for sophomores as for juniors. It is sometimes easier to fit study abroad into the first or second year than later, when the requirements of the major may be more constraining. Studying abroad as sophomores also enables students to engage in additional study abroad experiences in their junior or senior years if they wish. Since study abroad can lead to rethinking academic major and career goals (Dwyer & Peters, 2004), there is much sense to doing it earlier rather than later. Finally, studying abroad early enables students to apply and use what they have learned from the experience in the remainder of their educational career.

Returned study abroad students are also an asset to the campus community and can aid in its internationalization. They share perspectives based on their international experience and often encourage friends and peers to study abroad as well. Returned students also frequently reach out to international students on their home campuses, thereby facilitating their integration into the U.S. academic life.

Recommendations for Study Abroad During the Sophomore Year

As the Junior Year Abroad model continues to give way, study abroad enrollments are spreading across the undergraduate (and even graduate) years. It would be naïve, however, to assume that study abroad always works its magic, especially as it expands to new audiences. We must be intentional in making a connection between the developmental issues of sophomores and the study abroad programs in which they participate. The literature on best practices in study abroad has focused on duration, location, language preparation and use, housing, structured cultural and experiential learning, on-site mentoring, and self-reflection as key factors in program success (Dwyer, 2004b; Engle & Engle, 2003; Hulstrand,

2006). Because some of these ideas are tangential to the present discussion, the following recommendations focus on linking study abroad, specifically, to sophomore success.

Recognize Different Developmental Stages Among Study Abroad Students

Study abroad could benefit from closer attention to the literature on the stages of student cognitive and psychosocial development, such as those offered by Schaller (see Chapter Four). International educators have focused so much on cultural learning that we may have missed the fact that students are at different stages in their ability to engage in such learning (and that such learning may take different forms, depending on the stage). One size does not fit all. Different strategies are needed for students at different points on this trajectory. Students in random exploration may need more encouragement and modeling of the transition from absolutist to relativistic thinking than those further along. Students in focused exploration, many of whom are sophomores, are ready and even interested in examining the implications of their study abroad experience for career decisions and self-definition. In programs designed just for sophomores, such issues can be explicitly discussed. In programs designed for students from all levels, there is a need to develop multilevel strategies of cultural learning.

Develop Faculty-Led Programs Specifically Tailored to Sophomores

Although many sophomores can productively participate in more general study abroad programs, some will benefit from ones specifically designed to address the transitional issues they face. Group programs led by faculty who work closely with the students might be particularly appropriate. The faculty need not be from the home institution. Indeed, there is equal merit to having faculty from the host country. There should, however, be ample opportunity for students to engage in conversation and reflection with the faculty, as well as with each other. Sophomore-specific programs should explicitly raise issues of career definition and self-realization, and they should tie the learning back to particular majors and curricular requirements at the home institution, a movement that has been spearheaded by the University of Minnesota (Anderson, 2005). For first- and second-year students, such integration is just as likely to be with general education as with major requirements. Because sophomores rarely have the linguistic ability to take courses in another language, such programs should provide the opportunity for some language acquisition while playing up the aspects of intercultural learning that can be accomplished in English.

Too great an emphasis on language acquisition can block other forms of intercultural learning that are of equal (or greater) significance for sophomores.

Develop Effective Advising and Predeparture Programs

Early study abroad demands front-loading in several forms. Students should receive information on study abroad even before they arrive on campus. It should be incorporated into promotional and orientation materials. The possibility of study abroad must be integrated into advising early in a student's career. Studies have shown that most first-year students and sophomores have an interest in study abroad, but that few act on this (King & Young, 1994; Williams & Woodruff, 2005). Even though students should be assisted in planning to make study abroad a reality, two fifths of those who responded to the most recent NSSE survey reported that their advisors never mentioned study abroad (Kuh, 2007). Study abroad offices and advisors should work together to change this situation. They should also work together to establish criteria for determining whether particular students are ready for the experience. If not, the stresses of study abroad may only compound the stresses of the sophomore year. Once sophomores sign up for a study abroad program, they should be offered a comprehensive predeparture program that sets the tone for the learning that is to follow. The predeparture should include detailed information on travel basics but must go beyond this to incorporate an understanding of the host country's history and context, a discussion of how students can analyze and react to differences that they will experience abroad, encouragement for students to identify their own goals for their international experience, expectations of participants' behavior on the program, and a review of academic program and structure of assignments.

Support Sustained Reflection and Analysis

For sophomores to turn their study abroad experiences toward the issues of meaning and self-definition with which they are grappling, they need to record and reflect upon these experiences. And they need to be guided in doing this. Most study abroad programs, especially short-term ones, ask students to keep a journal. To prevent these from becoming mere travelogues with only superficial analyses, students must be given guidelines on what constitutes deep reflection and how to connect their experiences to the course material. They must also engage in group discussions and receive faculty feedback that draws out their learning, both while overseas and after they return (Gray, Murdock, & Stebbins, 2002; Hulstrand, 2006). Kalamazoo College and DePaul University have developed good models for such journaling and reflection that draw from the methodology of anthropological field notes (Sutton et al., 2007). The various publications of the International Partnership for Service and Leadership are also quite useful.

Build in Engagement with the Host Community

One of the most critical elements in student learning on study abroad programs is the degree to which students engage with the host community (Chisholm, 2005; Dwyer, 2004b; Hulstrand, 2006; Lewis & Niesenbaum, 2005). Research has shown that direct enrollment in classes or teaching by faculty at overseas institutions, living with host families, and participating in service-learning or internships are among the most effective methods for connecting U.S. students to individuals and organizations in the host country (see Parker & Dautoff, 2007, on the importance of "connective" learning). This connection, in turn, transforms a one-way endeavor into a two-way dialogue. New voices and sources of knowledge are opened, students develop skills of international networking and dialogue, they come to appreciate the assets of the host country, and the interaction engendered by these methods leads to direct, experiential learning about the host country. Because it intensifies the learning process, direct engagement with host communities is a particularly appropriate method for short-term programs.

Build in Experiences That Strengthen Student Competence and Confidence

Study abroad programs that operate simply as organized tours, with students being led from one site to another, do little to advance active learning and under use the power of study abroad. Study abroad offers multiple opportunities for experiential learning and for students to learn things that go beyond what is taught in the formal coursework. Students can become actively engaged in the production of knowledge. Programs aimed at sophomores should capitalize on this potential, for example, by asking students to explore neighborhoods, organizations, institutions on their own and then report back to the class. Students could also be engaged in conversations that explicitly help them identify how to learn from experience.

Develop a Thorough Reentry Program

Learning from study abroad does not end when students return to the United States. They will have had experiences that take time to understand fully and some they will ponder for years to come. Reentry programming includes opportunities for (a) guiding reflection on these experiences, (b) connecting students with others who have studied abroad, and (c) helping students talk about their experience. Many returned students are unable to articulate fully the transformations they have undergone and the skills they have gained through study abroad. Reentry programming can help students push beyond initial reactions—"I had the most amazing experience" or "I can't believe I saw the Taj Mahal!"—to recognize what they have gained in resourcefulness, flexibility, ability to work with people from diverse backgrounds, and language fluency.

Consider the Issue of Cost

As study abroad spreads to new audiences, the issue of cost frequently surfaces. For most private, residential institutions, study abroad costs are paid out of regular tuition, room, and board, so there is no (or minimal) additional cost. For public institutions, however, study abroad can present new financial demands. Even if tuition remains the same, there are travel costs. And for students who must work to finance their education, there is the loss of work time. As institutions commit to greater global learning for all students, they must take up this issue in several ways. Financial aid packages must be managed so as to support study abroad, particularly during the summer. Institutions must seek (or reallocate) funds to support study abroad scholarships and support faculty in developing programs. The cost-benefit ratio of studying abroad related to earnings potential should be explored. Of equal importance, institutions must integrate study abroad into curricular requirements. In a recent survey, 70 percent of the 700 students polled said that finances alone would not deter them from study abroad; institutional barriers are far more important (Raby, 2007).

Remember Community Colleges

With the large number of students who do not continue on to four-year institutions, it is important to recognize that if community colleges do not provide programs these students will not have access to study abroad (Green, 2007; Raby & Valeau, 2007) and the resulting personal and academic benefits. Community colleges face many of the same issues that four-year institutions do in enhancing study abroad on their campuses (Green, 2007), so the information presented here is relevant to all college types. One strategy that community colleges in particular have used to increase study abroad offerings for students is the creation of statewide study abroad consortia (Korbel, 2007). Sixteen states have found this an effective way to increase the availability of programs while minimizing investments from individual institutions (Korbel, 2007).

Conclusion

In conclusion, study abroad is not only possible for sophomores but also, if done well, a very good idea. One student put it this way after her sophomore experience in Spain:

> I had gone to Spain scared and alone. And I survived and returned with memories that changed who I am, changed my perspective, changed my life. I learned that the benefits to studying abroad are both professionally and personally immeasurable. I mean, not only did I get to add this amazing experience to my résumé, which I am hoping will help me with my current search for employment, but I received college credit for it. I got to learn about the amazing country of Spain, as well as my own country, my home, my prior education, and myself. I underwent a metamorphosis that has made me more confident, flexible, engaging, and tolerant. I feel better prepared to function academically, socially, and professionally. I feel better prepared for my life.

CHAPTER ELEVEN

UNDERGRADUATE RESEARCH

A Powerful Pedagogy to Engage Sophomores

Kathryn J. Wilson, Mary Crowe

A U.S. Department of Education study has shown that 90 percent of traditional-age first-year college students return to a school the following calendar year. However, "by the end of the students' second year a significant spread in credit generation, academic performance, and curricular participation has opened up between those who eventually completed bachelor's degrees and those who did not" (Adelman, 2006, p. 61). Adelman's data show that two major factors, credit hours earned in the first year and first-year GPA, relate negatively to students' persistence to graduation. In fact, by the end of the second year, those students who do not persist to earn their bachelor's degrees are already 25 credits behind those who do complete their degrees. Adelman (2006, p. xx) points out that success in the second year depends on the "quality of persistence" defined primarily by credit momentum (credits earned per year on time) and academic performance. He argues that the quality of a student's *first*-year record is extremely important, but the second year is *equally important* and is where a student can gain lost momentum. The challenge for institutions, then, is to adopt strategies that effect students' success by engaging them in activities that demand their own active participation in their education.

The Boyer Commission report, *Reinventing Undergraduate Education,* articulates the need for research-based learning as an integral component of undergraduate education (Boyer Report, 1998). Undergraduate research contributes to all five of the national benchmarks for student learning and development identified by the *National Survey of Student Engagement 2000 Report* (NSSE Report, 2000). The benchmarks include educational practices that provide academic challenge, an enriching educational experience, active and collaborative learning, student interactions with faculty mentors, and supportive social and learning environments. These practices address the issue of persistence for sophomores by increasing their engagement with research mentors to guide their learning and connect them intimately to their disciplines via disciplinary scholarship in science, technology, engineering, and mathematics (the STEM disciplines), the humanities and social sciences, fieldwork, overseas study, and community research. In this chapter, we advocate using undergraduate research as one strategy to help sophomore students maintain their momentum and actively engage in their educational experiences.

Undergraduate Research: Definitions

Participation in research may be a recognized goal of undergraduate education, but a consistent definition has yet to emerge. Hakim (1998) defines undergraduate research by four distinguishing attributes found in the literature and program Web sites: (a) student mentorship by a faculty researcher that includes serious interaction between the two, (b) a research project leading to a meaningful contribution by the student to the subject of inquiry, (c) a project conducted using techniques or scholarship adopted and widely recognized in the field of inquiry, and (d) a project resulting in a final product that can be disseminated and assessed.

At Wayne State University, the undergraduate research program promises that faculty-mentored research experiences will include "problem identification; creation and testing of a hypothesis; and presentation of results" ("Wayne State University Undergraduate Research and Creative Projects," 2008). On campuses with programs spanning multiple disciplines including the sciences, humanities, and fine arts, definitions are more useful if they are very broad. For example, Indiana University-Purdue University Indianapolis (IUPUI) offers more than 200 academic undergraduate research program options and thus its definition is very inclusive: Research includes any scholarly or artistic activity that leads to the production of new knowledge; to increased problem-solving capabilities, including design and analysis; to original critical or historical theory and interpretation; or to the production of art or artistic performance (IUPUI Undergraduate Research Web site).

In defining research and constructing undergraduate research programs and individual research experiences for students, institutions commonly note the importance of student learning as part of the overall experience. When student learning is included in the definitions, the advantage of adopting undergraduate research to infuse the "quality of persistence" (Adelman, 2006, p. xx) into the sophomore year becomes more apparent. The two most commonly cited goals for an undergraduate research experience are (a) that it contributes to a student's learning and (b) that the project results contribute to advancing knowledge in the discipline or to new scholarly and creative works. When an undergraduate researcher pursues these goals under the guidance of a faculty member, who deliberately connects research to "deep learning," additional advantages may be gained. Deep learning includes learning objectives such as critical thinking, integration of knowledge, and independent learning (Teagle Foundation Web site). In the 2005 and 2006 FSSE (Faculty Surveys of Student Engagement) and NESSE (National Surveys of Student Engagement) studies, Kuh and his colleagues (2007) sampled over 29,000 faculty and more than 65,500 seniors at 209 four-year colleges and universities. These studies indicated that the positive effects of research on student engagement are related to *both* the active engagement of the faculty member in research and the value a faculty member places on this activity to effect deep learning. The research also demonstrated a positive relationship between student engagement in "educationally purposeful activities" such as research participation, and outcomes including critical thinking and grades (Kuh, Chen, & Laird, 2007, see p. 42). Thus, the impact of undergraduate research experiences on student learning should be viewed with as much interest as the results produced in any one project.

Key Outcomes of the Undergraduate Research Experience

Students involved in undergraduate research report gains in a variety of areas. For example, students engaged in community-based research at DePaul University thought the experience enriched their education, influenced their career goals, and led to personal growth (Ferrari & Jason, 1996). First- and second-year students at Truman State University reported increased abilities in analytical and logical thinking, working independently, and pursuing ideas as a result of doing research with faculty members (Nnadozie, Ishiyama, & Chon, 2001). Students at Texas Tech University indicated increased confidence and motivation for further educational study (Campbell & Skoog, 2004). Additional studies report that students gain critical-thinking and problem-solving skills (Hathaway, Nagda, & Gregerman, 2002; Houlden, Raja, Collier, Clark, & Waugh, 2004; Ishiyama, 2002; Kardash, 2000; Lopatto, 2004; Seymour, Hunter, & Laursen, 2004).

Astin (1993a) reports that what matters most in keeping students engaged in college is (a) the nature of the students' peer groups, (b) the quality and quantity of student interactions with faculty members outside the classroom, (c) the level of student involvement, and (d) the amount of time students spend on task. Mateja (2006) explains that participation in undergraduate research touches on all these aspects of student engagement, especially the nature of peer-group interactions. Engaging students in undergraduate research means pulling them out of their usual social environment and into the faculty members' or graduate students' offices or laboratories to spend time. In the University of Minnesota Life Science Undergraduate Research Program, students of color reported that the most important element of this program, besides faculty contact, was peer group socialization (Wenzel, 2000).

If such experiences are offered to second-year students they can change students' relationships to course work from one that is passive within a classroom setting to one that fosters rich disciplinary engagement and encourages critical thinking. Also, because research is often carried out in interdisciplinary settings, these experiences invite students to think in interdisciplinary contexts early in their academic careers.

Transition to Graduation and Post-Baccalaureate Training

If sophomores lack "quality of persistence," then, not only is graduation with an associate or bachelor's degree less likely but also is the pursuit of advanced or professional degrees. The three primary problems preventing graduation or the pursuit of higher degrees after four years of college are (a) lack of basic skills, (b) financial problems, and (c) lack of substantive knowledge about and preparation for post-baccalaureate education (Adelman, 2006; Carey, 2004; Pascarella & Terenzini, 2005). However, for almost every problem we might identify as an obstacle for retention to graduation or for proceeding to post-baccalaureate training, we may find a solution, at least for some of our students, within a well thought-out undergraduate research program. In fact, studies show that students who undertake research projects are more likely to complete their undergraduate education (Ishiyama, 2001; Nagda et al., 1998) and are more likely to go on to graduate school or professional training compared to students who do not have a research experience (Alexander, Foertsch, Daffinrud, & Tapia, 2000; Bauer & Bennett, 2003; Chandra, Stoecklin, & Harmon, 1998; Foertsch, Alexander, & Penberthy, 2000; Nnadozie et al., 2001).

A Powerful Pedagogy Deserves an Early Start!

Questions arise about how early students are able to undertake meaningful projects and how long students should continue research. We would argue that students should engage in research as early as feasible, preferably beginning in their first year, and should then be encouraged to continue doing research until graduation. An early start fosters higher retention and a higher likelihood of pursuing a post-baccalaureate degree. A recent evaluation of National Science Foundation (NSF)–funded undergraduate research experiences recommends that students in science, technology, engineering, or mathematics (STEM) disciplines should be engaged in undergraduate research as first- or second-year students. The study showed that the longer undergraduates participated in research the more likely they were to pursue doctoral degrees (Russell, Hancock, & McCullough, 2007).

With a grant from the NSF's Science, Technology, Engineering and Mathematics Talent Expansion Program (NSF-STEM), Saint Francis University, a small liberal-arts school, established a model research program to support faculty-mentored research participation by science students completing their first and second years. Retention of participants was more than double that of non-research participants who had the same academic qualifications (for example, SAT scores) (Felix & Zovinka, 2008). A study at the University of Michigan (Nagda et al. 1998, see pp. 66–68) showed that participation in the university's Undergraduate Research Opportunities Program for first- and second-year students increased the retention rate the most for participating African American students, especially for low-achieving students and sophomores.

An early start provides time for students to complete experiments that are worthy of publication by the time the student is a senior. The IUPUI Diversity Scholars Research Program does just that. Students recruited directly from high school are assigned a faculty research mentor who introduces them to research and scholarship in his or her own discipline. By their sophomore year, students are independent partners in projects, developing hypotheses and pursuing scholarship more independently. By the time these students are seniors, they often resemble talented graduate students (IUPUI diversity scholars Web site).

Examples of Research Specifically for Sophomores

Nationally, undergraduate research is established in all types and sizes of colleges and universities, where it successfully engages students in the first two years (Rueckert, 2008). However, undergraduate research specifically targeting sophomores is surprisingly uncommon and is even rarer at community colleges. Of the 44 universities that the National Resource Center for The First-Year Experience and Students in Transition identifies as having dedicated sophomore programs, only one program focuses on undergraduate research (Duke University). A few institutions "lump" programs for first- and second-year students together to engage them in research early in their academic training. A more common approach is to group sophomore, junior, and senior students in research programs with no apparent recognition that sophomore students might possess different skill sets and mentoring needs than juniors and seniors.

In 2002–2003 only 8 percent of NSF-funded undergraduate researchers were sophomores versus 27 percent juniors and 64 percent seniors (Russell et al., 2007). However, NSF programs that specifically target underrepresented groups, such as the Historically Black Colleges and Universities Undergraduate Program (HBCU-UP) and Louis Stokes Alliances for Minority Participation Program (LSAMP), served more sophomores, 20 percent and 14 percent, respectively (Russell, 2006). Following are examples of undergraduate research programs.

Carnegie Mellon University piloted a sophomore program beginning in fall 2008. The Odyssey Program is designed to help sophomores take an active role in directing their education. During a three-day session, approximately 40 students interact with faculty, other students, and professionals as they learn to develop personal statements and craft research proposals. The Howard Hughes Medical Institute (HHMI) also supports students who have just completed their first-year credits (referred to as "rising sophomores") in science and engineering to participate full time in a sophomore-only program, the Summer Research Institute ("Summer Undergraduate Research Opportunities at Carnegie Mellon," 2008). The HHMI funded the Science for Life program at the University of Florida, targeting students in their first year to enroll in a course to prepare them to compete for undergraduate research grants. Then, as rising sophomores, they engage in faculty-mentored research in their first summer to qualify for grants to support research publications ("Science for Life," 2007).

A program originally supported by the NSF at Union College selects talented first-year students, designated as Honors Scholars. As sophomores, these students are required to complete projects that may be either empirical or library research projects ("Union Scholars Program: The Sophomore Project," 2006).

In 2007, the University of Wisconsin at Milwaukee began the Sophomore Research Experience (SRE), an eight-week summer research program for underrepresented minority sophomores in STEM fields. This is part of a well-coordinated set of experiences in the campus Access to Success program engaging beginning students through learning communities, a first-year transition course, and supplemental instruction. STEM students enter the SRE program their first summer (as rising sophomores) to do research with faculty members and to receive personal and academic counseling (UW Milwaukee Sophomore Research Experience Web site, 2007).

Wooster College has had a sophomore research program for 20 years. Each year, at least 20 student research projects are funded via a competitive process. These second-year students are engaged in independent research that provides them with knowledge and skills critical for junior and senior-level work (Wooster Sophomore Research Program Web site, 2008).

We have already stressed the importance of involving undergraduates early in research experiences. This effort is not just true for students in four-year institutions. Gaglione (2005) reviews numerous examples in which engaging in undergraduate research in community colleges increases enrollment and retention in both two- and four-year institutions. In 1999 and 2000, community colleges educated almost half of all undergraduate students who had earned baccalaureate degrees in science and engineering nationwide. Of science and engineering students, 34 percent of those earning master's degrees reported attending community colleges and 14 percent of undergraduates had earned associate degrees (NSF Web site). However, few of these students engaged in research in their community college because these institutions often lack laboratory facilities or sufficient faculty time for one-on-one student mentoring (Cejda & Hensel, 2008). They also lack potential peer mentors (such as juniors and seniors) who can offer advice and support or who can serve as models of success to younger students. Clearly community colleges are an important part of the picture as we seek ways to increase the number of second-year students who participate early in active learning. Recently Cejda and Hensel (2008) have identified four ways community colleges introduce undergraduate research: (a) including research topics in the course curriculum; (b) replacing standard laboratory exercises with case studies and inquiry-based exercises; (c) conducting community-based research projects, and (d) conducting basic research at the college or in a partnership with a research institution.

To overcome their obvious institutional disadvantages, community college partnerships with four-year colleges and universities have provided a number of creative solutions that capitalize on curriculum models incorporating a research-connected pedagogy. The NSF funded Undergraduate Research Collaboratives (URCs) at Purdue University, The Ohio State University, the University of South Dakota, and the City Colleges of Chicago. Each of these URCs, all in the chemical sciences or related interdisciplinary areas, specifically targets first- and second-year students, involves partnerships with two-year colleges, and integrates research experiences into large first- and second-year courses of 500 or 600 students (NSF news summary Web site). At the Purdue University URC, the Center for Authentic Science Practice in Education (CASPiE), the main construct is a six to eight-week lab-based research module, which engages students in a research topic that potentially generates publishable data (Purdue,

CAPSiE Web site). The URC at the City Colleges of Chicago facilitates 10-week summer research experiences for students using faculty members at research universities and small liberal arts colleges to inspire community college students to complete their associate of science degrees and pursue STEM degrees at baccalaureate-granting institutions (City Colleges of Chicago Web site). The NSF also supports participation of community colleges in its Alliances for Broadening Participation (ABP) in STEM programs. The Louis Stokes Alliances for Minority Participation (LSAMP) program within the ABP program serves first- and second-year undergraduates and *requires* participation in a research program. The purpose of these latter programs is to encourage first- and second-year underrepresented minority students, who begin in either community colleges or four-year institutions, to enter STEM careers and successfully graduate (NSF publications Web site) .

The National Institutes of Health (NIH) Bridges to the Baccalaureate Program supports partnerships between associate degree-granting institutions and those that offer baccalaureate degrees. Many of the institutions funded by this program engage students in research projects. The IUPUI School of Science Bridges Program, a partnership with Ivy Tech Community College, admits first-year Ivy Tech students into IUPUI science classes and engages them in a structured research program to introduce them to research practice. As rising sophomores the Ivy Tech students participate in full-time faculty-mentored summer research and continue to participate in research through graduation.

Undergraduate research is becoming more prevalent at two-year institutions and, even without external funding, community college faculty members find ways to involve students in their research. During the past decade, for example, the Community College of Southern Nevada has involved more than 60 research students in research, with 90 percent of those students pursuing advanced degrees (Petkewich, 2006).

How to Reinvent Undergraduate Education

If we are able to successfully integrate research into the undergraduate curriculum in the first and second years of college, we will finally realize Boyer's vision for reinventing undergraduate education. Simply put, we must find ways to incorporate research across the academic landscape to achieve our goals.

Inquiry-based courses reach more students than can otherwise be actively engaged by a limited number of faculty members. At Minnesota's University of St. Thomas (Chaplin, Manske, & Cruise, 1998), a January interim investigative research course is open to first- and second-year biology majors. In 1998, the university offered the course six times with 47 students (34 of whom were first-year students and sophomores). Fifty-four percent of students worked subsequently as researchers or teaching assistants, increasing their interaction with the major. Only two of the 47 students eventually changed majors, whereas eight students continued their research and presented their findings at a national meeting.

Engaging courses keep students in school because they increase understanding, improve skills, and make learning fun. Moravian College's Department of Chemistry has a sophomore course called Methods in Chemical Research specifically aimed at improving the knowledge and skills that sophomore students need to contribute to future research projects. The course dovetails with the department's goal to involve all students in original research during their undergraduate studies (Salter, 2007).

Recommendations

The success of a student's participation in an undergraduate research project is measured by whether and to what extent the student has learned from, or somehow has been transformed by, the experience. The following recommendations are ways to consider introducing undergraduate research programs effectively on your campuses:

Encourage Early Participation and Keep Second-Year Students Engaged

Starting early will improve the likelihood that any positive factor in the research experience will increase student success.

Encourage Faculty Members and Research Program Managers to Acquire Training in Best Practices Related to Working with Undergraduates. The Council on Undergraduate Research (CUR) (Council on Undergraduate Research, n.d.) and the National Conferences on Undergraduate Research (NCUR) (National Conferences on Undergraduate Research, n.d.) both provide information, workshops and training about research mentoring and undergraduate research programming. CUR has produced several very useful publications to guide faculty members in establishing best practices in programming both in the summer and during semester. These guides also provide help for faculty mentors in guiding student projects in various disciplines, individually and within a curriculum (see especially Hakim, 2000; Karukstis & Elgren, 2007; Kauffman & Stocks, 2003).

Nurture the Faculty Mentor–Student Relationship. Faculty members provide essential role models for student development and necessary guides for research. Descriptive studies suggest that it is the student-faculty interaction that plays a key role in enhancing student confidence (Blackburn, Chapman, & Cameron, 1981; Jacobi, 1991; Koch & Johnson, 2000), student retention, and academic growth (Astin, 1993a; Pascarella & Terenzini, 1991, 2005, Tinto, 1998). Programs should match students and faculty members according to student *and* faculty member preferences and monitor and assess these relationships over the course of a project so that students do not get lost. Programs or individual mentors should use a contract to insure that both the research mentor and the student understand their responsibilities over the course of a project. Programs can benefit by setting up small teams of research mentors to work together with students where less experienced mentors can learn from those with experience. On teams, less experienced students can benefit from mentoring by more experienced undergraduates, graduate students and post-doctoral researchers. Also, faculty members need to be cognizant that working with undergraduate researchers can be productive and rewarding but is not the same as working with graduate students.

Pay Attention to the Student's Research Environment. Many components of the research environment contribute to intellectual growth and determine student success. Some students work in teams in laboratory settings to accomplish research goals, whereas others pursue document-based scholarship independently with infrequent guidance. Student success may depend on whether a student is the same race or gender as others working on a project. The project's physical location may also be important. It is crucial that a student–mentor match is comfortable for both student and mentor. A campus must ensure research safety regulations are in place for students as well as for mentors. Program directors should work with the campus office in charge of international programs, as well as other academic and administrative offices that insure student safety.

Set Up Undergraduate Research Programs That Contribute to Learning and Success. The elements of an undergraduate research program should be carefully considered. Program design, whether embodied in a campuswide undergraduate research office or a department summer program, will make a difference to student persistence, career choice, and ultimately even to how a student views the institution after graduation. Students can pursue undergraduate research in formal programs during the summer or academic year or both, or may engage in research with faculty mentors on an independent, arranged, for-credit, or for-pay basis. Summer programs usually provide 8–10 weeks of intense engagement in a research project that cannot happen during a busy semester. Such intensity gives a student a real taste of conducting research. During the academic year, most faculty members recommend about 10 hours per week spent on research.

Make Faculty-Mentored Research Available to All Undergraduate Students. Adelman (2006) has identified the tragedy that befalls students who lose momentum by falling behind in accumulating credits in their first and second years and by poor academic performance. Clearly it is especially crucial to provide experiences for sophomores to encourage participation in the curriculum (taking rigorous courses and enrolling continuously). Undergraduate research is a powerful pedagogy to encourage this active participation, and it should be available to students in all disciplines because it promotes intellectual engagement and better student performance. As an intellectual endeavor requiring active learning and faculty-student relationships, it needs to be modeled to the entire campus community. Program administrators should carefully document the learning gains experienced by sophomore researchers as well as the programs' costs and benefits to be able to provide data about the effectiveness of these initiatives.

Conclusion

Although the impact of the undergraduate research experience on a student clearly is transformative, we cannot definitively pinpoint what characteristic(s) of the research environment are responsible for the transformation. Is it the overall environment or the personal connection with a mentor? Research is needed to reveal why sophomores and underrepresented minorities benefit the most from the undergraduate research experience and how we can improve our techniques and interventions with respect to mentoring and designing the research environment.

Still, much is known. Huber and her colleagues (2007) eloquently point out that a quality undergraduate education is one that fosters integrative learning, that is, it develops "the ability to make, recognize and evaluate connections among disparate concepts, fields or contexts" (p. 46). The Boyer Commission's blueprint exhorts research universities in particular to embrace inquiry-based education. One would expect research universities to be the best environments for undergraduate research activities but not the only place. Undergraduate research is a powerful pedagogy that accomplishes this goal and can do so in a variety of types and sizes of institutions. Capturing first- and second-year students through undergraduate research experiences is a compelling strategy to achieve what both the public and higher educators are looking for in our students. Too few programs specifically target students early in their academic careers. Colleges and universities would be well-served to develop programs to engage sophomore students in undergraduate research, being careful to understand that experiences and needs of sophomore students are different than that of junior and senior students.

CHAPTER TWELVE

RESIDENTIAL LEARNING
IN THE SOPHOMORE YEAR

Jimmie Gahagan, Mary Stuart Hunter

Residence halls are no longer places for students simply to sleep. They are places where specifically planned activities shape the academic and social experiences of students. When intentionally designed, campus residence halls are unique environments that enhance student learning and engagement. Pascarella and Terenzini (2005) found that "students living on campus are more likely to persist and graduate than students who commute" (p. 421). They also found that living in campus residence halls has a positive impact on students' esthetic, cultural, and intellectual values. A University of Michigan study also found that residential learning initiatives have a positive impact on students' academic achievement and intellectual engagement (Pasque & Murphy, 2005). In this chapter we examine the variety of ways that colleges and universities can employ the residential experience to facilitate sophomore student engagement and learning. We give specific attention to the history and current status of residential learning initiatives, institutional policies related to the sophomore experience, the impact of physical space, the role of the resident advisor, strategies for developing community, and residential learning initiatives that can be delivered in and through the residential nexus.

History and Current Status of Residential Learning Initiatives

Designing residence halls to promote student learning is not a new concept but rather one that has its roots in the centuries-old Oxford and Cambridge model of higher education transported from England to American colonial colleges. The Oxbridge model brought faculty and students together to a shared place of residence to engage in the intellectual (and social) life of the academy. As true today as it was at Oxbridge years ago, intentionally using students' places of residence to enhance learning is important. In *Student Success in College*, Kuh, Kinzie, Schuh, Whitt, and Associates (2005) reported that institutions with higher than predicted scores on the National Survey of Student Engagement intentionally designed their residence halls and residentially based initiatives to promote and support academic and intellectual vitality (p. 257). Their findings support the work of Klippenstein and James (2002), which described the residential nexus as a place "where students and faculty can often come together on more common ground, [and] can provide the co-curricular learning opportunities and programs that intentionally support and are connected to the curriculum" (p. 2).

Even though research has supported the educational value of a student's place of residence, the question remains: How can college educators more effectively utilize this residential nexus to support sophomore student success? Many institutions capitalize on the residential experience for first-year students by intentionally front-loading resources to create initiatives such as living and learning communities, academic success centers, and faculty involvement initiatives. In light of the unique developmental needs of sophomores as described in Chapter Four, colleges and universities are now reexamining the types of residential services they provide for second-year students.

At the same time that institutions were considering refinements with their educational programming in the residence halls, they were also considering the physical environments where such programs were situated. College students were attracted to new amenities in their living spaces, and institutions responded by building new facilities. Until the recession that began in late 2008, American higher education was in the midst of a boom in residence hall construction. As Agron (2007) states, a possible explanation for that expansion is that

> Residence hall construction at the nation's higher education institutions remains strong, as the benefits to students, parents, and the college are many. Students get a total college experience with easy access to classes and institution amenities; parents get the comfort of knowing their child is in an environment designed for their safety and personal growth; and the college improves

efficiency of auxiliary services while building better long-term bonds with students and their families. (n.p.)

But market forces also influence new construction. In an article in the *Chronicle of Higher Education*, Hoover (2008) observed that "as off-campus costs rise and college digs become cushier, many colleges report an increasing demand for on-campus residences among sophomores, juniors, and seniors" (n.p.). Economic trends also influence campus residence hall construction, and the impact on second-year students hangs in the balance. Quoted in *Inside Higher Education* in June 2008, columnist David Moltz commented:

> [W]hat some administrators see as a possible response to the recent downturn in the U.S. economy, some of these same institutions cannot keep up with the rising demand of upperclassmen who want to live on campus for a more practical purpose: to save money. Although it is too early to tell whether the economy is to blame for this newfound demand, some campus administrators find that it exacerbates an already strained housing system. This boom comes at a time when many colleges and universities are welcoming larger-than-average freshman classes, most of whom typically require housing. The challenge for these institutions then becomes which group of students to serve, under-classmen or upperclassmen. (n.p.)

In the midst of increased new construction, campus leaders now have the opportunity to shape the types of living and learning spaces in which students will engage. As Bonfiglio (2004) suggests, "what we should be focusing on is whether these facilities fulfill their potential for facilitating relational learning, strengthening community on campus, and contributing to the education of the whole person" (p. 28).

As sophomores move beyond their first college year and their living communities change, many face periods of uncertainty. Therefore, the experience of living on campus has tremendous potential to provide the type of emotional support and academic resources sophomores need in order to succeed. Institutional policies, physical space, staffing patterns, and programmatic goals all influence the experiences of second-year students in residence.

Institutional Policies

Many institutions strongly encourage or require traditional-age first-year students to live on campus. As Pascarella and Terenzini (2005) found in their meta-analysis of how college affects students, living on campus increases the likelihood of student persistence and has a positive impact on esthetic, cultural, and intellectual values. It is understood that encouraging or requiring students to live on campus helps students build relationships quickly and supports their transition from high school to college. It also allows institutions to front-load resources to support first-year student success and development.

According to data from the American Council on Education, "at four-year institutions, almost two thirds of beginning students live on campus" (King, 2002, p. 16). However, by their sophomore year, many students have begun to move off campus. There are many reasons contributing to student migration off campus. Some institutions lack the total bed space to house sophomores; others lack the amenities or privacy that this generation of students has come to expect from their place of residence. The style of room can also make a difference in where sophomores live. At some institutions, space to house second-year students is abundant, but priority in the assignments process is not given to sophomores. Such systems often reward special populations of students and all students based on number of credit hours earned, therefore pushing many sophomores off campus. In some cases, students may leave based on the perception of escaping institutional supervision, rules, and regulations.

In order to address these issues, institutions across the country have started to consider or implement second-year residency requirements. For example, Gordon Gee, the president of the Ohio State University, wants "all 6,000 second-year students to live in residence halls to help create a better learning environment" (Gray, 2008, n.p.). In fall 2008, Miami University of Ohio implemented a two-year residency requirement in order to "keep students engaged in ways that administrators hope first-year students are" (Powers, 2008).

A sophomore participant in Gansemer-Topf, Stern, and Benjamin's (2007) study highlights the difficultly with haphazard living arrangements for second-year students: "Last year, I had, I felt like I had a ton of friends. We were all really tight ... but now we live on different parts of campus, and that was really hard adjusting to ... " (p. 39). However, of the institutions surveyed (n = 371) by the National Resource Center for The First-Year Experience and Students in Transition, only 33.6 percent had sophomore-specific living arrangements (Tobolowsky & Cox, 2007b). In order to facilitate learning and success in second-year students, solid demographic information about where they live and what special needs they have must be incorporated into policy and process formation.

The Impact of Physical Space on Student Interactions

Relationships and community often change in the sophomore year, and nowhere is this more evident than in the residential setting. As Coburn and Treeger (1997) describe:

> Intimate relationships may suffer the strain of unexpected changes after a summer apart. Some sophomores, especially in large overcrowded universities, move off-campus into apartments, undertaking a whole new range of tasks and responsibilities. As one administrator put it, "No one is loving you up anymore, whether it is the RA, an advisor, or your parents; and at the same time you're betwixt and between in your academic life." (p. 267)

These feelings of isolation can be inflated based on the types of facilities in which students live and by the amount of regular casual contact they have with their peers. In a recent survey of chief residence life officers, "38% of campuses say they'll see a net increase in the number of beds in super suites [generally defined as two or more bedrooms that share a common bathroom and a small living space with no kitchen] or individual contract apartments" over the next five years (First-Year Housing, p. 1). This push for increased privacy can often undermine the development of community in a residence hall. As one University of South Carolina sophomore shared in a 2006 focus group:

> I think it's a lot different than when I was in a first-year residence hall. We would leave our doors open and people would just come by. I haven't really met anyone in our dorm this year. Everyone keeps their doors closed, because it's apartment style, I guess. I just haven't really met too many people in my building at all.

Technology also has an impact on housing design and, ultimately, the opportunities for face-to-face interaction in the residence hall. As Rybczynski (2004) states, "Since students have their own televisions, music systems, computers, internet access (the new [rooms] are fully wired), and cell phones, the opportunities for shared public experiences are drastically reduced" (para. 10).

The physical design of a residence hall has an impact on how students interact and can be an important starting point to begin examining how an institution supports second-year students. A careful analysis of both the variety of physical spaces available for student residences at an institution and also what is known about the needs of second-year students can assist institutional leaders in intentionally developing new initiatives for sophomores. Such analysis may lead administrators to an intentional and meaningful overhaul of residential assignments.

Redefinition of the Role of Resident Advisor

Educational event programmer, advisor, mentor, disciplinarian, friend, fellow-student, employee, and *peer-educator* are all words used to describe the work of resident advisors (RA). Functions of resident advisors at different institutions range from policy enforcement to intentional programming, yet no role is more important than that of peer mentor and advisor. Because the resident advisor to student ratios for sophomore or upper-class buildings vary widely, far too often high ratios of students to RAs can make it difficult for a resident advisor to develop meaningful relationships with their second-year residents.

There are many issues facing today's students that can complicate the work of a resident advisor with sophomore residents. As Willenbrock (2008) states, "what influences the lives of students today—helicopter parents, computer technology, and campus violence to name a few—not only creates a heavier workload for RAs but also forces them to juggle several different responsibilities at once" (p. 45). In addition, issues related to major and career decision making, changing relationship and social dynamics, and increasing financial concerns are examples of issues that increase the complexity for RAs working with sophomores. In order to maximize support for second-year students, institutions can transform the role of the resident advisor by focusing on a number of key areas: (a) moving from programming to mentoring, (b) connecting to campus resources, and (c) helping students reflect on their experience.

From Programming to Mentoring. Many campuses across the country empha-size the role of the resident advisor in developing and implementing programs for students. Institutions have developed complex educational programming models based on sound student development theories. As Kerr and Tweedy (2006) state:

> Programming in residence halls has typically involved offering a series of educational events on a variety of topics such as appreciating diversity, building healthy relationships, maintaining personal wellness, and developing leader-ship. In most cases, the success of the programming has been measured by the number of residents who attend the events. (p. 10)

As calls for assessment and accountability in higher education changed edu-cational practice, so also have these calls influenced educational practice in residence halls. In order to more meaningfully assess the educational outcomes and to truly maximize the peer influence between residence advisors and sophomore residents, the role of the resident advisor must be shifted from that of program and activity planner to mentor.

A similar shift was encouraged among university faculty and staff by Barr and Tagg (1995) in their landmark *Change* magazine article. They argued that a fundamental shift was under way in higher education from an "instruction paradigm" that emphasized teaching to a "learning paradigm" that emphasized active student participation in the educational process. A comparable change must occur in the role of the resident advisor. Yet as Kerr and Tweedy (2006) acknowledge, "we had directed resident assistant staff to plan a specified number of programs on these and other topics, but we had failed to consider key questions related to student learning" (p. 10). In order to better support sophomores, learning outcomes must be developed that are consistent with institutional mission and departmental goals. Then the resident assistants' role must be adjusted to address carefully crafted learning outcomes specific to second-year students. Attention must be given to training resident assistants to go beyond simply delivering programs for sophomores to intentionally engaging their second-year residents in developmentally appropriate conversations about their academic success, social integration, and major and career aspirations. Resident advisors will need coaching and guidance along the way; however, this paradigm shift redefines the work of resident advisors and allows them the opportunity to focus on individual student needs and facilitate student learning.

Connecting to Campus Resources. This shift from a teaching paradigm to a learning paradigm can also help promote residents' involvement in residence hall activities. Rather than expecting RAs to provide programs for students, having the RAs involve residents in planning their own learning activities and exploration of campus can increase student learning. At some institutions, programming responsibilities reside with hall governments or other groups and are not the responsibility of resident advisors. As Arboleda, Wang, Shelley, and Whalen (2003) found, "the first line of staff contact with the student—the RA—did play a role in the student's level of house involvement" (p. 528). This type of transformation is not without cost. Raising the expectations of RAs will also raise the expectations bar for the residents.

In sophomore-year experience programs at the University of South Carolina and Emory University (Georgia), the role of the resident advisor has changed and expanded to support second-year students. Resident advisors at USC have one intentional meeting every semester with each sophomore resident (see Appendix B, The Sophomore Student Success Initiative). During the meeting, the resident advisor asks questions and discusses topics based on specific needs of sophomores identified through research at the University of South Carolina (such as information on academic advising, academic support services, and campus engagement opportunities). The resident advisor takes notes about the conversation for two reasons: (a) to be able to follow up with the resident after the conversation and (b) to be able to communicate important information to his or her supervisor and other institutional service offices as needed. Emory University's Coke Conversation program provides similar support and encouragement for one-on-one meetings between the resident advisor and the student. Topics for these conversations include academic success, community involvement, goal setting, and feedback about the sophomore-year experience.

Helping Students Reflect on Their Experiences. The RAs at the University of South Carolina also encourage each resident to use The Sophomore Initiative calendar/planner. This resource was intentionally designed to be more than just a daily planner but rather a tool that can direct sophomores to specific resources on campus and can help them reflect on their experience. Along with the planner, an RA's supervisor provides the necessary encouragement and accountability the RA needs to help make these meetings more intentional and engaging.

Establishing and Developing Community in Residence Halls

Many sophomores may experience changes in their social community. Friends they made their first year may not be the people they want to spend time with as they return to campus for the second year. Romantic relationships begun in the first year may or may not have survived the summer, and thus many sophomores will be redefining their community of friends. The residence halls can be an important place to help sophomores establish or develop community. Living with other students can help them define their friendship groups but also define the type of community in which they want to live. This is true not only for second-year students but can also be true for all students.

Living in residence halls enhances the likelihood of the establishing community among sophomore residents. As Kuh, Kinzie, Buckley, Bridges, and Hayek (2007) suggest:

> That campus residence is relatively powerful is understandable because . . .
> living on campus puts students in close physical proximity so they cannot avoid
> interacting with on an almost daily basis others who have views and back-
> grounds different from their own. Living on campus helps students develop

social connections with peers who are dealing with similar challenges and difficulties. (p. 83)

Living in close proximity not only promotes learning but also can accentuate differences. These differences can sometimes lead to conflict arising between roommates or among members of a floor or residential community.

In 1990–1991, staff at the University of Nevada Las Vegas developed the Community Standards Model in order to address issues of empowering students to care and invest in their community. As Piper (1997) describes, "community standards are shared agreements that define mutual expectations for how the community will function on an interpersonal level, that is, how the members will relate to one another" (p. 22). Standards do not replace existing policies concerning health and safety or other university rules of governance; however, they do empower students to take responsibility for their own actions. If facilitated in the proper way, they give students the opportunity to voice their concerns and solve their own problems. According to Baxter Magolda (1992), this kind of buy-in and decision making can be especially important for sophomores as they progress from "absolute ways of knowing" to more complex patterns of thinking.

Residence hall staff play a critical role in the implementation of community standards, roommate contracts, and other community building activities. Therefore, it is important for colleges and universities to make the shift from the staff as programmers to the staff as mentors to emphasize the skills that will help them be successful during hiring and training staff. As Piper (1997) notes, "we now select [residence hall staff] who demonstrate attributes such as self-awareness, critical thinking, openness, and ability to listen—rather than more traditional traits such as assertiveness, confrontation skills, and programming ability" (p. 23).

In promoting the idea of the resident advisor as a mentor in the lives of second-year students, it is important to note that some sophomores serve as resident advisors. Special consideration should be given to these student leaders in order to help them be the most effective they can be. Schaller and Wagner (2007) describe the implications for second-year students who serve as hall staff. Often sophomore RAs face increased pressure during the first six weeks of school as they build relationships with new students, maintain important friendships, and manage their time effectively. If they are also undecided about their major, this may pose additional stress as they try to navigate a new academic year, make major and career decisions, and manage the responsibilities of their position.

In summary, in order to provide the intentional support for second-year students needed to help them succeed, examining the role of the resident advisor is a good starting point. Faculty and administrators may only see students for short periods either in class or on campus; however, the resident advisor has the opportunity to interact with sophomores 24 hours a day, addressing specific concerns and building the type of positive community and safety nets necessary to help second-year students reach their educational and personal potential.

Intentional Efforts to Support Second-Year Students

Resident advisors, in their role as peer leaders among sophomore residents, have a key responsibility in providing resources for them and encouraging them to participate in activities that will promote growth and development. But leaving this important work to resident advisors alone is insufficient. Institutions must develop a wide range of support for second-year students. Many students enter their second year of college expecting the same level of support from the institution they experienced during their first year. However, this is often not the case, as one University of South Carolina second-year student shared in a 2004 focus group: "I think my sophomore year kind of left me more stranded, . . . because your freshman year there were so many things that were reaching out to you that when you come back your sophomore it's just like you're on your own." By providing resources and expressing care, resident advisors can demonstrate the type of support second-year students need to be successful.

In recent years, residence life staff at many institutions have explored ways to connect the curricular and cocurricular. Residence halls are no longer thought of as places where students live and sleep but as true learning environments that can be intentionally designed to facilitate student learning and development. In designing efforts to support second-year students, two types of initiatives are employed by many campuses: (a) residential and linked course learning communities and (b) academic success and career development initiatives.

Learning Communities

The concept of learning communities can encompass a wide variety of structures at institutions across the country, from cohorts of students participating in linked courses to groups of students living in a residence hall around a common theme. Regardless of range of structures, Brower and Dettinger (1998) state that any type of learning community should develop a sense of group identity in which all participants recognize one another as learners, provide facilities or spaces in which people can come together to meet and engage in transformative learning activities, create a supportive environment, develop a seamless student experience that integrates social and academic experiences, develop connections among disciplines, provide the context for developing complex thinking skills, and continually evaluate both the process and the outcomes. (pp. 20, 21)

Inkelas, Zeller, Murphy, and Hummel (2006) define residential learning communities and living and learning programs as initiatives in which participants share the following characteristics: "(1) live together on campus, (2) take part in a shared academic endeavor, (3) use resources in their residential environment that were designed specifically for them, and (4) have structured social activities in their residential environment that stress academics" (p. 11). Residential learning communities can be extremely effective at engaging second-year students. Whether organized around an academic theme or designed as a cluster of linked courses, these types of communities promote increased faculty-student interaction, intellectual engagement, and academic achievement (Pasque & Murphy, 2005; Zhao & Kuh, 2004).

In 2004, the University of Central Arkansas (UCA) developed the Sophomore Year Experience (SYE) at Stadium Park Community for second-year students. The community supports the overall mission of the second-year experience program at UCA "to develop student leadership who are guided by the character values of respect, justice, service, honesty, and community, and to assist students with embracing their educational goals by engaging in academically oriented activities outside the classroom" (Files & Gahagan, 2007). With 12 buildings housing approximately 350 students, SYE at Stadium Park focuses on encouraging students' service in the local community and leadership development. A live-in faculty member provides the academic leadership for the community. Initial persistence data have shown that the community had a positive effect on sophomore-to-junior-year persistence: 84 percent of SYE community participants persisted to their junior year as compared to 78.5 percent of students not participating in the community (Files & Gahagan, 2007).

Emory University's Sophomore Year Experience (SYE) program offers second-year students the opportunity to live together and provides intentional resources to support their academic success and career development. Residents participate in a faculty dinner series, have intentional conversations with the resident advisor, and are able to drop in and meet with an academic and career advisor in their residence halls. Initial persistence data found that the SYE program had a positive impact on grades and retention (96.4 percent for

SYE participants versus 95.2 percent for non-SYE participants); however, not at statistically significant levels (The Sophomore-Year Experience: An Evaluation of Outcomes, 2006).

Academic Success and Career Development Initiatives

Expanding on its successful Freshman Interest Group (FIG) program, Iowa State University developed a sophomore learning community for women in science and engineering (WISE). The program includes a one-credit seminar facilitated by staff and peer mentors who

> provide opportunities for professional development, connections with professionals to reaffirm career decisions, continued career exploration, and development of leadership skills. In addition . . . students may take one or two designated courses with other women in the program. The program will also provide networking and social interactions among sophomore women in science, technology, engineering, and mathematics fields. (Iowa State learning community Web site)

Sophomore learning communities can also provide the opportunity to deliver services such as academic and career advising to students in their place of residence. The residential environment also provides opportunities to deliver academic success resources to second-year students. Institutions such as New York University, Emory University, Colgate University (New York), and others intentionally provide academic resources for sophomore residents. At Emory University, academic advisors have regular drop-in office hours in the residence halls to answer students' questions, such as how to change a major. Other institutions, such as Colgate University, host career exploration activities for their second-year students where they interact with alumni.

Promoting faculty-student interaction can also provide another important layer of support for second-year students. The University of Central Arkansas has a faculty member live in the SYE village and interact with residents. Emory University hosts a faculty dinner series in which each dinner focuses on an academic area (such as sciences and pre-med, business and economics, English and journalism, and so forth). Dinner invitations are extended to 15 sophomore students, five Emory faculty, and two academic advisors. The students and faculty invited represent the academic focus area being featured at the dinner. Students and faculty sit together during dinner to promote dialogue and questions regarding the discipline and career field (Emory housing activities Web site).

Recommendations

As discussed throughout this chapter, the residential environment can be intentionally designed as a powerful shaping influence for second-year students. However, in order for this to happen, many aspects of the residential environment must be critically examined. We encourage educators to consider the following recommendations for redesigning the sophomore-year experience for residential students.

Explore the Experience of Sophomores Who Live on Campus

Where do they live? What is their experience like? What types of learning outcomes result from their living on campus? What types of facilities best meet the needs of sophomores on your campus? What systems or processes need to be reevaluated based on their input? Collecting this type of information is extremely important in determining where to begin efforts to improve the second-year experience.

Examine Current Institutional Policies Affecting Second-Year Students

How do room assignment policies influence the geography and migration patterns for sophomores on and off campus? Are the results of these policies in the best interest of second-year students? Reexamining policies to uncover the rationale beyond tradition can be insightful.

Reevaluate and Redesign the Role, Selection, and Training of Resident Advisors

What is the current role of the RA on campus? What are current staffing ratios between RAs and second-year students? Do these ratios enable adequate educational outcomes? How can the RA job description be redesigned to provide intentional support for second-year students? What types of administrative changes need to be addressed to make this possible? The peer relationship is extremely important. Any significant residential initiative for sophomores must consider how to more effectively maximize this relationship.

Infuse and Integrate the Academic Experience into Sophomore Students' Places of Residence

What current academic resources are provided for students residentially? Are there first-year learning communities that could be expanded into the second-year experience? What partnerships need to be established to better facilitate learning in the sophomore year? How can faculty-student interaction be better promoted in the residence environment? A student's place of residence can be a powerful nexus for learning and engagement when developed intentionally.

Build Assessment into Institutional Efforts from the Start

What learning outcomes have been established for new and continuing programs? Are they being assessed? What strategies are employed to gather qualitative and quantitative data? How is what is learned about current initiatives used to improve future efforts? Assessment data can be used to both prove an initiative is effective and to improve institutional residential life programs.

Conclusion

We have reviewed several avenues colleges and universities can employ to facilitate sophomore student engagement and learning through the residential experience. Institutional policies, physical space, resident advisors, strategies for developing community, and residential learning initiatives can all be examined and shaped to meet institutional and departmental goals for sophomore student success.

As Dewey said in 1916, "we never educate directly, but indirectly by means of environment. Whether we permit chance environments to do the work, or whether we design environments for the purpose makes a great difference" (as cited in Bickel, 1998, p. 230). As educators who are concerned for second-year students, we have a tremendous opportunity to intentionally employ the residential nexus to support learning and development for second-year students.

CHAPTER THIRTEEN

SPIRITUALITY, MEANING MAKING, AND THE SOPHOMORE-YEAR EXPERIENCE

Jennifer A. Lindholm

Who am I? What do I want to do with my life? Is this the right place for me? What happens after college?

During their undergraduate years, traditional-age college students typically experience an intensive period of cognitive, social, and affective development. In refining their identities, formulating life goals, determining career paths, and testing their emerging sense of self-authority and interdependence, young adults often grapple with issues of meaning, purpose, authenticity, and spirituality. Although they generally experience a common set of developmental milestones during college, students are inclined to face somewhat unique challenges during each academic year. Sophomores, in particular, often encounter an especially daunting maturational period in which they must begin to clarify their personal priorities, academic plans, and vocational paths. The first year of college is a time of transitioning to a new life—learning to live apart from the family, making new friends. and learning how to organize one's time. The sophomore year, however, can be viewed as a time for reflection about questions such as, Who am I? What do I want to get out of college? What should my life's work be?

In the midst of this key transitional year, between their matriculation to college and their upper division curricular and cocurricular pursuits, some sophomores may experience an existential crisis of sorts in which they struggle to establish a purposeful sense of direction and to feel a genuine sense of belonging within the institution (See Chapter Four.) Juillerat (2000) contends that sophomores actually have the highest needs of any undergraduate class yet are the most likely to go unnoticed or not be attended to effectively by colleges and universities. In this chapter, we examine students' spiritual development during the college undergraduate years with some special attention offered to the sophomore year as a time when students' search for meaning and purpose appears to be of great importance. Building on findings from the UCLA Higher Education Research Institute's ongoing *Spirituality in Higher Education* study, we consider how students' spirituality may affect, and be affected by, their college experience, including the dilemmas they commonly face during their second year. We also consider what campuses can do to facilitate students' development during this key educational period.

Defining Spirituality

There are numerous definitions of spirituality but the key elements include transcendence, interconnectedness, authenticity, self-awareness, and wholeness. Although religious values may be connected to these central facets, spirituality may well exist apart from religion altogether in that religion is seen as "organized," "social," and "traditional" and spirituality is broadly conceived as "personal," "transcendent," and characterized by qualities of "relatedness" (Zinbauer, Pargament, & Scott, 1999, p. 901). In keeping with characterizations in the extant literature, the undergraduates we have interviewed as part of the *Spirituality in Higher Education* project most frequently conceptualize spirituality in terms of people's "morals," "philosophy of life," and "ultimate beliefs," which reflect the "values that you live by" and a "part of who you are." Many students we interviewed expressed conceptions that fit with one student's explanation that spirituality involves "asking questions about who you are and what you believe."

Although an individualistic theme was prominent in students' definitions, we also heard clearly from most that one's spirituality has important implications for relating to and connecting with others. As one student described, spirituality is about "what you're experiencing from the world and how you process that and send that back out into the world." Regardless of their religious faith, or lack thereof, students tended to view spirituality as an "every day" part of one's life that encompasses "emotional feelings" and an "individual connection" to "an intangible something larger than yourself."

The sense in which we are defining "spiritual development" within the study is also very broad: how students make meaning of their education and their lives, how they develop a sense of purpose, the value and belief dilemmas that they experience, as well as the role that religion, the sacred, and the mystical have in their lives. Each student, of course, will view his or her spirituality in a unique way. For many, traditional religious beliefs and practices may form the core of their spirituality. For others, such beliefs and practices may play little or no part.

It is also important to understand that, for the purposes of our work, *how* students define their spirituality, or sense of meaning and purpose in life, is not at issue, but rather the fact that our UCLA-based research team believes that academic culture has, for too long, caused its staff and students to lead fragmented and inauthentic lives. People act either as if they are not spiritual beings, or as if their spiritual side is irrelevant to their vocation or work. Academic work thus becomes divorced from students' most deeply felt values and students hesitate to discuss issues of meaning, purpose, authenticity, wholeness, and fragmentation with each other or faculty.

Meaning Making and the Sophomore Year

As indicated in our definition of spirituality, the search for meaning and purpose is central to how a person experiences spirituality. Writing about the inherent connections between meaning making, learning, and development, Mezirow (1991) speaks of how, developmentally, young adults are in the process of beginning to move toward more progressive meaning perspectives. The undergraduate years offer many opportunities to construct, and often reconstruct, meaning as students encounter new experiences and expectations, reflect on disparate perspectives and practices, and try to create a meaningful sense of place and purpose within the campus community and beyond.

Having successfully navigated the transition from high school and completed their first year of college, traditional-age sophomores are often faced with unique transitional challenges that may lead them to experience what Mezirow (1991) terms "disorienting dilemmas" (p. 168). These include learning to balance school, work, and social activities; confronting individual limitations and the "realities" of college; managing an emerging sense of independence; and contending with potential uncertainty about personal, academic, and professional interests and goals (e.g., Hagstrom & Schwartz, 2003). Such dilemmas tend to trigger a multistage, meaning-making process that involves introspection and reflection on one's preexisting assumptions. For some, this dynamic leads to what Freedman (1956) termed a "slump," characterized by academic disengagement and a generalized dissatisfaction with one's college experience. (For more on the sophomore slump, see Chapter Two.) Others have highlighted the phenomenon of a sophomore year "identity crisis," which Margolis (1976) characterized as involving academic self-conceptions, as well as social and personal identities.

As students struggle internally during their sophomore year and wrestle with motivations that may not be clearly defined, they tend to disengage academically and socially, exhibit prolonged indecisiveness in choosing a major, demonstrate a low level of commitment to the institution, and show a lack of cocurricular involvement (see e.g., Olcott & Kotovich, 2007; Pattengale & Schreiner, 2000). Lemons and Richmond (1987) have contextualized the sophomore slump, or identity crisis, as originating primarily from problems students are encountering in four of Chickering's (1969) vectors: achieving competence, developing autonomy, establishing an identity, and developing purpose. As elaborated in Chapter Four, students' optimal progression along each of these vectors is at least partially dependent on simultaneous growth along several others. At the heart of each are elements of both the maturation of selfhood and spirituality.

Addressing issues of selfhood by adopting educational frameworks that address the "whole person" may be especially important for helping sophomores make meaning of their college experience. So-called "transformational" education (see e.g., Kazanjian & Laurence, 2002; Keen, 2002; Walsh, 2002) is characterized by (a) promoting character development; (b) establishing an appropriate balance between challenge and support in curricular and cocurricular programming; (c) encouraging students to think "connectively"; and (d) providing mentoring that is accessible, accommodates students' diverse needs, and enables them to engage in open and honest dialogue with their mentors. Unfortunately, in keeping with larger social mores, the priorities and practices of modern-day colleges and universities have increasingly emphasized the cognitive, structural, and systemic dimensions of learning. In many cases, this emphasis has come at the expense of attending to students' so-called interior development and the nurturance of campus community. The resulting fragmentation undercuts the essence of who we are and compromises our capacities—both as individuals and as campus communities—to develop our full potential. For young adults who are in the midst of an especially formative developmental period, the effects of living and learning in such imbalanced environments can be especially damaging. For this reason, it is critical for campus personnel to consider how their institutional culture along with curricular and cocurricular programming may help or hinder students' holistic development.

Spirituality in Higher Education: Reconnecting Minds and Hearts

In the modern higher education era, students' interior development (i.e., that which pertains to the inner life, or that of the spirit) has been largely ignored in our colleges and universities. On the whole, faculty and staff have increasingly come to neglect students' "inner" development—the sphere of values and beliefs, emotional maturity, spirituality, and self-understanding. Within today's colleges and universities, the development of self-understanding, in particular, receives very little attention, even though most of the great literary and philosophical traditions that constitute the core of a liberal education are grounded in the maxim, "Know thyself." Apart from playing an instrumental role in charting life and career paths that resonate authentically with who we are and what we value, self-understanding is a necessary prerequisite to our ability to understand others and to resolve conflict.

Based on this observation and a shared belief that this condition is detrimental to individuals, institutions, and society as a whole, we began at UCLA in fall 2003 a multifaceted study that examines the spiritual development of traditional-age undergraduates. The *Spirituality in Higher Education* study, funded by the John Templeton Foundation, addresses a number of questions, including

- What role does spirituality play in the lives of today's college students?
- What is the connection between spirituality and religion?
- How many students are actively engaged in a spiritual quest?
- What are colleges and universities doing that either encourages or inhibits students in this quest?

The core component of the *Spirituality in Higher Education* study is a longitudinal analysis of students' spiritual development that was initiated in fall 2004 with a national survey of 112,000 entering first-year students at 236 colleges and universities. In spring 2007, at the end of their third year in college, we collected data again from approximately 15,000 of these same students. Based on the responses to survey questionnaire items, we developed a number of scales measuring traits such as various dimensions of spirituality (such as spiritual quest, equanimity, ethic of caring), and religiousness (such as religious commitment, religious struggle, religious/social conservatism), and related qualities (such as equanimity, ecumenical worldview, ethic of caring, global citizenship, compassionate self-concept, charitable involvement). Students also responded to questions about their activities while in college, their fields of study and career plans, and their college experiences. Emerging findings from this aspect of the study, coupled with findings gleaned from three earlier components of the research—a 2003 pilot study; group interviews conducted with second-, third-, and fourth-year undergraduates; and a national survey of college faculty in the 2004–2005 academic year—provide important insights and offer new understanding into this largely unexamined aspect of college students' lives. The driving questions of this study are how students change with respect to these qualities as they move through the college years and what role colleges and the college experience have in students' inner development. Although our key data collection efforts have focused specifically on students in their first and third years at baccalaureate institutions, the findings nonetheless provide at least some preliminary context for understanding students' spiritual development during the early part of their undergraduate careers. They may also help inform efforts that are uniquely tailored to supporting the specific developmental needs of sophomores.

Spirituality and Religiousness in the Lives of College Students

What do we know about the inclinations, aspirations, and expectations of today's traditional-aged college students? To be sure, utilitarian motives figure prominently in students' decisions to attend college. Fully three-quarters of the 2004 first-year students cited receiving training for a specific career as an "essential" or "very important" college-going motivation. The desire to be able to get a better job and to make more money also figured prominently for 72 percent and 70 percent, respectively. Nonetheless, students' most dominant reason for attending college is to learn more about things that interest them, cited as "essential" or "very important" by 77 percent of the 2004 entering college students. For nearly two-thirds (65 percent), the desire to gain a general education and appreciation of ideas was also of paramount importance. Moreover, fully half (52 percent) of first-year college students say that desiring to find their purpose in life was a compelling factor in their decision to attend college. Indeed, today's undergraduates emphasize the importance of enhancing both the interior and exterior dimensions of their lives.

Findings from the 2004 survey also reveal that entering college students generally report high levels of spiritual interest and involvement. For example, four-in-five express an interest in spirituality and believe in the sacredness of life, nearly two thirds say that "my spirituality is a source of joy," and more than two thirds say they pray. Many are also actively engaged in a spiritual quest, with nearly half reporting that they consider it "essential" or "very important" to seek opportunities to help them grow spiritually. Moreover, three fourths say that they are "searching for meaning and purpose in life," while similar proportions report that they discuss the meaning of life with friends.

How do students change as they progress through the college years? Seven in ten students at the end of their third year in college characterize themselves as a "spiritual" person, while nearly three fourths say that it is "essential" or "very important" for them to know their purpose in life. Fully half assign similar importance to integrating spirituality in their lives. The potential positive force originating from students' idealism is evidenced by the proportions who rate "helping others who are in difficulty" (74 percent) and "reducing pain and suffering in the world" (67 percent) as "essential" or "very important" life goals. Not only do many students hold these ideals, they act on them: nearly three fourths performed volunteer work during the past year; a similar proportion report that they are actively engaged in "trying to change things that are unfair in the world."

In comparing students' first-year to their junior-year responses on selected longitudinal survey items, we can see that students' proclivity to engage more intensively in questions of meaning, purpose, and spirituality tends to increase as they progress through their undergraduate careers. For example, the proportion of students for whom "developing a meaningful philosophy of life" is an "essential" or "very important" life goal increased from roughly four-in-ten to just over half. From the first year to the junior year, the proportion of students who prioritized "integrating spirituality in my life" and "seeking opportunities to grow spiritually" increased by similar margins.

Overall, as students progress through their undergraduate careers, their journey tends to become focused not just on outward pursuits and concerns but also on more inward considerations. Not unexpectedly, our findings also reveal that it is during times of uncertainty and struggle that students are most likely both to reflect privately and to engage publicly in conversation about life's "big questions" and the answers that they have or hope to find. And given what we know from the extant literature on sophomores, there is no question that the second year in college may be an especially pivotal time in students' transition to thinking more holistically about their lives and to engaging more intensively with existential questions.

For example, according to Chickering (1969), many sophomores are grappling with developing a sense of purpose and establishing a life plan that integrates their personal priorities with respect to vocational interests, lifestyle issues, and recreational pursuits. Simultaneously, sophomores are commonly confronted with intensified internal and external expectations for demonstrating both their academic and social competencies. Moreover, it is often during the sophomore year that students are first directly challenged with increasing their emotional and instrumental independence while recognizing and appreciating the necessity of their interdependence with others and their accountability to the broader community. As Chickering and Reisser (1993) have detailed, achieving competence in one's intellectual abilities, physical and manual skills, and social and interpersonal relationships is a critical developmental objective during the undergraduate years. Through the inevitable highs and lows of this developmental trajectory, our findings show that many students rely on their spiritual moorings. They also anticipate that their undergraduate experience will aid their integrative and meaning making capacities. But how are students' developmental needs being addressed by colleges and universities?

Meaning, Purpose, Spirituality, and the Campus Environment

Findings from the *Spirituality in Higher Education* study reveal that even as they enter college students tend to have high expectations for how their undergraduate experience will affect their emotional and spiritual development. Roughly two-thirds, for example, indicate that it is "essential" or "very important" for their college experience to enhance their self-understanding, prepare them for responsible citizenship, and provide for their emotional development. Nearly half have similarly strong expectations that their campus will encourage personal expressions of spirituality.

Our student interviews and results from the 2003 pilot survey that we conducted with third-year undergraduates underscored these sentiments. The conversations also revealed students' varied experiences with respect to addressing spiritual issues on campus. Given that the spiritual dimension of their lives is inherently personal, students reported that they are "cautious" about how they engage in related dialogue and with whom they have such discussions. There was also widespread agreement that initiating such conversations can be challenging. However, most students expressed their openness to addressing spiritual topics, both within and outside the classroom, provided that they felt safe within that environment, perceived that they would be listened to without judgment, and trusted that their perspectives would be valued.

Despite the high overall levels of spiritual interest, commitment, and engagement among today's college students, it appears from our work to date that most colleges and universities are doing little to help students explore these issues and support their search in the sphere of values and beliefs. For example, in 2003, more than half of the college juniors who participated in our pilot survey said that their professors "never" provide opportunities to discuss the meaning and purpose of life. Similarly, nearly two-thirds indicated that professors "never" encourage discussions of spiritual or religious matters. Although approximately four-in-ten students say that their religious or spiritual beliefs had been strengthened by "new ideas encountered in classes," just over half reported that classroom experiences have had no impact. Only slightly more than half were "satisfied" with how their college experiences have provided "opportunities for religious/spiritual reflection."

Our current study addresses just one group of educators' views—faculty. However, the findings from this aspect of our work offer important environmental perspective and provide a starting point for discussion about how to attend most effectively and appropriately to the spiritual side of college student development. Looking across all types of colleges and universities, nearly two-thirds of faculty consider themselves religious whereas just over eight in ten self-identify as spiritual.

Not unsurprisingly, being highly spiritual (as determined based on one's patterned responses to selected survey items) is also strongly correlated with faculty views about undergraduate education goals that pertain specifically to the importance of students' personal and spiritual development. In addition, faculty who are more spiritual—based on their own self-identification, the personal priority they place on seeking opportunities to grow spiritually, and the personal value they attribute to integrating spirituality in their lives—are much more likely to use "student-centered" pedagogical methods (such as class discussions, student self-evaluation, reflective writing, and journaling) when teaching undergraduates (see Lindholm & Astin, 2008). These faculty are also more likely to engage in civic-minded practice, such as using their scholarship to address local community needs. Overall, roughly half or more faculty across academic disciplines "disagree" that the spiritual dimension of their lives has "no place" within the academy. In addition, more than half of faculty believe that enhancing self-understanding, developing moral character, and helping students develop personal values are "essential" or "very important" goals for undergraduate education.

Faculty reticence to incorporate discussion of spirituality in the classroom tends to stem, most generally, from a feeling that such considerations are more appropriately the unilateral business of others on campus, namely offices of religious life, chaplains, and student affairs professionals. Other factors that mediate against faculty embracing the notion of addressing spirituality-related questions or concerns include concerns about proselytizing, fears about challenging academic norms or undermining one's intellectual status, lack of expertise in issues relating to spirituality, and simply the perceived challenge of addressing spiritual matters within disciplinary content (Bryant & Schwartz, 2007). Certainly in striving to create campus communities that optimally support students' holistic development and honor the presence and value of mind, heart, and soul, a wide range of considerations must be weighted. What may be "right" or "best" for one institution doesn't necessarily apply uniformly. However, there is a common concern for higher education institutions in that their traditional-age undergraduates are in the midst of a critical developmental period and many desire to establish and maintain connections between the so-called interior and exterior aspects of their lives.

As elaborated earlier, sophomores are often uniquely challenged intellectually, socially, emotionally, and spiritually. Moreover, until recently, their special developmental interests and needs have tended to be minimally researched and sporadically prioritized within institutional contexts. In the final section of this chapter, we highlight a few potentially promising avenues for integrating typically disparate elements of the undergraduate education.

Toward a More Integrative Approach to Undergraduate Education

Because the sophomore year is often a time of great internal transition, the challenge for campuses is to determine how to most effectively support students during this developmentally important period through curricular and cocurricular programming. Much of the literature on the second-year experience is focused specifically toward that end.

The most common recommendations center around residential life programs (such as creating living-learning communities) that help sophomores connect with each other and share common interests and concerns; academic courses that provide sophomores with mentoring experiences from faculty (through research involvement or other professional apprenticeship opportunities) or specialized opportunities to engage in interdisciplinary work or service-learning; and other more generalized educational experiences that promote students' interaction with campus professionals, whose insights and expertise can help support them in making informed personal, academic, and professional decisions (e.g., programming that reminds sophomores about available services on campus, events that encourage discussion about major and career choices).

Within any of these general categories of ideas for enhancing the sophomore-year experience, there is potential for providing students with opportunities to integrate questions of meaning, purpose, values, and spirituality during the sophomore year and beyond. Developmentally productive meaning-making processes that may promote emotional and spiritual maturity encompasses a range of subprocesses, including

- Recognizing that others have experienced similarly unsettling sentiments and have succeeded in negotiating positive outcomes
- Exploring possibilities for new roles, relationships, and behaviors; planning a course of action
- Acquiring the knowledge and skills needed to implement one's plans
- Provisionally trying out new roles
- Building competence and self-confidence in new roles and relationships
- Reintegrating new perspectives into one's existing worldview (Mezirow, 1991, pp. 168–169)

In an effort to begin thinking about how campuses can attend more purposefully to the interior aspects of students' lives, our research team hosted in fall 2006 a National Institute on Incorporating Spirituality into the Curriculum and Co-curriculum. Teams of faculty and administrators from ten diverse campuses across the country spent three days discussing the inherent structural and cultural complexities of such initiatives, as well as the tremendous range of possibilities for making minor modifications to existing perceptions and practices. From a curricular standpoint, ideas centered on ways to introduce faculty to students' interest and engagement in this realm and to help them feel better prepared to address comments and questions that may arise within classroom discussions or academic advisement meetings. Cocurricular efforts included creating theme residence halls and providing opportunities within convocation and selected other institutional gatherings for campus community members to consider fundamental questions. Also promising are efforts to create new partnerships and promote open dialogue among all of those on campus whose work plays a key role in various student development dimensions, but who may not necessarily communicate regularly with each other (such as student affairs professionals, chaplains, faculty, career counselors, psychological services professionals). Others (such as Braskamp, Trautvetter, & Ward, 2006 and Chickering, Dalton, & Stamm, 2006) have also considered avenues for aiding students' search for meaning and purpose and developed an excellent set of broadly based recommendations for encouraging authenticity, spirituality, and purposeful student development within undergraduate education.

The design and implementation of these and other curricular and cocurricular efforts can be facilitated by conducting additional research that focuses more specifically on the spiritual interests and needs of sophomore students. From our current longitudinal research, we see evidence of notable change in students' perspectives during the first three years in college. Additional empirical efforts that focus specifically on how the sophomore-year experience affects and is affected by students' spiritual inclinations and engagement (or lack thereof) will no doubt provide valuable further information that can inform institutional practice.

Both qualitative and quantitative approaches can serve these interests well. For example, the existing surveys and scales we have developed as part of the ongoing *Spirituality in Higher Education* study are available to researchers who are interested in focusing specifically on the sophomore experience. Similarly, we encourage others to design qualitative studies employing interviews to explore in-depth how second-year students conceive of their spirituality, the extent to which they are struggling with various aspects of developing meaning and purpose in their lives, and how they perceive the respective roles of campus ministers, faculty, student affairs professionals, administrators, peers, and others on campus with respect to potentially facilitating their spiritual growth during this specific phase of their undergraduate careers.

Also important would be studies that look beyond students who are attending four-year colleges and universities. For example, how do the perceptions and experiences of students at two-year colleges compare with those of their peers at baccalaureate institutions? What unique challenges do second-year students at two-year colleges encounter as they prepare to complete their associate degree and possibly transfer to continue their undergraduate education? These are just a few of the many potentially fruitful avenues of research that can ultimately serve to inform institutional efforts aimed at enhancing this often overlooked, yet critical, aspect of undergraduate student development.

Conclusion

Given previous literature on the sophomore-year experience and the insights offered in this volume, it is of paramount importance that colleges deliberately focus their efforts in assisting students in their search for meaning and purpose. The sophomore year is a developmentally critical year for students who experience pressure to make vocational decisions and who go through a process of self-exploration about who they are and what choices will match best their intellectual and career interests. We hope that the insights reported in this chapter will prove useful as we learn more about sophomores and how colleges can contribute to their academic and personal development.

PART THREE

CAMPUS PRACTICE AND IMPLICATIONS

In Part Three we focus on issues of implementation and planning. We look more broadly at programmatic approaches to offer step-by-step guides to developing or strengthening offerings for sophomore students.

Specifically, in Chapter Fourteen Julie Tetley, Barbara F. Tobolowsky, and Edward K. Chan discuss how to go about getting a program up and running. They offer goals to consider when creating a holistic program and steps to take to turn those ideas into reality. In Chapter Fifteen Ann M. Gansemer-Topf and Jerry A. Pattengale offer a guide to assessment, which is an element critical to the development and institutionalization of any effort. Finally, in the book's concluding chapter, the book editors provide a synthesis of some of the key recommendations that emerged from the individual chapters. The hope is that these suggestions will help educators better understand their students, build their case for attending to second-year students, form productive partnerships across campus, and, most important, empower their second-year students to succeed.

CHAPTER FOURTEEN

DESIGNING AND IMPLEMENTING NEW INITIATIVES FOR SOPHOMORES

Julie Tetley, Barbara F. Tobolowsky, Edward K. Chan

Early research on college attrition found that approximately 85 percent of students who drop out of college do so within the first two years of college (Astin, 1977). In response to this, research beginning in the 1980s and continuing to the present investigated the unique developmental needs and experiences of first-year students. As a result, American colleges and universities developed intentionally designed programs and courses that have contributed to increased academic engagement and end-of-first-year retention rates across the country (Upcraft, Gardner, & Barefoot, 2005).

The same history has not surrounded the creation of developmentally appropriate second-year programs. Pattengale and Schreiner (2000) concluded, "sophomores received the least attention of any class" and that "continued programming and services are thought to be no longer necessary as students move successfully into their second year of college" (p. v). The unintended result is that, until recently, sophomores, in comparison, have been largely ignored at many institutions.

Research supports these views. In a national study of second-year students, Jullierat (2000) found that among all college students, sophomores are significantly less satisfied with their college experience in four main areas that they also rank as highly important: (a) the approachability and concern of their advisors, (b) the registration process being free of scheduling conflicts, (c) the receipt of timely feedback from faculty in a course, and (d) the caring nature of faculty members.

Furthermore, Flanagan (1991) found in his study of small liberal arts colleges that second-to-third-year attrition was as great as first-to-second-year attrition. Though this finding may not be true in other types of institution, it does suggest a potential issue and a need to devote greater attention to second-year students.

Designing institutional programs to address the unique needs of sophomore students is complex and challenging but is clearly needed. This chapter presents the common challenges for sophomores, discusses components of second-year programs, offers steps for creating initiatives aimed at second-year students, and ends with a summary and recommendations for practitioners.

Second-Year Challenges

Sophomore issues are inextricably tied to the specific institutional environment: commuter versus residential, small versus large, traditional versus nontraditional student populations, two-year versus four-year, open versus selective admission, urban versus rural. Nevertheless, given the constellation of variables, a number of experiences present common challenges for sophomore students. These challenges and experiences of second-year students often include the following:

1. Questioning beliefs and values
2. Searching for meaning, purpose, and identity
3. Exploring and selecting an academic major and possible vocational choices
4. Dealing with pressures related to future plans including internships, study abroad, and life after college
5. Questioning whether to remain at the institution of original matriculation or transfer

Regardless of institutional type, second-year students must resolve these issues to feel connected to their academic interest area or major, to the faculty and students within the major department, and, in turn, to the institution. Sophomore students who fail to make these connections may question their purpose for continuing at a particular institution or even college in general.

There are a number of programmatic approaches available to help students address these concerns. One such approach is a sophomore-specific seminar or course. These seminars look very different depending on the institution, its history, and its mission. For example, according to a survey of institutional initiatives for sophomore students conducted by the National Resource Center for The First-Year Experience® and Students in Transition (NRC), Oglethorpe University (Georgia) offers an optional "Sophomore Choices" course that helps students "develop a greater awareness of their [future] options such as internships, majors, and graduate school." Crown College in St. Bonifacius (Minnesota) offers a spiritual formation and leadership course for second-year students to help "prepare students to grow spiritually and in their leadership skills." Even though these courses have unique objectives tied to the institutional mission, each is a vehicle to intentionally address various challenges of the second year.

Two-year institutions represent a large portion of higher education; nearly half (1,848) of the 4,392 institutions listed by the Carnegie Foundations are two-year schools (Carnegie Classification, 2005). Clearly, addressing sophomore needs at two-year colleges requires a different approach, because the first- to second-year transition is inherently different. In an effort to acknowledge these unique transition issues, Joe Cuseo at Marymount College (California), proposed a two-year model that equates the first semester with the first year, the second semester with the sophomore year, the third semester with the junior year, and the fourth semester with the senior year (J. Cuseo, 2007, personal communication). Using this model as a framework, it is likely that many students at two-year colleges would experience pressures to make decisions about an academic interest area or major during the second semester of college. This compressed schedule may require community colleges to begin focusing more attention on students at the end of their first semester through the second and third semesters of college. In addition, it is evident that many two-year institutions have put in place processes to help their second-year students transfer to four-year campuses. For example, the Marymount College Advisement Center offers the "Transfer Access Program" (TAP) to support students transferring to four-year institutions (Marymount College, n.d.). Therefore, although the timing may vary, sophomores at two-year institutions may face many of the same challenges as students at four-year campuses and may benefit from greater academic support as they make their next transition either to a vocation or a four-year college.

Components of Second-Year Programs

At any institution, regardless of type, sophomore programs will ideally go beyond retention and progression issues and connect directly to student learning, engagement, and the institutional mission. This connection is perhaps even more important for sophomore programs than it is during the first year when the needs of students are more clearly focused on the transition to college life. The link between sophomore programs and the institutional mission should bear a direct relationship on where the program is located (student affairs, academic affairs, or a partnership between the two) and what shape the program takes (curricular or cocurricular). At four-year institutions, a sophomore program should exist as one link in a continuous chain of transitions from the first year to graduation; at two-year institutions, the second year should be an endpoint from which sophomores will take the next step either to a four-year program or full-time employment. Moreover, institutions should tailor the program to their particular population of students based on a comprehensive needs assessment.

A review of literature on the topic and the findings from the survey conducted by the NRC revealed that sophomore programs and initiatives include a variety of components, each designed to address an area of sophomore students' development needs. (See Chapter Four for more information about sophomore student development.) These components present students with opportunities to

- Be academically engaged (e.g., curricular and living-learning communities)
- Build a sense of community and class identity (e.g., class councils, sophomore-specific dinners, lectures, residential hall programs, large social events)
- Interact with faculty outside of class (e.g., co-teaching and research opportunities)
- Conduct critical self-assessment (e.g., sophomore-focused Myers-Briggs or Holland Self-Directed Search workshops, advising programs)
- Plan for their immediate and long-term future (e.g., study abroad and internships)
- Explore potential majors and interests (e.g., major and career fairs)
- Interact socially with peers (e.g., retreats, sophomore residence halls)
- Become involved in campus activities and leadership development, (e.g., service-learning, peer teaching, leadership in campus organizations)

Given the unique challenges and issues that sophomores encounter, these programmatic opportunities provide a template for college and university faculty and administrators as they provide support for and develop interventions for their second-year students.

Steps for Creating a Second-Year Program

As with any new student initiative, program developers (that is administrators, staff, and faculty) need to complete a number of steps when creating a comprehensive second-year experience. Although each step should be accomplished, this process almost certainly does not happen sequentially. Rather, some steps will be taken in conjunction or simultaneously with others. However, for purposes of clarity, the steps are outlined individually here with practical suggestions for each step in the process. The steps are as follows:

Step 1. Ensuring commitment by the institution
Step 2. Building support from key campus stakeholders
Step 3. Creating partnerships between academic and student affairs
Step 4. Gathering local campus data
Step 5. Surveying and adapting what already exists on campus
Step 6. Identifying the gaps and creating new initiatives
Step 7. Intentionally packaging and marketing the product
Step 8. Assessing the program from the outset
Step 9. Using assessment to improve existing initiatives and to suggest new ones

Each of the steps are discussed in detail below. The provided examples are derived from institutional Web sites and findings from the National Resource Center for The First-Year Experience® and Students in Transition's 2005 Survey of Sophomore-Year Initiatives. All of the quotations come directly from the survey's narrative data.

Ensuring Commitment by the Institution

Institutions can demonstrate their commitment to helping sophomores succeed in a number of ways from offering sophomore-appropriate courses to designing programs specifically for second-year students (such as sophomore residence halls). In some instances, campuses have decided that student interests are best served by appointing an individual to coordinate initiatives and act as a liaison between campus constituents.

A sampling of positions that focus on sophomores includes the following:

- Deans (Colgate University, New York; College of the Holy Cross, Massachusetts)
- Directors of sophomore-specific advising programs (University of Washington; Colorado College)
- Sophomore program directors and coordinators (Texas Southern University)
- Sophomore seminar directors (Bridgewater State College, Massachusetts)
- Sophomore-specific faculty advisors (University of Central Arkansas)

By charging an individual or a group of people to monitor and support sophomores, an institution creates an advocate and sets a priority for this student population. Nevertheless, sustainability may be an issue, because professional turnover can threaten the existence of any program, especially a program that is tied to a charismatic leader. Therefore, it is critical that institutions create a permanent structure around sophomore initiatives to ensure that the program continues beyond the presence and energy of a single individual.

In addition to these sophomore-named positions, there are countless other positions for which sophomore issues are one of several areas of responsibility. For example, at New York University, the assistant vice president for residence education "advises the class councils as one part of his responsibilities." The director of residential life and assistant dean of campus life at St. John's University (Minnesota) "spend part of their time working with faculty residents and resident assistants in planning activities and discussion of sophomore specific issues."

Although creating a position is one very visible way that institutions signal commitment to sophomores, another way that an institution shows its commitment to serving this population is by linking sophomore programs to its institutional mission and strategic plan. The more connected a sophomore program is to the institutional mission and the more it directly addresses its student demographic, the more likely it is to survive its initial piloting. For example, as part of the larger institutional strategic plan, Grinnell College (Iowa) targets the sophomore year by encouraging students to focus on the values and benefits of a liberal arts education. Grinnell's three-day sophomore retreat entitled "Creating My Liberal Arts Life" included testimonials from alumni about how their liberal arts experience has affected their career and life choices (*Inside Higher Education*, 2005). In order to serve its nonresidential population, the University of Central Florida's Sophomore & Second Year Center "provid[es] academic advising and support services to targeted populations, programs that guide students towards declaration of a major, and services connecting students to campus resources" (UCF Student Success Center, n.d.).

Like any program, sophomore initiatives require funding. Not surprisingly, these efforts are more likely to receive funds allocated to improving retention and progression rates. In some cases, external funds provide the initial seed money to begin new programs, so it might be appropriate to seek support from funding agencies. Eastern University (Pennsylvania) and Texas Southern University, for example, developed their sophomore programs partially through FIPSE (Fund for Improvement of Post-Secondary Education) grants. If these programs are shown to have an impact by improving retention rates and actively engaging sophomore students, they are more likely to become a supported budget item. By creating a sophomore-named position, allocating funding, and thoughtfully connecting the programs to the institutional mission, colleges and universities show commitment to addressing the needs of second-year students.

Building Support from Key Campus Stakeholders

Building campus support for any new initiative is vital. One important step in this process is determining the primary and secondary stakeholders for the new program and consulting these stakeholders during the development phase. These stakeholders will vary from campus to campus but might include key academic and student affairs administrators (e.g., the vice presidents for student affairs and for academic affairs, department chairs, deans), academic advisors, faculty, staff, and students. Having representation from all sectors of the campus not only provides a richer vision for the sophomore year but also helps ensure participation and collaboration.

One mechanism to encourage conversations about developing a second-year program is to invite constituent groups to participate together in a professional development experience. A growing number of companies and organizations offer conferences, courses, teleconferences, or webinars focused on second-year students (e.g., PaperClip Communications, Academic Impressions, Noel-Levitz, and the National Resource Center for the First-Year Experience® and Students in Transition). Participating as an institutional team builds a synergy, common language, and support for developing second-year programs.

It is important to highlight academic advisors as critical stakeholders to include in these discussions. Whether they are full-time professionals or faculty members, advisors play a key role in helping sophomores gain a better understanding of their sense of self and an academic major, plan for domestic or study abroad opportunities, and investigate internships. Light (2001) argued, "Good advising may be the single most underestimated characteristic of a successful college experience" (p. 81). Therefore, gaining support from academic advisors and providing those advisors with sophomore-specific faculty and staff development opportunities is important to the success of a comprehensive second-year program.

Family members also play an important role in assisting second-year students. As is often the case with the millennial generation, traditional-aged students communicate frequently with their parents and family members to seek advice when making important decisions, such as choosing an academic major. Therefore, it is important to inform family members of the resources and programs designed to address second-year issues so that they might act as effective referral agents for their student. Many colleges and universities have parent relations staff who communicate with parents through newsletters, e-mail, and other means. Including an article in the parents' newsletter describing the major challenges of the sophomore year and the campus programs designed to address these challenges increases the likelihood that parents will recommend these programs to their son or daughter. The University of South Carolina's Sophomore Initiative sends a brochure designed for sophomore students to their permanent address late in the summer between the first and second year, knowing full well that the students' parents are as likely to see the brochure as the student. Actively involving parents in the process of assisting second-year students helps solidify the support system for sophomores.

Students are perhaps the most critical member of the team when developing and supporting sophomore programs. Most colleges and universities have student government organizations and class officers who could assist in program development, advertising of events, and provide feedback about the program and the needs of the sophomore class. Colgate University has a sophomore class council composed of nine second-year students. One of their purposes is to create programs for sophomore students at the college. The council introduced a lecture forum where students present research done in the classes, a debating society, as well as dances and dinners. From these examples, it is evident that institutions will be better able to achieve and sustain any efforts if they build support from all the key campus stakeholders, including students and their families.

Creating Partnerships Between Academic and Student Affairs

Over the past 10 years, in an effort to achieve an integrated approach to student learning, greater emphasis has been placed on creating partnerships across departmental and divisional boundaries. *Learning Reconsidered: A Campus-Wide Focus on the Student Experience* defined learning as "a complex, holistic, multicentric activity that occurs throughout and across the college experience" (Keeling, 2004, p. 5). Similarly, Baxter Magolda and King (2004) in *Learning Partnerships* advocated for an integrated approach to promote greater cognitive, interpersonal, and intrapersonal gains during the college years. Partnerships between student and academic affairs must be forged to most effectively meet the complex and holistic needs and issues of sophomore students.

Schroeder, Minor, and Tarkow (1999) describe the essential principles to building effective partnerships between student and academic affairs. They suggest that effective partnerships

- Develop from a common reference point or common purpose
- Involve cross-functional teams, joint planning and implementation, and assessment of mutually agreed-on outcomes
- Require thinking and acting systematically by linking, aligning, and integrating a variety of resources (e.g., human, fiscal) to achieve desired results

- Require senior administration in academic and student affairs to be strong champions and advocates for innovation and change, who make visible their commitment to developing, nurturing, and sustaining partnerships

A number of institutions have initiated the type of partnerships mentioned above when creating second-year initiatives. At Colorado College, collaboration between Residential Life, the Office of First-Year and Sophomore Studies and Advising, and the Partnership for Civic Engagement led to the creation of a sophomore living-learning community. Drawing on the model of Freshman Interest Group (FIG) housing and other residentially based learning communities from across the country, Colorado College opened the sophomore living-learning community in 2005. The living-learning community engages second-year students in a process of critical self-reflection and application of theory. Students put theory into practice, not only in their own residential community, but also in the larger Colorado Springs community. In addition, students engage in a series of workshops designed to enhance civic competencies and leadership skills. Anderson & Schreiner (2000) underscore the value of service:

> By asking sophomores to commit to service, we are increasing the potential for their learning experiences to engage their whole person. In addition, by focusing beyond themselves, sophomores can derive meaning and purpose in a year, which may have otherwise been only endured as a necessary step to graduation. (p. 61)

Responses to the NRC's survey on institutional initiatives for sophomores indicated that over a third of sophomore programs are housed in residence life offices (for example, New York University; Emory University, Georgia) (Tobolowsky & Cox, 2007a). If resident assistants are required to offer programming for their residents, there might be opportunities to include activities directed toward sophomore issues. These types of collaborations can help bridge student life and academic affairs. Additional suggestions for programming for second-year students are found in Chapter Twelve of this volume.

Another partnership that has proven helpful when developing second-year programs is with directors of college and university career centers. Most career centers across the nation provide resources for students to explore their interests, personality characteristics, and values. Two common self-assessments include the Holland Self-Directed Search and the Myers-Briggs or TypeFocus© personality inventory. Although not designed specifically for second-year students, these assessments do help sophomores learn more about their personalities and academic and career interests. Some schools use an assessment called the

StrengthsQuest that focuses on strengths rather than deficits and encourages motivation and an understanding of one's natural talents. When used appropriately, all of these personal assessments can empower second-year students to discover who they are and bring greater focus, meaning, and purpose to their academic studies. Creating partnerships between student and academic affairs divisions encourages buy-in from across campus and helps ensure an integrated approach to addressing the needs and issues of second-year students.

Gathering Local Campus Data

Although many campuses participate in national surveys to gain a better understanding of their first-year students in comparison to peer institutions or a national profile [for example, National Survey of Student Engagement (NSSE), the Cooperative Institutional Research Project (CIRP) Freshman Survey, and its follow-up Your First College Year survey (YFCY) or the College Senior Survey (CSS)], few national instruments survey students during the second year of college. (For more information on the Sophomore Experience Survey, see Chapter Three.) Although national data can be extremely valuable in providing a baseline for comparison, it is also very important to gather institution-specific data about second-year students.

An initial step in the data collection process is to determine retention figures on your campus. Do you lose as many students after their second year as you lose after the first year? If so, are there any data from exit surveys or departure interviews to suggest reasons for this attrition? Often retention data can act as a leveraging tool for resources when advocating for new programs and gaining support from multiple constituencies.

Although examining reasons for departure is important, it is also essential to understand the experiences and levels of engagement of second-year students who remain at the college or university. One effective way to gain this understanding is through conducting focus groups. Building upon Schaller's (2000) work, Gansemer-Topf, Stern, and Benjamin (2007) studied the experiences of second-year students at a small, liberal arts college in the Midwest. They conducted focus groups with both sophomores and juniors to examine the needs and experiences of the students in their second year. The juniors were able to provide retrospective information about the year, which was a powerful complement to the data from the sophomores in the middle of their experience. Qualitative approaches such as this are invaluable in providing insight into students' personal needs. Moreover, they underscore how students' perceptions of the "campus environment can lessen or compound the challenges of the second year," which is of particular interest to college personnel (Gansemer-Topf et al., 2007, p. 44).

In addition to conducting focus groups, another relatively easy way to get feedback from students is to attach additional sophomore-specific questions to an existing questionnaire or survey that is being conducted on campus. If there is a specific residential building or housing area with a high proportion of second-year students, using resident assistants to do informal interviews of their residents can also be an effective strategy. Gathering data from commuter students is a constant challenge; however, their input is crucial especially at larger campuses where they often represent a significant part of the population. At these campuses, practitioners often must make inroads into understanding the commuter mentality or culture that defines standard practice as going to classes and then rushing off to work or off-campus life. Student centers provide a common space for capturing the attention of commuters (and free food is a conventional draw). Setting up a dedicated space for sophomores (such as San Antonio College's Transfer Center) can also provide a "captive," targeted pool of students while offering a support system for this population.

Maintaining a reliable database of postal and e-mail addresses for students is also important, especially because e-mail addresses change quite often. Specialized Web sites are an easy and relatively inexpensive way to create a portal of information that is otherwise scattered and not readily accessible on an institution's main Web site. These sites can also be used as a way to target and to solicit feedback from second-year students. Whatever the method, gathering local campus data and then comparing it to the national data is important in order to create a program that best suits the students' needs and culture of individual campuses.

Surveying and Adapting What Already Exists on Campus

Initiating a second-year program might at first seem overwhelming and extremely costly; however, resources can often be re-allocated and programs repackaged to create a sophomore program without securing new funding or significantly changing the campus culture. Thus, it is very important to find out what types of support structures already exist on campus (for example, advising workshops in residence halls), even if these are not currently directed toward sophomores. Courses that sophomores typically take might be enhanced to address sophomore issues (for example, self-exploration or connection to the major). Those who are in the position of developing initiatives for sophomores need to investigate offerings of both student affairs offices and academic departments to find out what sophomore-oriented, or potentially oriented, programs and courses exist.

In some cases, an existing program or office may be well-positioned to offer sophomore initiatives (for example, residential life learning communities). If this is not the case, events or programs such as a campus activities night, study abroad opportunities, internships, and job fairs often exist on many college campuses and may be packaged as part of a sophomore-specific program. These opportunities are beneficial for any student, but they are developmentally appropriate opportunities for second-year students and can be advertised to second-year students as such.

As mentioned earlier, many career centers offer workshops for students to explore majors and careers through self-assessment and may provide opportunities for cooperative education and internships. Creating sophomore-only workshops sends the message to second-year students that self-assessment is important. Across many campuses, study abroad offices offer information sessions to assist students who are considering international study during the second-semester of their sophomore year or during the junior or senior years. Efforts should be made to advertise these information sessions specifically to sophomores. Another collaboration might include recruiting honors students or students enrolled in senior seminars to work as mentors or peer advisors for sophomores (and using program or course requirements to compensate the mentors).

It should be noted that some institutions might be able to take an existing program for all students and advertise it to second-year students (for example, a major or career fair). In other cases, it might be necessary to make some modifications to workshops and programs already offered by various campus offices—such as, residence life and career services—in order to intentionally support sophomores. These efforts require minimal new financial resources and could be the beginnings of a sophomore-specific program. Other campuses leverage existing first-year programs to create seamless transitions from the first to the second year. Beloit College, for example, expanded their first-year programs to address student transition issues for the first two years of college. The two-year model, developed by William Flanagan (2002), Beloit's vice president for student affairs and dean of students, begins at pre-entry; progresses to the junior year; and examines key variables such as students' academic integration, development of relationships and social integration, ability to pay for college, and assessment of students' skills and abilities. The model also accounts for influences of the campus environment such as policies and procedures regarding financial aid and housing and how those environments affect the experiences of students. This model suggests that although first-year programs have been enormously successful in helping students transition to college, perhaps an integrated two-year model would better serve students. In addition, there may be components of first-year experience programs that are more developmentally appropriate in a second-year program than during the first year of college.

Most important, campuses must consider their own specific student populations when initiating programs. However campuses proceed, it is prudent to know what is currently being offered to students on the campus to avoid duplicating efforts. Then whether institutions choose to adopt an approach similar to Beloit's or address the sophomore year in a different way, it may make financial, developmental, and programmatic sense to market (and adapt, as needed) existing programs to better address your students' needs.

Identifying the Gaps and Creating New Initiatives

After determining what already exists on campus, using the program components listed earlier in this chapter as a template (such as opportunities to build class identity, interact with faculty outside the classroom), practitioners should identify gaps between sophomore needs and existing institutional structures and begin to identify necessary additions. For example, after completing a campus audit of existing programs it may become apparent that there are no existing opportunities for sophomores to build a unified class identity. This might lead to the creation of a sophomore welcome-back barbeque or more formal sophomore pinning ceremony.

In addition, faculty and administrators who are developing sophomore programs can save time and, perhaps, some frustration by drawing on existing best practices from across the country. A valuable resource for practitioners who have identified gaps in their institutions' programming and may be looking for models for developing sophomore-specific program components is the sophomore listserv (SOPH-LIST) housed at the NRC. This listserv is an active community of colleagues who are eager to share ideas and assist those who are in the early stages of development.

Investigating what has worked at other institutions provides campuses that are in the planning stages some exemplary models to consider adapting for their own campuses. For example, dating back to the mid 1990s, Beloit College was one of the first to create a sophomore program and retreat. Beloit's program includes a welcome-back dinner, a two-day retreat at a Lake Geneva resort, and a major exploration and declaration fair in the spring. Retreats help sophomores reconnect to campus life, especially those who are now forced to reevaluate their first-year experiences and need to figure out where they fit. Stanford's Sophomore College offers second-year students the opportunity to study in small groups with faculty during the summer between their first and second year; this type of program can help bridge the gap between the first and second year by easing re-integration issues after the summer break, as well as facilitating connections between sophomores and faculty (Sophomore College, 2006). Although different in their approaches, these programs serve as helpful models to consider when identifying the gaps in programming and developing new second-year programs.

Intentionally Packaging and Marketing the Product

Packaging and marketing are essential to the success of a second-year program. Simply creating sophomore programs is insufficient. Without a thoughtful marketing plan, institutions run the risk of losing support for their program due to lack of participation by students. Traditional-aged, millennial-generation students expect a colorful, interactive product, whereas nontraditional students and commuters often look for programs whose objectives and benefits are clear and tangible and fit easily into their limited time on campus.

The use of technology is one way to attract millennials to sophomore programs. Brandeis University (Massachusetts) has an extensive Sophomore Year Experience Web site that includes dates for important events (such as council meetings and study abroad information sessions), leadership opportunities, and four overarching goals to address in the sophomore year (such as competence, autonomy, identity, and purpose) and steps to take to achieve these objectives. Other institutions may consider using social networking sites and podcasts as ways to connect with millennial students.

One way to package a sophomore program for nontraditional students and commuters is to set up a physical space housing resources and services addressing their specific needs, such as the Sophomore Center at the University of Central Florida. In addition to providing a space for sophomores to congregate in between classes, this approach also allows sophomores to wander in on their own schedule for academic advising.

Brochures, such as those used by Sacred Heart University and elsewhere, can be effective for marketing programs to all types of students. Sacred Heart's brochure offers information on career development, student activities, study abroad, residential life, workshops targeted to sophomores, and a list of strategies for avoiding the sophomore slump. All of these program examples provide evidence of how important it is to consider institutional populations when deciding how to package and market programs.

Assessing the Program from the Outset

The assessment of sophomore programs can and should draw on the many lessons learned from first-year program assessment and from assessment more broadly defined. Upcraft, Ishler, and Swing (2005) offer a "beginner's guide" to assessing first-year programs, whereas Upcraft (2005) provides a succinct overview of comprehensive assessment for the first year of college (see also Schuh & Upcraft, 2001). Many of these assessment and accountability practices can be adapted and applied to the second year of college and sophomore programs.

Of the seven reasons Upcraft (2005) offers on the need for assessment, three are notable in their application to sophomore programs. First, it is incumbent on sophomore programs to conduct meaningful assessment and show impact, because it is a relatively new area of emphasis at most institutions. Second, it is critical for practitioners to be intentional and clear "in linking goals to outcomes, helping define quality, and determining if efforts to promote first-year student [read: sophomore] success are of the highest quality" (Upcraft, 2005, p. 473). Third, cost-effectiveness is crucial, especially for those programs that might need to compete for funds allocated to first-year programs or demanding new funds altogether. Without data, these programs may never gain support for their continuation and improvement. Therefore, to the highest degree possible, "comprehensive assessment" (as outlined by Upcraft, 2005) will help ensure that sophomore programs are targeting the appropriate set of students' needs and achieving their identified goals and outcomes.

Engaging in this best practice, the University of Washington established student outcomes for their Individualized Second-Year Advising Program and used an "Academic Advising Syllabus" as a means for conveying these goals to the students in the program. Based upon these student objectives, they conduct an annual evaluation of their program. Building in assessment and accountability when developing a new sophomore-specific program is not only wise but it is also essential for the program's long-term sustainability. Therefore, assessment needs to be an inherent element of these programs.

Programmatic Challenges

Attempting any new program is fraught with challenges. In addition to any barriers that might be campus specific, there will undoubtedly be budgetary issues. Few campuses have readily available funds that can be used to create new structures. It is notable that the more comprehensive programs exist at selective, private universities where there may be fewer funding challenges. This does not mean that other types of institutions should not attempt to provide programs like those mentioned here. In fact, more large research institutions are offering second-year programming. This suggests that it is important to be able to justify the need for programs, so that the campus leadership will more readily allocate funds for a new initiative.

The survey conducted by the NRC provided a snapshot of what campuses across the United States were doing specifically, and intentionally, for their second-year students. Survey findings show that these programs are often new and unassessed, thus confirming that many campuses, for whatever reason, are just beginning conversations on second-year issues. Some institutions noted that questions of feasibility, which may be tied to resource allocation (for example, monetary limitations), are still under discussion. Retention concerns were central to the development of first-year programs and may be the best arguments to higher-level administration to support second-year students as well.

It cannot be overstated that without assessment, programs may always be in danger of extinction. Empirical evidence that a program is meeting institutional goals and student learning outcomes helps its continuation. In addition, it can aid in securing administrative and faculty buy-in, which is critical in establishing and institutionalizing any efforts. Leadership is key to the creation, adoption, and ongoing support of these programs.

We next offer strategies to help campus leaders develop programs and secure buy-in so that second-year students receive the support they need to succeed.

Recommendations

The following recommendations should be considered when developing a comprehensive approach to assisting second-year students:

- Provide an appropriate balance of challenge and support (Sanford, 1962). Supporting students during periods of disequilibrium and confusion is particularly important; however, it is equally important to allow students to discover their own answers to difficult questions. In doing so, students are more likely to advance their cognitive, intrapersonal, and interpersonal development (Baxter Magolda & King, 2004).
- Strengthen academic advising for second-year students by educating advisors about their needs and issues. During the sophomore year, academic advisors are positioned to pose questions that will push students to think about an academic plan and the relationship of their academic work to their personal lives. Advising students toward courses that engage them in self-actualization and reflection about "Big Questions" can be particularly valuable for second-year students.
- Encourage students to learn about their academic and career interests, talents, strengths, and learning styles by using various self-assessments mentioned earlier in this chapter.

- Encourage self-reflection through workshops, structured academic advising, and service-learning courses.
- Push students to set goals and to continuously reexamine those goals.
- Help sophomore students understand that others are experiencing the same issues that they are facing.
- Be ready to talk about "Plan B"—especially in highly competitive majors.
- Inform students of their resources and act as an active referral agent.
- Encourage sophomore students to consider study abroad and cooperative education and internship options.
- Connect sophomore students with juniors, seniors, and alumni in their areas of interest.
- Encourage internships, job shadowing, experiential learning, and community-based research (service-learning).

Conclusion

The sophomore year presents a host of challenges and issues for students. Only within the past five years have many institutions devoted resources, both financial and human, to examining the second year of college. Increased research in this area is vitally important. Most four-year institutions, and some two-year institutions, have comprehensive first-year programs to assist students in their transition to college. However, many fail to continue to support students during their second year, when students are experiencing a host of internal transition issues, including questioning of their own identity and their academic connection (Schaller, 2005). By drawing on the institutional models and examples presented here, as well as the steps for creating a holistic and comprehensive second-year program, higher education practitioners and researchers may combine their efforts to support second-year students.

CHAPTER FIFTEEN

ASSESSMENT

Evaluating Second-Year Programs

Ann M. Gansemer-Topf, Jerry A. Pattengale

A s the other contributors to this book have described, the second year of college is a time of unique challenges and new transitions. In response, institutions increasingly are investing time and resources in programs and strategies to meet the specific needs of second-year students. Unfortunately, in many cases, little time and resources are being devoted to assessing whether these additional efforts are meeting their intended goals (Tobolowsky & Cox, 2007b). The question remains: Did the resources and experiences provided to assist students in achieving the desired outcomes actually achieve those results? In this chapter we focus on assessment, a critical aspect of second-year programs.

Assessment challenges us to evaluate our assumptions about the second-year experience. Although research has provided some theories and generalizations regarding the second year, each institution has its own culture, services, and resources that may either intensify or mitigate some of the challenges of the second year. Thus, each campus needs to ask these questions: Do the research and theory that support the second year apply to our campus? What are we doing or what can we do to improve the second-year experience at this institution, and how can we best use assessment to achieve that overall objective?

In what follows we first define assessment and then discuss multi-level and multi-purpose aspects of assessment as they relate to the second-year experience. By integrating the research on assessment and infusing examples from other institutions, we seek to provide readers with practical approaches for assessing the varied aspects of the second-year experience.

Defining Assessment

Are second-year assessment efforts different from other assessments that focus on other transition periods? The simple answer is "no." The principles guiding effective assessment activities for the second year are in line with other effective assessment practices. [See, for example, American Association for Higher Education's (AAHE) "The Principles of Good Assessment" (1996) included in Appendix C.] In spite of the widespread use of the word, there is some confusion about what assessment entails. To clarify what we mean by assessment, we provide three commonly used, although slightly different, definitions. Each definition highlights an important component of assessment.

Definition 1

Assessment is the systematic collection, review, and use of information about educational programs undertaken for the purpose of improving student learning and development (Palomba & Banta, 1999). This definition reminds us that second-year assessment must be planned, formalized, and ultimately used to improve the learning and development of second-year students.

Definition 2

Assessment is any effort to gather, analyze, and interpret evidence, which describes institutional, departmental, divisional, or agency effectiveness (Upcraft & Schuh, 1996). Assessment for second-year students can take place in a variety of ways and levels. It can be used to assess a new welcome-back program for sophomores, evaluate changes in the second-year curriculum, or even used to evaluate—on a national level—the efforts geared toward second-year students. Although student learning can be an outcome, this definition suggests that other measures (such as cost effectiveness, staff development, retention) may be important also.

Definition 3

Assessment is the process of gathering and discussing information from multiple and diverse sources in order to develop a deeper understanding of what students know, understand, and can do with their knowledge as a result of their educational experience; the process culminates when assessment results are used to improve learning (Huba & Freed, 2000).

The second-year experience can most clearly be understood by using a variety of assessment methods. Each approach brings insight into the student experience. For example, surveys provide valuable data about the campus population (or subgroup) as a whole, whereas interviews and focus groups offer in-depth information about individual students' experiences. Both are valuable tools for educators to better understand sophomores. These approaches allow us to determine whether our articulated outcomes were achieved. Those outcomes will vary by institutional mission. This is especially the case at two-year institutions where the second year takes on different meanings, leading to different questions. How is the second-year experience for students who are about to graduate and enter the workforce different from the experience of second-year students who are about to transition to a new institution or into a baccalaureate major? What is the experience for older, part-time students who are responsible for caring for family members in comparison to traditional-aged, full-time community college students? The answers to these questions help educators learn how to develop and revise initiatives to assist these students on their educational journeys.

Planning for Sophomores with Assessment in Mind

Despite an increasing awareness of the importance of conducting assessment on many campuses, assessment is often still an afterthought. Programs are created and curriculum is revised because a need has been identified. Unfortunately, little thought may be given to understanding whether these programs or curricula met their intended goals. Assessment efforts of second-year programs and policies are similar in this respect. In their national survey, Tobolowsky and Cox (2007b) found that of the responding institutions with sophomore initiatives, only 29.5 percent had assessed their efforts.

As faculty, staff, and administrators begin to examine the second-year experience and develop programs and policies related to the second year, we hope that assessment activities are an aspect of this planning. Anyone given the task of assessment knows that it is much easier to conduct an effective assessment if it is developed during the planning process. Although somewhat time consuming, discussions about assessment that are held in conjunction with program development are necessary because they will assist in clarifying the goals and objectives of new programs (Huba & Freed, 2000; Palomba & Banta, 1999). In addition to providing guidelines for measuring the effectiveness of a program, assessment can also serve as a roadmap for implementing a new program or policy. Grinnell College (Iowa), for example, used assessment to better understand the experience of sophomores at their institution. Focus groups of sophomores and juniors illuminated several of the challenges of second-year students. The data from these focus groups were used in the development of a new second-year retreat—an initiative designed to assist students in the development of their academic and career goals. The focus group data also were incorporated into academic advising workshops so that faculty members had an opportunity to begin to discuss ways to improve academic and career advising for second-year students (Gansemer-Topf, Stern, & Benjamin, 2007).

Qualities of Effective Assessment for Second-Year Students

In working on a variety of assessments, we have noticed that the most effective assessments possess five broad qualities that we believe speak to the process of self-discovery critical for sophomore students. Incorporating these "best practices" can help ensure that assessment activities will be effective and useful.

Assessment Is Intentional

As mentioned earlier, assessment takes planning, foresight, and resources. Good assessment just does not simply "happen" but is the result of lengthy discussions about the goals, purposes, and plans for assessment. Faculty, staff, and administrators juggle a variety of activities, and, until recently, very few institutions were able to devote time and resources to the assessment of second-year students and programs that support them. Without intentionality, assessment efforts will never begin.

Assessment Requires Involvement

Assessment requires involvement from a variety of administrators, faculty, staff, and students. A full-time staff member devoted solely to assessment will find little success without the support of campus leadership. The best assessment methods will fail if students are not appropriately consulted or encouraged to participate. The most successful assessment approaches involve collaborations among various departments, faculty, staff, and institutional leadership. The challenges of the second year may be academic, social, interpersonal, or financial (Schreiner & Pattengale, 2000). Faculty and staff with expertise in these areas will need to collaborate in order to fully understand and address these various challenges.

Assessment Requires Interpretation

Assessment is quite often focused on a specific population for a specific purpose at a specific institution. As mentioned earlier, although there are commonalities in the second-year experience, differences in institutional mission, curricular requirements, and campus cultures may significantly affect the sophomore experience. Any information gleaned from assessment practices developed elsewhere must be interpreted within these contexts.

Assessment Requires Incorporation

Too often data are collected, analysis is conducted, and recommendations are listed, but nothing is done with the results. The assessment appears to be "completed," and faculty and staff go on to the next item on their "to do" list. This need for incorporation may be one of the reasons individuals are reluctant to engage in assessment in the first place. Although a significant amount of work went into the assessment, it may stop short of answering the question, "So what?" What should we continue or change based on the results? What more do we need to know about this program to make better judgments? In order to keep faculty, staff, and students engaged and willing to undertake more assessment, it is critical that they can see that results are used.

Assessment Is Infinite

As we will discuss, assessment is best represented as a cycle or a spiral (Maki, 2004; Wehlburg, 2007). There is neither a clear beginning nor an end. This reality can be both overwhelming and comforting. It is important to recognize that no one assessment method will answer all questions about the second year, or any other aspect of the undergraduate experience for that matter, but it can provide insight into at least one question. From there, other questions may be generated; that is, after all, the essence of continuous improvement. Also, the assessment focus can change over time, so it is important to be flexible. Assessment requires adaptation over perfection.

What Should We Be Assessing in the Second Year?

Perhaps the most difficult aspect of assessment—at least in the beginning stages of the assessment process—is narrowing and clarifying the focus: What should we assess? Although this sounds rather simplistic, it is not uncommon for institutions to send out surveys, organize focus groups, and begin to analyze data before they have agreed on a common assessment focus. Since each institution has its own culture, challenges, and organizational style, each institution must decide—on its own terms—what should be assessed in the second year. This section provides some frameworks to help focus second-year assessment activities.

Needs Assessment

Institutions that are just beginning to look at the sophomore experience may benefit by starting with a needs assessment. The purpose of a needs assessment is to evaluate whether a problem (need) exists and to better understand and describe the problem (Fitzpatrick, Sanders, & Worthen, 2004). What is the retention rate of second-year students? What is the most challenging aspect of the second year for students at our institution? Are there certain groups of students (based on gender, ethnicity, academic major, and such) that struggle more than others? What resources (personnel, space, funding) currently exist, and what would be necessary to enhance the second year? However, as Schuh and associates (2008) advise, "It is important to remember . . . that needs are not the same as wants" (p. 12). An effective needs assessment must align with the institution's mission and, in this case, must also align with the goals of the second-year experience.

What Others Are Doing

Another assessment avenue to be explored is to simply review what others have been doing. AAHE's (1996) *9 Principles of Good Practice for Assessing Student Learning* provides direction and guidelines for conducting assessment activities. As more institutions implement programs and strategies targeted to second-year students, more information is available about what is working. The National Resource Center for The First-Year Experience® and Students in Transition provides programming, research, and professional development opportunities for educators working with second-year students. Comparing an institution's retention rate for sophomores with those at peer institutions can help campuses pinpoint areas of strengths and areas of opportunities.

Astin's Input-Environment-Outcome Model

Astin's (1991) Input-Environment-Outcome (I-E-O) model provides another conceptual framework for categorizing several aspects of the second-year experience that can be assessed. Inputs refer to specific student characteristics. These may include aspects related to academic preparation, motivation, mental health issues, or expectations. Outcomes pertain to the skills, talents, or changes we want to develop through our programs, policies, or curriculum. Environment takes into account the many experiences of the student within the educational context.

Large-scale surveys, such as College Board's Admitted Student Questionnaire (ASQ) and the Cooperative Institutional Research Program (CIRP) Freshman Survey, can be useful for understanding students at your institution. Although these surveys are conducted on first-year students, it can provide valuable information regarding students' previous experiences, their expectations and perceptions of their college environment, and to what extent they are connected with faculty and their peers. Using these data is another way to assess the "inputs" that may affect students in their second year of college. For instance, if the Freshman Survey data indicate that students are interested in research opportunities or community service, an institution may develop second-year programming that integrates these experiences.

Environmental characteristics can also impact the sophomore experience. As Gansemer-Topf et al. (2007) reported, students find that the college environment changes from the first to the second year. Many institutions put resources into first-year programs such as new student orientation, learning communities, and first-year seminars, which have been found to positively enhance the first-year experience. However, most of these programs and resources are not continued in the second year; therefore, students may experience the college environment differently than they did in their first year (Gansemer-Topf et al., 2007).

Institutional efforts focused on assessing the campus environment and the campus culture may also yield important information about the second-year experience (Upcraft & Schuh, 1996; Whitt, 1996). What support services exist for sophomores? How do residence hall policies, study abroad, and research opportunities address the needs of second-year students? In their recent study of community colleges, Gross and Goldhaber (in Jaschik, 2009) found a positive relationship between the percentage of tenured faculty members and the likelihood that students will transfer to a four-year institution. Although it is impractical to suggest a cause and effect, it is likely that the presence of tenured faculty members has an impact on the culture and environment on the community college campus that results in an increase in students pursuing bachelor's degrees.

Outcomes, as summarized by Terenzini and Upcraft (1996), focus on "the desired effects of college" (p. 222). These characteristics can be relatively simple such as students' cumulative GPA or student persistence, or they can be more complex and encompass students' cognitive, moral, psychosocial, and interpersonal growth (Astin, 1993b). Without examining the outcomes, an institution will not be able to determine whether the time, money, and energy devoted to these activities met their intended goals.

In explaining his I-E-O model, Astin (1991) emphasizes the importance of considering all three elements when conducting assessment. He cautions against focusing on only one or two of these elements as this approach can often lead to incorrect or invalid interpretations. An outcomes-only approach examines only specific outcomes without considering inputs. In this case, assessments would not consider the unique backgrounds of the students, even though different students respond differently to programs and initiatives. An environment-only approach may focus on specific resources without measuring outcomes. For instance, an institution may decide to provide a Welcome Back Days event for second-year students or develop specific academic advising sessions geared to meet the advising needs of second-year students, but then never assess whether these strategies had any impact.

Beloit College's second-year campus audit (Flanagan, 2002) exemplifies a broad approach to assessing the second year. William Flanagan, vice president of student affairs at Beloit College, designed a campus audit as a way for faculty, staff, and administrators to conceptualize the second year. To understand the second-year experience, the campus audit requires college personnel to view the second year in relationship to the first and third years. In addition, it takes into account the many factors that are unique to the second year. The audit requires faculty and staff to first define the emotional, academic, social, and financial challenges and then to outline how different campus offices are addressing these challenges. This process provides an effective vehicle for thinking about and discussing the second-year experience at the institutional, departmental, and program level.

Systematic Cycle of Assessment

As mentioned earlier, assessment should be viewed as a continuous cycle rather than a linear formula with a right or wrong answer. Maki (2004), in her book, *Assessment of Learning*, provides an illustration of this cycle. The nature of a book chapter forces us to present the information in a somewhat linear fashion; however, in reality, a reader should be able to jump into the "cycle" at any point.

At the heart of the assessment cycle is an institution's mission, goals, and purposes. Any assessment work needs to be grounded within the educational mission of the college or university. Therefore, an institution with a strong connection to a religious tradition may expect to assess learning outcomes related to student spirituality. A public or non-religious institution might look at assessing learning in relation to standards of good citizenship. Carleton College (Minnesota) is a small, private, selective, liberal arts institution that stresses the importance of writing throughout their curriculum and has developed a formalized program to assess writing. At the end of their second year, each student must submit a writing portfolio, which is then reviewed by faculty and staff at the college. Although this assessment requires a significant amount of time, it has received institutional support because it is integrally tied to the college's goal of developing effective writers (AAC&U, 2004).

Identify Learning Outcomes. Effective assessment begins with identifying appropriate learning outcomes "at the course, program and institutional levels" (Huba & Freed, 2000, p. 94). If you develop a new residence hall program for second-year students, what do you hope they gain from the initiative? Perhaps you want to evaluate the entire second year. What do you expect students to be able to do at the end of the second year that they were not able to do at the end of their first year?

Baxter Magolda (2006), using Keeling's (2004) work, identified outcomes that are especially relevant for sophomores: (a) cognitive complexity, (b) knowledge integration and application, (c) humanitarianism, (d) civic engagement, (e) interpersonal and intrapersonal competence, (f) practical competence, and (g) persistence and academic achievement. These outcomes can provide a guide to help frame the second-year experience and its assessment.

Experts in the assessment literature offer a variety of tips for developing strong learning outcomes. Perhaps the most important quality of effective learning outcomes is that they be measurable. Palomba and Banta (1999) recommend using action verbs. Verbs such as *construct, critique,* and *analyze* can be easier to measure than verbs such as *understand* or *appreciate.* After writing a learning outcome, it can be helpful to answer these questions: How will I know if the student has met this outcome? What would it look like? How would I measure it? If you have specific answers to these questions, it is likely that you have developed an effective learning outcome.

As Huba and Freed (2000) remind us, "Intended learning outcomes focus on the learning resulting from an activity rather than on the activity itself" (p. 99). The following learning outcomes demonstrate this difference:

Learning Outcome 1: Second-year students will be able develop a three-year course of study.

Learning Outcome 2: Second-year students will be able to demonstrate their knowledge of university requirements through the development of their three-year course of study.

Whereas the first learning outcome focuses solely on what the student would do, the second learning outcome communicates what the student should learn as a result of the activity.

Gather Evidence. When learning outcomes have been developed, it is time to begin to gather evidence. There are a variety of quantitative and qualitative methods that can be used to assess the second-year experience, programs, and policies. Other publications have listed examples of a variety of possible qualitative and quantitative techniques (see, for example, Allen, 2004; Angelo & Cross, 1993; Palomba & Banta,1999; Upcraft & Schuh, 1996). We have provided suggestions to assist you deciding upon your specific method.

Document What You Already Know or Should Know About Your Students. Before disseminating a new survey or inviting students to participate in focus groups, find out what data your institution currently has about students (such as gender, race/ethnicity, GPA, credit status). Surveys such as the Community College Survey of Student Engagement (CCSSE) or Cooperative Institutional Research Program (CIRP) do not target second-year students, but they do provide information about first-year students that can be used as baseline data for future studies. Other institutionwide surveys, such as those about health or wellness, may provide data that allow administrators to make comparisons among classes. Trinity University (Texas) administers a Quality of Life Survey to all residence hall students but is able to make distinctions between first-year and upper-class students, which, in turn, can be used to target specific programmatic efforts for these different areas (Tuttle, 2006).

Identify the Methods Appropriate for Measuring Specific Learning Outcomes. Assessment plans are used for different purposes—both formative and summative—and employ a variety of techniques. The key to successful assessment planning is to align the assessment purposes with the methods to best address the learning outcomes. Formative assessment activities are conducted for purposes of improvement, whereas summative assessments are used for determining a program's worth (Fitzpatrick et al., 2004). The purpose or goal of the assessment may alter the types of questions you seek to answer. For example, formative assessment conducted on a second-year residence hall program would seek to answer the question, "What can we do differently to enhance the social interaction of second-year students?" Summative assessment may wonder, "Does the increased benefit to the students who participate in this program justify the added cost of staffing?"

In the inaugural year of Grinnell College's second-year retreat, less than one-third of the sophomore class chose to participate. As a part of the assessment plan, a paper survey was conducted immediately following the retreat and then, several months later, focus groups were conducted with retreat participants. Students almost unanimously agreed that the retreat was valuable and that it should be continued in the future. They also offered suggestions for ways to improve attendance and the retreat itself. If Grinnell had embraced the assessment paradigm of quantity equals quality, the second-year retreat would have been regarded as a failure. Incorporating the survey findings (quantitative) as well as the focus group data (qualitative), retreat planners received support for the continuation of the program, as well as feedback on ways to improve it.

A variety of quantitative and qualitative methods exist for evaluating learning outcomes. The following explanation by Upcraft and Schuh (1996) offers a concise explanation of the differences between quantitative and qualitative methods:

> Making meaning of what respondents have to report is a key concept in qualitative methods. Quantitative methods, on the other hand, tend to be concerned with identifying statistical relationships. . . . In very simplistic terms, on the whole quantitative methods are well suited to answer the "what" questions, while qualitative methods are best at answering the "why" questions. (p. 55)

There are also direct and indirect measures of assessment. Direct measures of assessment ask students to "display their learning and skills as they relate to the instrument" (Palomba & Banta, 1999, p. 11). Examples of direct measures, such as those used at Carleton College, are objective tests, portfolios, and most in-class exams. Indirect measures of assessment ask students to reflect on their learning, their attitudes, and beliefs. This can be achieved through satisfaction surveys, focus groups, and reflection papers. Colgate University (New York) utilized all three of these indirect methods in its study of its sophomore males (Bellani, 2007).

Acknowledge Methodological Limitations Up Front, But Focus on Results.
Assessment methods, similar to other research designs, are rarely perfect (Upcraft & Schuh, 1996). Thus, acknowledging the limitations, developing plans to address the limitations in the future, and resisting the temptation to allow methodological concerns to monopolize the conversations on assessment can prevent roadblocks to assessment and use of assessment results.

Imagine this scenario: You have collaborated with faculty and staff to create a new program for second-year students as well as an assessment plan to evaluate it. Both were implemented. At the request of the college leadership, you were asked to present the results and implications at the upcoming faculty meeting. You arrive at the meeting prepared to discuss how assessment results can be used to improve the student experience, but instead, all of the questions focus on the validity and reliability (or lack thereof) of the methodology of the assessment.

Unfortunately, this scenario is all too common. The reasons for this behavior may vary and, frankly, may not be worth trying to pinpoint. Therefore, do not let them overshadow the key findings of the assessment, acknowledge the methodological limitations in your reports and presentations, but focus on what you have learned.

Interpret Evidence. In reviewing many assessment reports, it is interesting to note that although authors may spend significant amounts of time analyzing the data, they may fall short in interpreting or making sense of it. They may fail to answer the basic question, "So what?" What are the implications of what the data tell us? Do the data suggest that we expand or limit the scope of the program? For example, if an assessment of a community college mentoring program found that participants were twice as likely to receive their associate's degrees as nonparticipants, should this program be expanded or required?

Implement Change. Assessment begs for action. Using the results of assessment is what is commonly referred to as closing the loop (Maki, 2004). Closing the loop may occur in a variety of ways. It may include making programmatic or policy changes or aid in decision making. It may involve decisions on where to align staff and fiscal resources or guide decisions.

In *Assessment Update*, Wehlburg (2007) proposed the "assessment spiral" as a new way of interpreting the assessment cycle (p. 2). This approach challenges us not to think of it as a unidimensional "closing the loop" but as a three-dimensional spiral. As the spiral moves upward, it also widens. As assessment continues, it can encompass more outcomes. Although an assessment effort in its infancy can be very focused, subsequent assessment can incorporate additional activities and provide a more comprehensive understanding of the second year.

This approach echoes what Kuh, Kinzie, Schuh, Whitt, and Associates (2005) also uncovered in their research in *Student Success in College*. Institutions that had higher than expected levels of student engagement had an improvement-oriented ethos. They were not satisfied with the status quo but were constantly motivated to improve.

Recommendations

We hope this chapter assists you in addressing the challenges of assessment (Wehlburg, 2007) in the second-year experience. As you examine the environment for second-year students or develop programs or policies targeting sophomores, we encourage you to plan for assessment. What outcomes do you want to achieve? How will you know whether these outcomes are achieved? What methods will you use to measure these outcomes? What will you do with the results? In closing, we offer these recommendations.

View the Second-Year Experience as a Continuous Process

This book focuses on the second-year experience as a discrete, unique time in the life of a student. But as Astin's (1991) model illustrates, this experience and the assessment of this experience cannot be fully realized without an understanding of what happens before and after the second year of college. This experience may differ based on an institution's mission and goals. Therefore, although one can focus efforts on assessing the second year, these efforts must be done in conjunction with assessment activities for first-, third-, and fourth-year students and must be in line with institutional mission and goals.

Share Information with Colleagues Within and Outside the Institution

In contrast to the information we have available on first-year students, research and assessment on the second-year experience is limited. Most of the data we have are based on students at four-year institutions. Very little is known about second-year students at two-year institutions, and this information may be critical in understanding the sophomore year as a developmental process. Thus, we would encourage individuals working on assessment to share their results with peers at other institutions. Although assessment results may be very institution specific, the methods and process used to embark on assessment activities may be adapted across various types of institutions.

Develop Priorities

Examining the second year is a significant task. Higher education environments are complex. Students are complex. All institutions are limited at least somewhat by the amount of time, financial resources, and personnel that can be dedicated to assessment. Therefore, take small steps. It is imperative that you build on previous efforts to develop a more comprehensive understanding of the second year.

Keep "Purpose" in Focus

The second year is a year when students focus on purpose. As you assess the second-year experience, what will be your purpose? Both the student embarking on a search for purpose or a faculty member beginning their assessment plan will find that there are more questions than answers. These activities require intentionality, involvement, interpretation, incorporation, and a willingness to revisit tasks repeatedly. Neither of these processes is linear or straightforward. In this sense, perhaps individuals doing assessment can more wholly appreciate the struggle of the second-year student. Fortunately, successful sophomores who have wrestled with these questions are rewarded with a renewed sense of commitment to pursuing their goals. Knowing that assessment-driven initiatives have contributed to such success may also leave faculty, staff, and administrators with a renewed sense of purpose.

CHAPTER SIXTEEN

RECOMMENDATIONS TO IMPROVE SOPHOMORE STUDENT SUCCESS

John N. Gardner, Barbara F. Tobolowsky,
Mary Stuart Hunter

We began this book by raising a number of guiding questions as a focus for this new work and by discussing the primary objectives for the sophomore year as selecting a major, developing a sense of purpose, and, for some students, especially in two-year institutions, the decision to transfer. We also grappled with defining the sophomore student and year and declared our intent to provide a wide range of academic and programmatic options to assist this unique and important student population. We hope, and trust, that the reader now has a better understanding of the issues of the sophomore year, a wide range of approaches that help address second-year students' challenges and goals, and the tools to develop and implement second-year programs.

Most chapters in this book provide detailed recommendations. In this conclusion, we combine and synthesize many of these specific suggestions, especially those that were presented in multiple chapters. We refer to those chapters parenthetically to guide you to additional information on the following suggestions. Our goal here is to provide a manageable set of recommendations for consideration and action. After all, it is the application of these ideas that leads to student success, which is the ultimate goal.

One of the key lessons from the first-year movement is that the most successful approach is a comprehensive one. Although there were strides made in helping entering students with individual programmatic efforts, the most effective approaches have had a holistic, comprehensive, and integrated focus.

Therefore, the recommendations offered in this chapter are designed to support comprehensive efforts on behalf of second-year students. The suggestions are organized around five primary themes that emerged from the specific chapters: (a) understand the importance of the second year, (b) build a case, (c) develop partners, (d) engage, empower, and recognize students, and (e) extend lessons from other transitions.

Understand the Importance of the Second Year

The first step in helping sophomores is recognizing the uniqueness of this student population and their issues and concerns. Here are a few suggestions on how to gather this type of information as you begin to focus on second-year students.

Create an Institutionwide Task Force on the Sophomore-Year Experience

One of the simplest, most cost-effective, and constructive steps a campus can take to move this issue forward is to establish a standing committee or task force to discuss, problem solve, monitor, and advocate for second-year issues and students. Colleges and universities create their standing committees about and around those components of the educational process and overall institutional life that they most value. Such a task force would bring together old and new stakeholders and partners, engage in stimulating intellectual discourse about the roles and purposes of the second year, and bring forward new initiatives for consideration. A very important first step for such a task force could (and we think should) be to undertake the self-study of second-year students. (Chapter Fourteen)

Explore the Experience for Your Second-Year Students

You need to know how your students are performing during this period. What are their issues and concerns? How do your policies and programs affect them? One way to answer these questions is to conduct a self-study of the second-year experience. This recommendation is offered with full cognizance that the most dreaded words in the higher education lexicon are "self-study." Nevertheless, if many institutions are having the challenges and problems with second-year students that are presented in this book, they certainly cannot hope to move forward unless they thoroughly understand their own unique dynamics. The keys here are to study both student outcomes and institutional policies and practices, and then to affirm what is working well and make recommendations to change what is not working well. (Chapters Fourteen and Fifteen)

Survey Your Current Offerings

As a part of that self-study, institutional representatives must determine what is currently offered on campus. Many of the programs mentioned in this book (such as undergraduate research, study abroad, service-learning) may exist on your campus. However, such programs are frequently decentralized and operate independently from one another. Take stock of what you offer and consider repackaging them as a part of a more comprehensive program. This approach helps communicate the importance of the second year to students and other stakeholders. (Chapter Fourteen)

Be Intentional About Providing What Sophomores Need

Part of an institutional self-study should focus on a comprehensive needs analysis of the second-year population. Whatever it is that sophomores need but may not currently be receiving must not be left to chance; this argues for intentionality as opposed to serendipity. A needs analysis allows institutions to identify what is and is not being addressed intentionally. There are many implications of this for accountability and administrative responsibility centers, just as we have seen in first-year improvement efforts. (Chapters Fourteen and Fifteen)

Make Assessment a High and Early Priority

Assessment is critical to building support, making the case, and converting skeptics. All too frequently, we see assessment as an afterthought, after initiatives have been developed, or in response to the accreditation process. These initiatives cannot hope to receive greater claims to attention, resources, and respect without more practice of assessment and the application of what is learned from those assessments. The result of a culture of evidence is a more intentional and focused approach to the second year. (Chapter Fifteen)

Build a Case

After you have a firm grasp on the second-year experience at your institution, it is critical to begin to bring campus stakeholders on board. The first step in achieving that goal is to be able to explain why this focus is necessary. Here are some ideas of how to build a convincing case.

Develop a Compelling Intellectual Rationale, Not a Business Model

An intellectual argument must be presented to your campus as to why the second year matters. It cannot be assumed that this case is obvious or inherently logical. The first-year movement was sold, perhaps oversold, on a nonintellectual rationale: retention and enhanced revenue. This lack of an intellectual rationale explains in part why many faculty have not become engaged in the first-year movement. We must not make this mistake again, even though the high stakes of public accountability for retention are now more pressing than ever. For faculty investment in new or alternative strategies in working with second-year students, there must be an argument for academic purposes and an intellectual vision. A business model is simply not going to be sufficient to motivate significant numbers of faculty to change certain practices in the academic units where many second-year students now find themselves. (Introduction)

Develop an Argument That Goes Beyond Helping Students Develop a Sense of Purpose

As readers will have noted, a primary rationale for this work and for paying more attention to second-year students has been to help them develop and solidify a sense of purpose. This is important because purpose relates to motivation, goal setting, commitment, personal investment, and institutional fit, and hence learning, retention, and revenues. These are all important, but they are insufficient. The central argument for more attention to the second year has to go further than helping students develop and solidify a sense of purpose. A greater intellectual and academic case must be made: What do we want students to learn and experience, and how best can these outcomes be delivered? (Chapters One, Two, Three, and Four)

Connect New Sophomore Initiatives to Institutional Mission

As with any legitimate and new educational undertaking, proponents must make the case for ties to institutional mission. How does paying more attention to sophomores increase the probability of institutional mission attainment? A mission-related focus is also essential for institutional acceptance, assessment purposes, and is an emphasis of interest to regional accreditors. (Introduction, Chapter Fourteen)

Consider Using Mechanisms Now Provided by Regional Accreditors

All colleges must be reaccredited periodically. Regional accreditors provide mechanisms to select special areas of institutional investment for improvement, such as the Southern Association of Colleges and Schools' Quality Enhancement Plan; the Higher Learning Commission's Academic Quality Improvement Program (AQIP) action projects and options for "special emphasis" self-studies; and the Middle States Association's options for self studies "with emphasis" and "selected topics." This approach provides us with a unique opportunity to link something we have to do, obtaining reaccreditation, with something we do not have to do, confer significantly more attention, status, and resources to second-year students. (Introduction)

Position the Improvement of the Sophomore Year in Strategic Plans

For the second year to have greater potential of more attention and more success, it should be placed in the institution's strategic plan. After all, these are the institution's highest, public, and resourced priorities. Upon examination, it is likely that enhancement of the sophomore year would be a natural educational and aspirational fit with other elements of the strategic plan. (Introduction, Chapter Fourteen)

Develop Partners

Sustainable and supported efforts are the result of a dedicated number of people's time and energy. Here we offer a few ideas of how to find and nurture a team of advocates.

Develop Partnerships Across Campus

Students will be more successful in the second-year transition if they are recipients of thoughtful and intentional curricular and co-curricular initiatives that are delivered through a partnership among faculty, academic and student affairs administrators, institutional researchers, and students. Multiple new and existing partnerships must be cultivated. It is axiomatic that one of the biggest lessons learned from the reform effort on the first year is that greater institutional commitment and change for a cohort of students in transition can come only when such partnerships exist and are encouraged, even demanded, at all levels of the institution. These partnerships are essential to execute the kind of strategies called for in this work: improved academic advising and career planning, service-learning, study abroad, second-year learning communities, and more. (Chapters Five, Six, Nine, Ten, and Twelve)

Give Priority to the Academic Experience and the Associated Critical Role of Faculty

Many improvement efforts often start at the periphery (outside the curriculum). But for increased support, status, and probability of institutionalization, they must move toward the center and bring the focus to the classroom and the curricular requirements. This means that faculty investment in the second year is of critical importance in moving this issue to a higher level of institutional commitment. Proponents must make the case to faculty colleagues and their academic departments for why there is a need for more attention on second-year students, what kind of attention is needed, and what has been and might be the educational results of greater investments. Because much of the work of the second year focuses on choosing and becoming integrated into a major, faculty, of necessity, must be more involved in efforts surrounding this transition. Ultimately, this may bode well for greater long-term faculty ownership of second-year initiatives. In turn, the work on the second year must have deeper roots, more ownership in the academic departments, where students are really going to do their most focused academic work. (Chapters Seven, Eight, and Eleven)

Bring Students on Board

Students may be your most important stakeholders. The greatest influence on students during the college years is the influence of other students. Therefore, we must intentionally engage them in the second-year efforts. If the students believe you are earnest in your interest, they will be more likely to give of their time to help and encourage other students to be involved as well. Remember student buy-in is as critical as other campus partners. (Chapters Fourteen and Fifteen)

Engage, Empower, and Recognize Students

All the suggestions require the involvement of students to succeed. Here are several recommendations of ways to develop those critical connections between the students and learning.

Engage Students Outside the Classroom

Engaged students learn and develop on campuses. Service learning is a transformational effort outside of the classroom that helps connect students to their sense of purpose, interests, and the needs of the community. Learning opportunities in the residence halls are another important way to integrate the academic experience outside the classroom. (Chapters Nine and Twelve)

Develop Initiatives to Connect Students with Faculty

Students who are engaged in meaningful and rewarding work with faculty are more likely to be successful students. Undergraduate research programs or living-learning communities that focus on sophomores are two ways to engage students with faculty that result in helping students develop critical thinking skills. (Chapters Seven, Eight, Nine, Ten, and Eleven)

Build Purpose Through Peer Relationships

As previously stated, the greatest influence on students during the college years is that of other students. Harnessing this peer influence can be a terrific tool for addressing students' issues in the second year. Educators must take full advantage of the opportunity this reality offers. For example, because students recognize that success is the ultimate goal, use peer interactions to build a sense of purpose. Successful seniors in particular majors could mentor sophomores interested in those disciplines, thus giving students more support as they tackle the inherent challenges of the second year, such as major declaration and career exploration. (Chapters Two, Three, and Four)

Use Traditions to Reward and Recognize Student Advancement

It is helpful to create traditions that honor student success or acknowledge students as they declare their majors. Pinning ceremonies and welcome back events are potential traditions that may be tied to the fundamental goals of the second year. (Chapter Fourteen)

Extend Lessons from Other Transitions to the Second Year

Over the past thirty years, the institutional focus has been on first-year and senior students. Much can be learned from these previous efforts. Following are some ways to adapt these learned lessons to address the unique needs of sophomores.

Learn from Other Important Student Transitions

In the process of adapting American higher education to our changing student population, what we learn from helping one unique student population sheds light on the needs of other students. The more we have learned about first-year and senior-year students in transition, the more we have learned about other student transitions. This knowledge is the basis for the argument to pay more attention to the students who are no longer first-year but still very far away, educationally, developmentally, and chronologically, from senior-year status: America's sophomore students. For example, one important outcome of a campus-based focus on sophomore students would be a better understanding, and thus more support for, transfer students. (Introduction)

Consider Extending First-Year Student Support Programs and the Scope of Administrative Units to Second-Year Students

Most colleges and universities do a good job of orienting and welcoming students during the first term to the institution. But we have to take this process further. Think of the second year as part of a continuous process of student development. Let traditional first-year supports evolve to address second-year issues. Similarly, extend the focus of the units responsible for those supports, such as university and general colleges, to include second-year students in their individual missions. (Introduction, Chapters Seven and Fourteen)

Do Not Focus Early Efforts on Marginal Students

Given the desirability of gaining respect for early adoption and institutionalization of sophomore initiatives and the realities of academic politics, it is generally not advisable to focus pilot initiatives on at-risk, low-achieving students. Although such students are worthy of and definitely need more attention, it is a reality that institutional leaders will be less willing to invest in such initiatives, particularly at the outset if they perceive the initiatives as being remedial in nature. Instead, early adoption and institutionalization will be more likely if proponents argue that what is needed is for all second-year students, not just a subset. Focus on the common good, the most desirable common experiences. The programmatic initiatives espoused in this book are intended to address the developmental needs of all second-year students, not just those at risk.

Don't Look for the Silver Bullet

As with efforts to improve the first year, there are no silver bullets. Many worthwhile strategies for enhancement are presented in this book, but no one single effort is transformative. Taken together, multiple, coherent, integrated, educational philosophy-based initiatives have greater potential to be more influential, particularly if they are linked with assessment of outcomes. (Chapter Fourteen)

Conclusion

Much has been learned from the research on the first-year and senior-year experiences. This book on the sophomore year is a descendent of those important groundbreaking efforts. Because we are only at the beginning of what we hope is the second-year movement, we encourage our readers to increase our understanding of this population through engaging in empirically based research. Notions such as the sophomore slump may exist on individual campuses, but it is clear much more research is needed to understand whether it is only an isolated experience or a broader phenomenon. Also, much more work needs to be done to understand the issues for students at two-year institutions. Do they confront similar issues seen in sophomores on four-year campuses? If so, when do they occur? When is their equivalent to the second-year experience?

Although these questions remain, the book offers foundational insights into the sophomore year. Most important, the individual chapter authors provide valuable guidance to help educators forge a new path in assisting students. The recommendations in this chapter summarize the many ideas and suggestions cited throughout the book. We believe these are the keys to building a successful, comprehensive sophomore program. Sophomore students have too often told us that they felt invisible on campus—caught between the first-year students who receive many types of support during their transition to campus and juniors who have found themselves settled in a disciplinary home. This book spotlights second-year students and provides the intellectual and programmatic tools for a campus to build a comprehensive, institutional response to their issues and concerns. We ask you to heed this clarion call and join us in furthering institutional accountability for second-year student learning and success.

SUMMARY OF HIERARCHICAL REGRESSION ANALYSES IN PRIVATE INSTITUTIONS: 2007 SURVEY OF SOPHOMORES

TABLE A.1. SUMMARY OF HIERARCHICAL REGRESSION ANALYSES FOR VARIABLES PREDICTING DESIRED OUTCOMES OF SOPHOMORE EXPERIENCE IN PRIVATE INSTITUTIONS

	Tuition Worth	Intent to Reenroll	Intent to Graduate	Overall Satisfaction	Second Year Better Than First	College Grades
Variable	β	β	β	β	β	β
Step 1						
High school grades	.06	−.03	.01	.00	.06	.22***
Living on campus	.00	.03	.01	−.04	.00	.07**
Working off campus	−.01	−.10*	−.07*	.02	.00	.03
Major certainty	−.01	.02	.08*	−.01	.00	.08**
Asian	.02	.00	−.03	.02	.01	−.10***
Black	.02	−.01	.01	−.05	−.02	−.12***
Hispanic	.08*	.00	.02	−.01	.02	−.11***
Grad school aspirations	.01	.04	.06	−.04	.02	.13***
First choice at entrance	.03	.01	.05	.09***	−.02	.01
R²	**.07**	**.06**	**.06**	**.10**	**.03**	**.22**

(*Continued*)

TABLE A.1. (*Continued*)

	Tuition Worth	Intent to Reenroll	Intent to Graduate	Overall Satisfaction	Second Year Better Than First	College Grades
Step 2						
Engaged learning	.10**	.03	.04	.08**	.02	.00
Academic self-efficacy	.06	−.01	.00	.05	.04	.46***
Hope	.01	.02	.03	−.01	.07	.13***
Strengths	.22***	.07*	.10**	.11***	.00	.13***
Growth mindset	.00	.06	.02	−.05*	.03	−.07**
R² change	**.13**	**.04**		**.10**	**.04**	**.22**
Step 3						
Involvement in student organizations	.06	.01	.02	.07*	−.06	.12**
Fraternity/sorority involvement	.07*	−.01	−.03	.00	−.01	−.04
Community service involvement	−.07*	−.03	.01	−.02	.02	−.04
Involvement in campus activities	.06	.02	.02	.08**	−.02	−.03
Religious involvement	.06	.01	.01	.08**	.00	.04
Met with advisor	−.09*	.00	.05	.06	−.03	.03
Advising satisfaction	.21***	.16***	.13***	.12***	.11**	.02
Faculty interaction (office hours)	.05	−.01	−.04	−.01	.00	−.08*
Faculty interaction (social)	−.03	−.01	−.07*	−.01	.01	.11**
Faculty interaction (discuss academic issues)	−.07	−.05	.00	−.08*	−.09*	−.06
Faculty satisfaction	.12***	.09*	.07*	.13***	.06	.00
Peer satisfaction	.13***	.17***	.17***	.48***	.28***	−.07*
R² change	**.10**	**.07**	**.07**	**.32**	**.10**	**.03**
Total R²	**.30**	**.17**	**.17**	**.53**	**.17**	**.48**

Note: Only those predictor variables significant in at least one equation are included in the table.

N = 1,924; * p < .05; ** p < .01; *** p < .001

TABLE A.2. SUMMARY OF HIERARCHICAL REGRESSION ANALYSES FOR VARIABLES PREDICTING INTENT TO REENROLL AND GRADUATE IN PRIVATE INSTITUTIONS WHEN VALUE OF TUITION AND OVERALL SATISFACTION WITH COLLEGE ARE ADDED AS PREDICTORS

	Intent to Reenroll	Intent to Graduate
Variable	β	β
Step 1		
Hours working off campus	.03	−.07*
Major certainty	.03	.09*
R² change	**.06**	**.06**
Step 2		
Strengths	.02	.10**
R² Change	**.04**	**.04**
Step 3		
Met with advisor	.03	.09*
Advising satisfaction	.12**	.06
Tuition worth	.13***	.19***
Overall satisfaction	.24***	.29***
R² change	**.13**	**.15**
Total R²	**.23**	**.25**

Note: Only those predictor variables significant in at least one equation are included in the table.

N = 1908; * p < .05; ** p < .01; *** p < .001

TABLE A.3. SUMMARY OF HIERARCHICAL REGRESSION ANALYSES FOR VARIABLES PREDICTING DESIRED OUTCOMES OF SOPHOMORE EXPERIENCE IN PUBLIC INSTITUTIONS

	Tuition Worth	Intent to Reenroll	Intent to Graduate	Overall Satisfaction	Second Year Better Than First	College Grades
Variable	β	β	β	β	β	β
Step 1						
First generation	.09**	.06	.05	.05	.04	.02
Gender (Male)	.04	−.03	−.04	−.06*	.00	−.08*
Age	−.01	−.02	−.07	.02	−.04	.11***
High school grades	−.02	.01	−.01	−.02	−.01	.21***
Major certainty	.00	.05	.06	.03	.09*	−.01
Asian	−.08*	−.03	−.03	.00	.06	.01

(Continued)

TABLE A.3. (*Continued*)

	Tuition Worth	Intent to Reenroll	Intent to Graduate	Overall Satisfaction	Second Year Better Than First	College Grades
Black	−.04	−.03	−.01	−.03	−.05	−.17***
Hispanic	.06	−.06*	−.05	.02	−.05	−.09**
Grad school aspirations	.02	.11*	.11*	.05	.03	.13***
First choice at entrance	.02	.15***	.16***	.10***	.02	−.03
R²	**.09**	**.09**	**.09**	**.12**	**.07**	**.24**
Step 2						
Engaged learning	.15***	.12**	.10*	.13***	.11*	.02
Academic self-efficacy	−.10*	−.13**	−.08	.00	.00	.37***
Hope	.11*	.05	.03	.03	.01	−.06
Meaning in life	.01	−.09*	−.11**	.02	−.03	.00
Strengths	.16***	.18***	.16***	.02	.05	.12**
Growth mindset	−.01	.03	.04	.01	−.07	−.08*
R² change	**.13**	**.07**	**.06**	**.11**	**.05**	**.16**
Step 3						
Fraternity/sorority involvement	.04	.03	.01	.01	.04	−.11**
Student govt. involvement	−.05	−.07	.05	.00	−.04	−.07*
Faculty interaction (office hours)	−.07	.07	.11**	.02	.00	.05
Faculty interaction (discuss career)	.00	.02	.00	−.06	−.02	.09*
Faculty interaction (social)	.02	.10*	.08	.01	.00	.04
Faculty interaction (discuss academic issues)	.03	−.16***	−.14**	.01	−.06	−.05
Met with advisor	−.03	.00	.03	−.04	.12**	−.05
Service-learning courses	−.02	−.01	.00	−.06*	−.01	.00
Learning community	.02	.01	.02	.04	.14***	−.01
Advising satisfaction	.10**	.11**	.10*	.12***	.02	−.04
Faculty satisfaction	.12**	.03	.04	.15***	.13**	.13***
Peer satisfaction	.14***	.17***	.19***	.46***	.20***	−.07*
R² change	**.07**	**.07**	**.10**	**.28**	**.10**	**.04**
Total R²	**.29**	**.23**	**.22**	**.52**	**.22**	**.43**

Note: Only those predictor variables significant in at least one equation are included in the table.

$N = 932$; * $p < .05$; ** $p < .01$; *** $p < .001$

TABLE A.4. SUMMARY OF HIERARCHICAL REGRESSION ANALYSES FOR VARIABLES PREDICTING INTENT TO REENROLL AND GRADUATE IN PUBLIC INSTITUTIONS WHEN VALUE OF TUITION AND OVERALL SATISFACTION WITH COLLEGE ARE ADDED AS PREDICTORS

	Intent to Reenroll	Intent to Graduate
Variable	β	β
Step 1		
Hispanic	−.07*	−.06
Graduate school aspirations	.10***	.10*
First choice at entrance	.12***	.13***
R² change	**.09**	**.09**
Step 2		
Academic self-efficacy	−.12**	−.06
Meaning in life	−.10**	−.12**
Strengths	.16***	.14***
R² change	**.07**	**.06**
Step 3		
Faculty interaction (office hours)	.07	.11**
Faculty interaction (discuss academic issues)	−.16***	−.14**
Tuition worth	.09*	.12**
Overall satisfaction	.25***	.22***
R² change	**.11**	**.12**
Total R²	**.28**	**.28**

Note: Only those predictor variables significant in at least one equation are included in the table.

$N = 932$; * $p < .05$; ** $p < .01$; *** $p < .001$

Notes for Tables in Appendix A:

In order to save space, the tables contain only those predictor variables which were significant in at least one of the equations. Before conducting any of the regression analyses, the data were separated by private and public institution and weighted for gender, leadership participation, and race. All scale scores in Block 2 were standardized before entering the regression.

The regression analyses were conducted with the following variables entered at each block:

BLOCK 1

Gender	Age
First-generation status	High school grades
College grades	Choice of institution at entrance
Anglo	Asian
Black	Hispanic
Residence	Athlete status
Major certainty	Hours worked off campus

BLOCK 2

Engaged Learning Index
Hope Scale
Academic Self-Efficacy Scale
Meaning in Life Questionnaire
Growth Mindset Scale
Use of Strengths for Academic Success

BLOCK 3

Participation in student organizations	Student leadership
Community service	Student government
Fraternity/sorority involvement	Being a peer leader
Religious activities involvement	Faculty interaction (office hours)
Faculty interaction (social outside of class)	Faculty interaction (discuss career issues)
Faculty interaction (discuss academic issues)	Met with advisor
Service-learning courses	Learning community participation
Advising satisfaction	Faculty satisfaction
Peer satisfaction	

THE SOPHOMORE STUDENT SUCCESS INITIATIVE: QUESTIONS FOR DISCUSSION BETWEEN RESIDENT ADVISOR AND SOPHOMORE STUDENTS

Fall Semester Meeting

(Complete by the end of September)

Here are potential questions to ask and suggested resources to guide your conversation. Before you begin the first meeting, please start by asking questions to make the student feel comfortable such as: How did move-in go? Have you met anyone new? What do you think about your schedule?

Academic Success

- How do you feel about your choice of major?
- What courses do you think you will do well in? Which will be difficult?
- How do you study?
- When you did well in class freshmen year, what study skills did you use?
- Do you know the academic requirements for your major, college, or school?
- Would you be interested in a study group? What subject?
- Do you know your academic advisor?

Leadership

- What organizations are you involved with on campus?
- Are there other organizations you are interested in getting involved with?
- Would you like to be involved in residence hall activities?
- What programs would you like to see this semester?
- How would you specifically contribute to making programs happen?

Community Responsibility

- How will you contribute to the community this year?
- Why did you choose to live on campus, and what do you hope to gain from this experience?
- What do you expect from me, your Resident Advisor?
- How well do you know your hall mates?

Self-Responsibility

- How do you balance your academic and social life?
- Do you have a part-time job? How are you balancing with your job, school, etc.?
- Are you on scholarship(s)? Are you meeting their requirements?
- How have you changed since your first year?
- Have you thought about getting further work experience in your career choice?
- Do you maintain a budget?

Character

- What are some challenges you anticipate for your sophomore year? What is your plan to deal with those challenges?
- How have you given back to your neighborhood community in the past?
- Please explain experiences that have made you feel uncomfortable.
- What do you struggle with most?
- What do value about the Carolinian Creed, and does that match what you personally value?

Conclusion

- Summarize what you have discussed, outline an action plan for the semester, and ask the student whether there is anything else he or she would like to talk about or needs help with.

Spring Semester Meeting

(Complete by the end of January)

Here are potential questions to ask and suggested resources to guide your conversation. Before you begin the meeting, please start by asking questions to make the student feel comfortable such as: How was break? Where did you go? What do you think about your schedule?

Academic Success

- How do you feel about your choice of major?
- Have you considered studying abroad?
- How have your major classes been going?

Leadership

- What are some challenges you have faced your sophomore year?
- How have you handled those challenges?
- How have you gotten involved on campus?
- Are there other organizations you have thought of looking into?
- Are you meeting your goals from our first meeting? How?
- What are your goals for this semester? How will you meet those?

Community Responsibility

- Why did you choose to live on campus?
- What are you hoping to gain out of the experience this year?
- What input did you give in the formation of your floors community charter?
- Why is this important to you?

Self-Responsibility

- Have you thought about gaining further work experience in your intended career field?
- Have you visited the Career Center to explore internship and job opportunities?
- Do you have financial aid/scholarships ready for next year?
- How have you balanced your social and academic lives?
- What are your summer plans? Will you be working?

Character

- What are some concerns you have about your junior year?
- How do you think those concerns will change next year?
- What are you doing to prepare for those changes?
- How has the transition to your sophomore year been? (Academically, socially, etc.)
- What do you struggle with most?

Conclusion

- Summarize what you have discussed, outline an action plan for the semester, and ask the student whether there is anything else he or she would like to talk about or needs help with.

APPENDIX C

PRINCIPLES OF GOOD ASSESSMENT

1. *The assessment of student learning begins with educational values.* Assessment is not an end in itself but a vehicle for educational improvement. Its effective practice, then, begins with and enacts a vision of the kinds of learning we most value for students and strive to help them achieve. Educational values should drive not only *what* we choose to assess but also *how* we do so. Where questions about educational mission and values are skipped over, assessment threatens to be an exercise in measuring what's easy rather than a process of improving what we really care about.

2. *Assessment is most effective when it reflects an understanding of learning as multidimensional, integrated, and revealed in performance over time.* Learning is a complex process. It entails not only what students know but what they can do with what they know; it involves not only knowledge and abilities but also values, attitudes, and habits of mind that affect both academic success and performance beyond the classroom. Assessment should reflect these understandings by employing a diverse array of methods, including those that call for actual performance, using them over time so as to reveal change, growth, and increasing degrees of integration. Such an approach aims for a more complete and accurate picture of learning and therefore firmer bases for improving our students' educational experience.

3. *Assessment works best when the programs it seeks to improve have clear, explicitly stated purposes.* Assessment is a goal-oriented process. It entails comparing educational performance with educational purposes and expectations—those derived from the institution's mission, from faculty intentions in program and course design, and from knowledge of students' own goals. Where program purposes lack specificity or agreement, assessment as a process pushes a campus toward clarity about where to aim and what standards to apply; assessment also prompts attention to where and how program goals will be taught and learned. Clear, shared, implementable goals are the cornerstone for assessment that is focused and useful.

4. *Assessment requires attention to outcomes but also and equally to the experiences that lead to those outcomes.* Information about outcomes is of high importance; where students "end up" matters greatly. But to improve outcomes, we need to know about student experience along the way—about the curricula, teaching, and kind of student effort that lead to particular outcomes. Assessment can help us understand which students learn best under what conditions; with such knowledge comes the capacity to improve the whole of their learning.

5. *Assessment works best when it is ongoing, not episodic.* Assessment is a process whose power is cumulative. Though isolated, "one-shot" assessment can be better than none, improvement is best fostered when assessment entails a linked series of activities undertaken over time. This may mean tracking the process of individual students, or of cohorts of students; it may mean collecting the same examples of student performance or using the same instrument semester after semester. The point is to monitor progress toward intended goals in a spirit of continuous improvement. Along the way, the assessment process itself should be evaluated and refined in light of emerging insights.

6. *Assessment fosters wider improvement when representatives from across the educational community are involved.* Student learning is a campuswide responsibility, and assessment is a way of enacting that responsibility. Thus, while assessment efforts may start small, the aim over time is to involve people from across the educational community. Faculty members play an especially important role, but assessment's questions can't be fully addressed without participation by student-affairs educators, librarians, administrators, and students. Assessment may also involve individuals from beyond the campus (alumni/ae, trustees, employers) whose experience can enrich the sense of appropriate aims and standards for learning. Thus understood, assessment is not a task for small groups of experts but a collaborative activity; its aim is wider, better-informed attention to student learning by all parties with a stake in its improvement.

7. *Assessment makes a difference when it begins with issues of use and illuminates questions that people really care about.* Assessment recognizes the value of information in

the process of improvement. But to be useful, information must be connected to issues or questions that people really care about. This implies assessment approaches that produce evidence that relevant parties will find credible, suggestive, and applicable to decisions that need to be made. It means thinking in advance about how the information will be used and by whom. The point of assessment is not to gather data and return "results"; it is a process that starts with the questions of decision makers, that involves them in the gathering and interpreting of data, and that informs and helps guide continuous improvement.

8. *Assessment is most likely to lead to improvement when it is part of a larger set of conditions that promote change.* Assessment alone changes little. Its greatest contribution comes on campuses where the quality of teaching and learning is a priority and visibly valued. On such campuses, the push to improve educational performance is a visible and primary goal of leadership; improving the quality of undergraduate education is central to the institution's planning, budgeting, and personnel decisions. On such campuses, information about learning outcomes is seen as an integral part of decision making and is avidly sought.

9. *Through assessment, educators meet responsibilities to students and to the public.* There is a compelling public stake in education. As educators, we have a responsibility to the publics that support or depend on us to provide information about the ways in which our students meet goals and expectations. But that responsibility goes beyond the reporting of such information; our deeper obligation—to ourselves, our students, and society—is to improve. Those to whom educators are accountable have a corresponding obligation to support such attempts at improvement.

Authors. Alexander W. Astin; Trudy W. Banta; K. Patricia Cross; Elaine El-Khawas; Peter T. Ewell; Pat Hutchings; Theodore J. Marchese; Kay M. McClenney; Marcia Mentkowski; Margaret A. Miller; E. Thomas Moran; Barbara D. Wright. This document was developed under the auspices of the AAHE Assessment Forum with support from the Fund for the Improvement of Post Secondary Education with additional support for publication and dissemination from the Exxon Education Foundation. Copies may be made without restriction.

REFERENCES

ACT (1999). *Fewer college freshmen drop out, but degree rate also falls.* Available from http://www.act.org/news/releases/1999/04–01b99.html

Adelman, C. (1999). *Answers in the tool box: Academic intensity, attendance patterns, and bachelor's degree attainment.* Washington, DC: National Institute on Postsecondary Education, Libraries, and Lifelong Learning (ED/OERI).

Adelman, C. (2005). *Moving into town—and moving on: The community college in the lives of traditional-age students.* Washington, DC: US Department of Education.

Adelman, C. (2006). *The toolbox revisited: Paths to degree completion from high school through college.* Washington, DC: U.S. Department of Education.

Agron, J. (2007, June 1). 18th Annual residence hall construction report. *American School & University.* Available from http://www.printthis.clickability.com/pt/cpt?action=cpt&title=Residence+Hall+Construction+Report&expire=&urlID=22757496&fb=Y&url=http://asumag.com/Construction/res_halls/university_th_annual_residence/index.html&partnerID=99516

Alexander, B. B., Foertsch, J., Daffinrud, S., & Tapia, R. (2000). The "spend a summer with a scientist" (SaS) program at Rice University: A study of program outcomes and essential elements 1991–1997. *CUR Quarterly, 20*(3), 127–133.

Allen, J. M., & Smith, C. L. (2008). Faculty and student perspectives on advising: Implications for student dissatisfaction. *Journal of College Student Development, 49*(6), 609–624.

Allen, J., Robbins, S.B., Casillas, A., & Oh, I. (2008). Third-year college retention and transfer: Effects of academic performance, motivation, and social connectedness. *Research in Higher Education, 49,* 647–664.

Allen, M. (2004). *Assessing academic programs in higher education.* Bolton, MA: Anker.

Almanac Issue (2007–2008). *The Chronicle of Higher Education, 54,* 1.

American Association of Community Colleges. (n.d.). Horizons Service-Learning Project. Available from http://www.webadmin.aacc.nche.edu/Resources/aaccprograms/horizons/Pages/default.aspx

American Association of Community Colleges. (2007). CC Stats. Available from http://www2.aacc.nche.edu/research/index.htm

American Association of Higher Education (AAHE). (1996). *9 Principles of Good Practice for Assessing Student Learning*. The AAHE Assessment Forum. Retrieved June 11, 2009 from http://www.assessment.tcu.edu/assessment/aahe.pdf

Anderson, E., & Schreiner, L. A. (2000). Advising for sophomore success. In L. A. Schreiner & J. Pattengale (Eds.), *Visible solutions for invisible students: Helping sophomores succeed* (Monograph No. 31) (pp. 55–77). Columbia, SC: University of South Carolina, National Resource Center for The First-Year Experience® and Students in Transition.

Anderson, L. C. (Ed.). (2005). *Internationalizing undergraduate education: Integrating study abroad into the curriculum*. Minneapolis: University of Minnesota, Learning Abroad Center.

Angelo, T. A., & Cross, K. P. (1993). *Classroom assessment techniques: A handbook for college teachers* (2nd ed.). San Francisco: Jossey-Bass.

Arboleda, A., Wang, Y., Shelley, M. C., & Whalen, D. F. (2003). Predictors of residence hall involvement. *Journal of College Student Development, 44*(4), pp. 517–531.

Arce, E. M. (1996). *Minorities in higher education: 1992 eleventh annual status report*. Washington, D.C.: Author

Arendale, D. (1997). Supplemental instruction (SI): Review of research concerning the effectiveness of SI from the University of Missouri–Kansas City and other institutions from across the United States. In S. Mioduski & G. Enright (Eds.), *Proceedings of the 17th and 18th Annual Institutes for Learning Assistance Professionals, 1996 and 1997*. Tucson: University Learning Center, University of Arizona.

Aronson, J., Fried, C., & Good, C. (2002). Reducing the effects of stereotype threat on African-American college students by shaping theories of intelligence. *Journal of Experimental Social Psychology, 38*(2), 113–125.

Association of American Colleges and Universities (AAC&U). (2004). *Portfolios transform writing assessment at Carleton College*. AAC&U Newsletter. Available from http://www.aacu.org/aacu_news/AACUNews04/December04/feature_print.cfm

Association of American Colleges and Universities (AAC&U). (2007). *College learning for the new global century: A report from the National Leadership Council for Liberal Education and America's Promise*. Washington, DC: Association of American Colleges and Universities.

Astin, A. W. (1977). *Four critical years*. San Francisco: Jossey-Bass.

Astin, A. W. (1991). *Assessment for excellence: The philosophy and practice of assessment and evaluation in higher education*. New York: Macmillan.

Astin, A. W. (1993a). *What matters in college? Four critical years revisited*. San Francisco: Jossey-Bass.

Astin, A. W. (1993b). What matters in college. *Liberal Education, 79*(4), 4–15.

Astin, A. W. (1998). The changing American college student: Thirty-year trends. *Review of Higher Education, 21*(2): 115–135.

Astin, A. W. (1999). Student involvement: A developmental theory for higher education. *Journal of College Student Development, 40*, 518–529.

Astin, H. S., & Antonio, A. L. (2004). The impact of college on character development. *New Directions for Institutional Research, 122*, 55–64.

Attewell, P., Lavin, D., Domina, T., & Levey, T. (2006). New evidence on college remediation. *Journal Higher Education, 77*(5), 886–924.

Bain, K. (2004). *What the best college teachers do.* Cambridge, MA: Harvard University Press.

Barefoot, B. O. (2005). Current institutional practice in the first year of college. In M. L. Upcraft , J. N. Gardner & B. O. Barefoot (Eds.), *Challenging and supporting the first-year student: A handbook for improving the first year of college* (pp. 47–63). San Francisco: Jossey-Bass.

Barr, R. B., & Tagg, J. (1995). A new paradigm for undergraduate education. *Change.* Available from http://critical.tamucc.edu/~blalock/readings/tch2learn.htm

Bauer, K. W., & Bennett, J. S. (2003). Alumni perceptions used to assess undergraduate research experience. *The Journal of Higher Education, 74*(2), 210–230.

Baum, S., & Payea, K. (2004). *Education pays 2004: The benefits of higher education for individuals and society.* Washington, DC: The College Board.

Baur, E. J. (1965). *Achievement and role definition of the college student.* U.S. Department of Health, Education, and Welfare Cooperative Research Project No. 2605. Lawrence, KS: University of Kansas.

Baxter Magolda, M. B. (1992). *Knowing and reasoning in college.* San Francisco: Jossey-Bass.

Baxter Magolda, M. B. (1999). *Creating contexts for learning and self-authorship: Constructive-developmental pedagogy.* Nashville, TN: Vanderbilt University Press.

Baxter Magolda, M. B. (2006). *The forgotten student: Understanding and supporting sophomores.* Tele-conference sponsored by The National Resource Center for The First-Year Experience® and Students in Transition.

Baxter Magolda, M. B., & King, P. M. (Eds.). (2004). *Learning partnerships: Theory & models of practice to educate for self -authorship.* Sterling, VA: Stylus.

Bean, J. P. (1985). Interaction effects based on class level in an explanatory model of college student dropout syndrome. *American Educational Research Journal, 22,* 35–64.

Bean, J. P. (2005). Nine themes of college student retention. In A. Seidman (Ed.), *College student retention: Formula for student success* (pp. 215–244). Westport, CT: Praeger.

Bean, J. P., & Metzner, B. (1985). A conceptual model of nontraditional undergraduate student retention. *Review of Educational Research, 55,* 485–540.

Bellani, R. N. (2007). *Sophomore men: Their growth, relationships and search for life direction at Colgate University.* (Doctoral Dissertation. University of Pennsylvania, 2007). Dissertations Abstracts International, A68, 03.

Beloit College. (2007). Sophomore year initiatives @ Beloit College. Available from http://www.beloit.edu/~syi

Beloit College. (2007a). Venture grants for the class of 2009. Retrieved June 27, 2007 from http://www.beloit.edu/~syi/venture_grants/venture_2009.php

Beloit College. (2007b). Venture grants for the class of 2008. Retrieved June 27, 2007 from http://www.beloit.edu/~syi/venture_grants/venture_2008.php

Bennett, M. (1993). Towards ethnorelativism: A developmental model of intercultural sensitivity. In R. M. Paige (Ed.), *Education for the Intercultural Experience* (pp. 21–71). Yarmouth, ME: Intercultural Press.

Berkner, L., He, S., & Forrest, E. (2002). *Descriptive Summary of 1995–96 Beginning Postsecondary Students: Six Years Later* (NCES 2003–151). U.S. Department of Education. Washington, D.C.: National Center for Education Statistics.

Berrios-Allison, A. C. (2005). Family influences on college students' occupational identity. *Journal of Career Assessment, 13*(2), 233–247.

Bhandari, R., & Chow, P. (2007). *Open Doors 2007: Report on International Education Exchange.* New York: Institute of International Education.

Bhandari, R., & Chow, P. (2008). *Open Doors 2008: Report on International Education Exchange*. New York: Institute of International Education.

Bickel, S. L. (1998). The future of residential colleges: Responding to demographic changes. In F. K. Alexander & D. E. Robertson (Eds.), *Residential colleges: Reforming American higher education* (pp. 225–231). Murray, KY: Murray State University.

Biddle, S. (2002). Internationalization: Rhetoric or Reality? *American Council of Learned Societies Occasional Paper, 56*.

Birney, R. C., Coplin, H. R., & Grose, R. F. (1960). *The class of 1959 at Amherst College: A preliminary report*. Amherst, MA: Committee on Guidance and Counseling, Amherst College.

Bisese, S. D., & Fabian, D. J. (2006). Sophomore men: The forgotten class, the forgotten gender. *Recruitment & Retention in Higher Education, 20*(3), 1–4.

Blackburn, R. T., Chapman, D. W., & Cameron, S. M. (1981). "Cloning" in academe: Mentorship and academic careers. *Research in Higher Education, 15*(4), 315–327.

Blair, D., Phinney, L., & Phillippe, K. A. (2001). International programs at community colleges (American Association of Community Colleges No. AACC-RB-01–1). Annapolis, MD; Community College Press.

Boivin, M., Fountain, G. A., & Baylis, B. (2000). Meeting the challenges of the sophomore year. In L. A. Schreiner & J. Pattengale (Eds.), *Visible solutions for invisible students: Helping sophomores succeed* (Monograph No. 31) (pp. 1–18). Columbia, SC: University of South Carolina, National Resource Center for The First-Year Experience® and Students in Transition.

Bolen, M. C. (Ed.). (2007). *A Guide to Outcomes Assessment for Education Abroad*. Carlisle, PA: Forum on Education Abroad.

Bonfiglio, R. A. (2004). What the building boom says about campus values, *About Campus, 9*(5), 27–29.

Boswell, K., & Wilson, C. D. (Eds.). (2004). *Keeping America's promise: A report on the future of the community college*. Denver: Education Commission of the States.

Boyer Report (1998). Available at www. Reinventioncenter.miami.edu/The BoyerReport.html

Boysen, G. A. & McGuire, S. (2005). Assessment of a study skills course using academic performance and self-efficacy. *Learning Assistance Review, 10*(2), 5–16.

Brandeis University. Available at http://my.brandeis.edu/groups/sye/

Bransford, J. D., Brown, A. L., & Cocking, R. R. (Eds.). (1999). *How people learn: Brain, mind, experience, and school*. Washington, DC: National Academy Press.

Braskamp, L. A., Trautvetter, L. C., and Ward, K. (2006). *Putting students first: How colleges develop students purposefully*. Boston, MA: Anker.

Braxton, J. M., Hirschy, A. S., & McClendon, S. A. (2004). *Understanding and reducing college student departure*. ASHE-ERIC Higher Education Report, Vol. 30, No. 3. San Francisco: Jossey-Bass.

Bridges, W. (1980). *Transitions: Making sense of life's changes*. Reading, MA: Addison-Wessley.

Bridges, W. (2003). *Managing transitions: Making the most of change* (2nd ed.). Cambridge, MA: Perseus.

Bridgewater State College. (2007). Second year seminar. Available from http://webhost. bridgew.edu/sholton/SecondYearSeminar2.2.htm

Brint, S., & Karabel, J. (1989). *The diverted dream: Community colleges and the promise of educational opportunity in American, 1900–1985*. New York: Oxford University Press.

Brookfield, S. D. (1995). *Becoming a critically reflective teacher*. San Francisco: Jossey Bass.

Brookfield, S. D. (2006). *The skillful teacher: On technique, trust, and responsiveness in the classroom*. (2nd ed.). San Francisco: Jossey Bass.

Brower, A. M., & Dettinger, K. M. (1998). What is a learning community: Toward a comprehensive model, *About Campus, 3*(5), pp. 15–21.

Brown, S. D., & Krane, N.E.R. (2000). Four (or five) sessions and a cloud of dust: Old assumptions and new observations about career counseling. In S. D. Brown & R. W. Lent (Eds.), *Handbook of counseling psychology* (3rd ed., pp. 740–766). New York: Wiley.

Brown, S., Krane, N. R., Brecheisen, J., Castelino, P., Budisin, I., Miller, M., & Edens, L. (2003). Critical ingredients of career choice interventions: More analyses and new hypotheses. *Journal of Vocational Behavior, 62*, 411–428.

Bruff, D. (2009). *Teaching with classroom response systems: Creating active learning environments.* San Francisco: Jossey-Bass.

Bryant, A. N., & Schwartz, L. M. (2007). *National institute on spirituality in higher education: Integrating spirituality into the campus curriculum and co-curriculum.* Los Angeles, CA: University of California, Los Angeles, Higher Education Research Institute.

Cabrera, A., Castaneda, M., Nora, A., & Hengstler, D. (1992). The convergence between two theories of college persistence. *Journal of Higher Education, 63*, 143–164.

Campbell, A., & Skoog, G. O. (2004). Preparing undergraduate women for science careers: Facilitating success in professional research. *Journal of College Science Teaching, 33*(5), 24–26.

Campus Compact. (2007). *2006 Survey statistics: Highlights and trends of Campus Compact's annual membership survey.* Providence, RI: Campus Compact.

Campus Compact. (2008). *How can engaged campuses improve student success in college?* Research Brief. Providence, RI: Campus Compact.

Carey, K. (2004). *A matter of degrees: Improving graduation rates in four year colleges and Universities, A Report by the Education Trust.* Washington, DC: Education Trust.

Carlson, J. S., Burn, B. B., Useem, J., & Yachimowicz, D. (1990). *Study abroad: The experience of American undergraduates.* Westport, CN: Greenwood Press.

Carnegie Classification (2005). Available at http://www.carnegiefoundation.org/classifications/index.asp?key=800

Carsello, C., & Creaser, J. (1976). How college students change during study abroad. *College Student Journal 10*: 276–278.

Casner-Lotto, J. (2006). *Are they really ready to work?: Employers' perspectives on the basic knowledge and applied skills of new entrants to the 21st century U.S. workforce.* Washington, DC: Partnership for 21st Century Skills.

Cejda, B. D., & Hensel, N. (2008). Undergraduate research in community colleges: A summary of the CUR/NCIA conversations. *CUR Quarterly, 29*(1), 7–11.

Chandra, U., Stoecklin, S., & Harmon, M. (1998). A successful model for introducing research in an undergraduate program. *Journal of College Science Teaching, 28*(2), 116–118.

Chaplin, S., Manske, J., & Cruise, J. (1998). Introducing freshman to investigative research: A course for biology majors at Minnesota's University of St. Thomas. *Journal of College Science Teaching, 27*(5), 347–350.

Chartrand, J. M., Martin, W. F., Robbins, S. B., McAuliffe, G. J., Pickering, J. W., & Calliotte, A. A. (1994). Testing a level versus an interactional view of career indecision. *Journal of Career Assessment, 2*, 55–69.

Chemers, M. M., Hu, L., & Garcia, B. F. (2001). Academic self-efficacy and first-year college student performance and adjustment. *Journal of Educational Psychology, 93*(1), 55–64.

Chickering, A.W. (1969). *Education and identity.* San Francisco: Jossey-Bass.

Chickering, A.W., Dalton, J. C., and Stamm, L. (2006). *Encouraging authenticity and spirituality in higher education.* San Francisco: Jossey-Bass.

Chickering, A. W., & Gamson, Z. F. (1987). Seven principles for good practice in undergraduate education. *AAHE Bulletin, 39*(7), 3–7.

Chickering, A. W., & Reisser, L. (1993). *Education and identity* (2nd ed.). San Francisco: Jossey-Bass.

Chieffo, L., & Griffiths, L. (2004). Large-scale assessment of student attitudes after a short-term study abroad program. *Frontiers 10*, 165–177.

Chisholm, L. (Ed.). (2005). *Knowing and doing: The theory and practice of service-learning*. New York: International Partnership for Service Learning.

Chung, Y. B., & Sedlacek, W. E. (1999). Ethnic differences in career, academic, and social self-appraisals among incoming college freshmen. *Journal of College Counseling, 2*(1), 14–24.

City Colleges of Chicago Web site. CCC Notebook CCC Spearheads a Science Research Initiative [Electronic Version]. *Winter 2007*. Available from http://www.ccc.edu/aboutccc/files/ccc_winter07.pdf

Clark, E. C., & Kalionzes, J. (2008). Advising students of color and internationl students. In V. Gordon, W. Habley, T. Grites, & Associates, *Academic advising: A comprehensive handbook* (2nd ed.) (pp. 204–225). San Francisco: Jossey-Bass.

Clifton, D. O., Anderson, E. C., & Schreiner, L. A. (2006). *StrengthsQuest: Discover and develop your strengths in academics, career, and beyond* (2nd ed.). Washington, DC: The Gallup Organization.

Coburn, K. L., & Treeger, M. L. (1997). *Letting go: A parents' guide to today's college experience* (3rd ed.). Bethesda, MD: Adler & Adler.

Coelho, G. V. (1962). Personal growth and educational development through working and studying abroad. *Journal of Social Issues*, 55–67.

Cohen, E. R. (1982). Using the defining issues test to assess stage of moral development among sorority and fraternity members. *Journal of College Student Personnel, 23*, 324–328.

Colgate University. (n.d.). Sophomore-year experience. Available from http://www.colgate.edu/DesktopDefault1.aspx?tabid=1269&pgID=7215

Coll, J. E. (2008–2009). A study of academic advising satisfaction and its relationship to student worldviews. *Journal of College Student Retention, 10*(3), 391–404.

Colorado College. (2007). Your sophomore year. Available from http://www.coloradocollege.edu/academics/sophomore/

Community College National Center for Community Engagement, Mesa, AZ. Retrieved, from www.mc.maricopa/other/engagement

Côté, J. E., & Levine, C. (1997). Student motivations, learning environments, and human capital acquisition: Toward an integrated paradigm for student development. *Journal of College Student Development, 38*(3), 229–243.

Council on Undergraduate Research. (n.d.). "Learning Through Research." Available from http://www.cur.org

Covington, M. V. (2000). Goal theory, motivation, and school achievement: An integrative review. *Annual Review of Psychology, 51*, 171–200.

Cox, M. D. (2004). Introduction to faculty learning communities. In M. D. Cox & L. Richlin (Eds.), *Building faculty learning communities* (pp. 5–23). New Directions for Teaching and Learning, No. 97. San Francisco: Jossey-Bass.

Creamer, D. G. (2000). Use of theory in academic advising. In V. N. Gordon & W. R. Habley (Eds.), *Academic advising: A comprehensive handbook*. San Francisco: Jossey-Bass.

Cross, P. K. (1998). Classroom research: implementing the scholarship of teaching. *New Directions for Teaching and Learning, 75*, 5–12.

Dalton, J. C. (2001). Career and calling: Finding a place for the spirit in work and community. *New Directions for Student Services, 95*, 17–25.

Damon, W. (2008). *The path to purpose: Helping our children find their calling in life.* New York: Free Press.

D'Augelli, A. R. (1989). Lesbians' and gay men's experiences of discrimination and harassment in a university community. *American Journal of Community Psychology, 17*, 317–321.

D'Augelli, A. R. (1992). Lesbians' and gay male under undergraduates' experiences of harassment and fear on campus. *Journal of Interpersonal Violence, 7*, 383–395.

Daugherty, T. K., & Lane, E. J. (1999). A longitudinal study of academic and social predictors of college attrition. *Social Behavior & Personality, 27*, 355–362.

Deardorff, D. K. (2006). Identification and assessment of intercultural competence as a student outcome of internationalization. *Journal of Studies in International Education, 10*(3), 241–266.

DiRenzo, G. J. (1965). *Student imagery at Fairfield University, 1963–1964.* Social Psychology Laboratory, Department of Sociology, Fairfield University. (Mimeo).

Dolby, N. (2007). Reflections on nation: American undergraduates and education abroad. *Journal of Studies in International Education, 11*(2), 141–156.

Donaldson, J. F. & Townsend, B. K. (2007). Higher education journals' discourse about adult undergraduate students. *Journal of Higher Education, 78*, 27–50

Douglas, C., & Jones-Rikkers, C. (2001). Study abroad programs and American student worldmindedness: An empirical analysis. *Journal of Teaching in International Business, 31*(1), 55–66.

Dowd, A. C., & Coury, T. (2006). The effect of loans on the persistence and attainment of community college students. *Research in Higher Education, 47*(1), 33–62.

Drews, D. R., Meyer, L. L., & Peregrine, P. N. (1996). Effects of study abroad on conceptualizations of national groups. *College Student Journal, 30*(4), 452–462.

Duffy, R. D., & Sedlacek, W. E. (2007). The work value of first-year college students: Explaining group differences. *The Career Development Quarterly, 55*(4), 359–364.

Durrant, M. B., & Dorius, C. R. (2007). Study abroad survey instruments: A comparison of survey types and experiences. *Journal of Studies in International Education, 11*(1), 33–53.

Dweck, C. S. (2006). *Mindset: The new psychology of success.* New York: Random House.

Dweck, C. S., & Molden, D. C. (2005). Self-theories: Their impact on competence motivation and acquisition. In A. J. Elliot & C. S. Dweck (Eds.), *Handbook of competence and motivation* (pp. 122–140). New York: The Guilford Press.

Dwyer, M. M. (2004a). Charting the impact of studying abroad. *International Educator, 13*(1), 14–20.

Dwyer, M. M. (2004b). More is better: The impact of study abroad program duration. *Frontiers, 10*, 151–163.

Dwyer, M. M., & Peters, C. K. (2004). The benefits of study abroad: New study confirms significant gains [Electronic version]. *Transitions Abroad, 5*, 56.

Dym, C. L. (2006). The terrible two's. *ASEE Prism, 15*(7), 64.

Eastern University. Available at http://www.eastern.edu/academic/strengths/index.html

Eccles, J. S., & Wigfield, A. (2002). Motivational belief, values, and goals. *Annual Review of Psychology, 53*, 109–132.

Edgerton, R. (1997). *Higher education white paper.* Philadelphia: Pew Charitable Trusts.

Edgerton, R., & Schroeder, C. (2003, May/June). What's going on in higher education?: Charles Schroeder talks to Russell Edgerton. *About Campus, 8*(2), 8–15.

Educating for Global Competency: America's Passport to the Future. (1997). Washington, DC: American Council on Education.

Eisner, R. (1991). *Travelers to an antique land: the history and literature of travel to Greece*. Ann Arbor: University of Michigan Press.

Emory University. (2007). SYE at Emory. Available from http://www.emory.edu/HOUSING /SYE/index.html

Engle, L., & Engle, J. (2003). Study abroad levels: Toward a classification of program types. *Frontiers, 9*, 1–20.

Engle, J., & O'Brien, C. (2007) Demography is not destiny. Available from http://www .publicagenda.org/Research/research_reports_details.cfm?list=6

Eyler, J., & Giles, D. E. (1999). *Where's the learning in service-learning?* San Francisco: Jossey-Bass.

Fairfield University. (2007). Ignatian residential college. Available from http://www.faculty.fair field.edu/jmayzik/irc/index.htm

Farrell, P., & Suvedi, M. (2003). Studying abroad in Nepal: Assessing impact. *Frontiers, 9*, 175–188.

Favazza, J. A. & Talentino, K. (2008, January). *Supporting collaborative teaching: A tale of two colleges*. Presentation at the meeting of American Conference of Academic Deans, Washington, DC.

Feldman, K. A., & Newcomb, T. M. (1994). *The impact of college on students*. New Brunswick, NJ: Transaction.

Felix, A., & Zovinka, E. P. (2008). One STOP: Enhancing student retention through early introduction of research for STEM majors. *CUR Quarterly, 29*(2), 30–35.

Ferrari, J. R., & Jason, L. A. (1996). Integrating research and community service: Incorporating research skills into service learning experiences. *College Student Journal, 30*(4), 444–451.

Files, T., & Gahagan, J. (2007, April). *Sophomore year success: Building programs to help sophomores succeed*. Audio conference presented by PaperClip Communications, Little Fall, New Jersey.

Finnie, B. (1967). *Satisfaction and its relationship to other variables: A preliminary report*. Paper presented at the American College Health Association Conference.

First-year housing: Should we give students what they want or what they need? (2006). *Student Affairs Leader, 34* (8), 1. Retrieved June 5, 2009 from 222.magnapubs.com

Fischer, M. J. (2007). Settling into campus life: Differences by race/ethnicity in college involvement, college satisfaction, and outcomes. *Journal of Higher Education, 78*(2), 125–161.

Fisher, I. S. (1996). Integrating service-learning experiences into postcollege choices. In B. Jacoby (Ed.), *Service-learning in higher education: Concepts and practices* (pp. 208–228). San Francisco: Jossey-Bass.

Fitzpatrick, J. L., Sanders, J. R., & Worthen, B. R. (2004). *Program evaluation: Alternative approaches and practical guidelines* (3rd ed.). New York: Longman.

Flanagan, W. J. (1990). *Sophomore retention: The missing strategy in small college retention efforts*. Unpublished dissertation. University of Wisconsin–Madison.

Flanagan, W. J. (1991). *Sophomore retention: The missing strategy in small college retention efforts*. (Doctoral Dissertation. University of Wisconsin–Madison, 1991). Dissertations Abstracts International, 52, 03A.

Flanagan, W. J. (2002). In PaperClip Communications. (2007). *Sophomore Year Success*.

Flanagan, W. J. (2002). *First and second year program model*. Retrieved February 15, 2008, from http://www.beloit.edu/syi/images/model_lg.gif

Flanagan, W. J. (2007). The Sophomore-Year Initiative (SYI) program at Beloit College. In B. F. Tobolowsky & B. E. Cox (Eds.), *Shedding Light on Sophomores* (Monograph

No. 47, pp. 49–61). Columbia: University of South Carolina, National Resource Center for The First-Year Experience® and Students in Transition.

Floyd, C. J., & Gordon, E. G. (1998). What skills are most important?: A comparison of employer, student, and staff perceptions. *Journal of Marketing Education, 20*(2), 103–109.

Foertsch, J. A., Alexander, B. B., & Penberthy, D. (2000). Summer research opportunity programs (SROPs) for minority undergraduates: A longitudinal study of program outcomes 1986–1996. *CUR Quarterly, 20*(3), 114–119.

Foubert, J. D., & Grainger, L. U. (2006). Effects of involvement in clubs and organizations on the psychosocial development of first-year and senior college students. *NASPA Journal, 43*(1), 166–182.

Foubert, J. D., Nixon, M. L., Sisson, V. S., & Barnes, A. C. (2005). A longitudinal study of Chickering and Reisser's vectors: Exploring gender differences and implications for refining the theory. *Journal of College Student Development, 46*, 461–470.

Franco, R. (2002a). The Community College Conscience, Educational Commission of the States (Denver, CO); reprinted in the *Campus Compact Reader, 2*(3), 4. Providence, RI: Campus Compact.

Franco, R. (2002b). The civic work of community colleges: Preparing students for the work of democracy. *The journal of public affairs, 6* (Suppl. 1), 119–138.

Franco, R., Duffy, D., Baratian, M., Hendricks, A., & Renner, T., (2007). *Service-learning course design for community colleges*. Providence, RI: Campus Compact.

Fredrickson, R. H. (1972). The multipotential as vocational decision-makers. In R.H. Fredrickson & J.W.M. Rothney (Eds.), *Recognizing and assisting multipotential youth*. Columbus, OH: Merrill.

Freedman, M. B. (1956). The passage through college. *Journal of Social Issues, 12*, 13–27.

Friedman, T. L. (2005). *The world is flat: A brief history of the twenty-first century*. New York: Farrar, Straus, & Giroux.

Fry, G. W., Jon, J.-E., Josic, J., LaBrack, B., & Stallman, E. M. (February, 2009). *Study abroad for global engagement: Results that inform research and policy agendas*. Roundtable session presented at the meeting of the Forum on Education Abroad, Portland, OR.

Furr, S. R., & Gannaway, L. (1982). Easing the sophomore slump: A student development approach. *Journal of College Student Personnel, 23*, 340–341.

Gahagan, J., & Hunter, M. S. (2006, July/August). The second-year experience: Turning attention to the academy's middle children. *About Campus, 11*(3), 17–22.

Gaglione, O. (2005). Underground existence of research in chemistry in two-year college Programs. *Journal of Chemical Education, 82*(11), 1613–1614.

Gallup Organization. (1999). *Clifton StrengthsFinder*. Washington, DC: The Gallup Organization.

Galotti, K. M. (1999). Making a "major" real-life decision: College students choosing an academic major. *Journal of Educational Psychology, 91*(2), 379–387.

Gansemer-Topf, A. M., Stern, J. M., & Benjamin, M. (2007). Examining the experiences of second-year students at a private liberal arts college. In B. F. Tobolowsky & B. E. Cox, Eds.) (2007). *Shedding light on sophomores: An exploration of the second college year* (Monograph No. 47). Columbia, SC: University of South Carolina, National Resource Center for the First Year Experience® and Students in Transition.

Gardner, J. N., Pattengale, J., & Schreiner, L. A. (2000). The sophomore year: Summary and recommendations. In L.A. Schreiner & J. Pattegale (Eds.), *Visible solutions for invisible students: Helping sophomores succeed*. (Monograph No. 31) (pp. 89–93). Columbia, SC: University of

South Carolina, National Resource Center for The First-Year Experience® and Students in Transition.

Gardner, J. N., Van der Veer, G., & Associates (1998). *The Senior Year Experience: Facilitating Integration, Reflection, Closure, and Transition.* San Francisco: Jossey-Bass.

Gardner, O. S., Keller, J. W., & Piotrowski, C. (1996). Retention issues as perceived by African-American university students. *Psychology—A Quarterly Journal of Human Behavior, 33,* 20–21.

Gardner, P. D. (2000). From drift to engagement: Finding purpose and making career connections in the sophomore year. In L. A. Schreiner & J. Pattengale (Eds.), *Visible solutions for invisible students: Helping sophomores succeed* (Monograph No. 31) (pp. 67–77). Columbia, SC: University of South Carolina, National Resource Center for The First-Year Experience® and Students in Transition.

Global Competence & National Needs: One Million Americans Studying Abroad. (2005). Washington, DC: Commission on the Abraham Lincoln Study Abroad Fellowship Program.

Gmelch, G. (1997). Crossing cultures: Student travel and personal development. *International Journal of Intercultural Relations, 21*(4), 475–490.

Gordon, V. N. (2006). *Career advising: An academic advisor's guide.* San Francisco: Jossey-Bass.

Gordon, V. N. (2007). *The undecided college student: An academic and career advising challenge.* Springfield, IL: Charles C. Thomas.

Gordon, V. N., Habley, W. R., & Associates. (2000). *Academic advising: A comprehensive handbook.* San Francisco: Jossey-Bass.

Gordon, V. N., & Sears, S. J. (2009). *Selecting a college major: Exploration and decisionmaking.* Upper Saddle River, NJ: Prentice Hall.

Gordon, V. N., & Steele, G. E. (2003). Undecided first-year students: A 25-year longitudinal study. *Journal of the First-Year Experience, 15*(1), 19–38.

Gore, J. (2005). *Dominant beliefs and alternative voices: Discourse, belief, and gender in American study abroad.* London: Routledge.

Gore, P. A. (2006). Academic self-efficacy as a predictor of college outcomes: Two incremental validity studies. *Journal of Career Assessment, 14,* 92–115.

Gore, P. A., Jr., & Hitch, J. L. (2005). Occupational classification and sources of occupational information. In S. D. Brown, & R. W. Lent (Eds.), *Career development and counseling: Putting theory and research to work* (pp. 382–413). Hoboken, NJ: Wiley.

Gore, P. A., Jr., & Keller, B. (2007, July). *Promoting academic and career success: Critical concepts and strategies.* Professional Development Institute presented at the annual meeting of the National Career Development Association, Seattle, WA.

Gore, P. A., Jr., Leuwerke, W. C., & Turley, S. (2006). A psychometric study of the college self-efficacy inventory. *Journal of College Student Retention: Research, Theory and Practice, 7,* 227–244.

Gottlieb, K., & Robinson, G. (2006). *A practical guide to integrating civic responsibility into the curriculum* (2nd ed.). Washington, DC: Community College Press.

Graunke, S. S., & Woosley, S. A. (2005). An exploration of the factors that affect the academic success of college sophomores. *College Student Journal, 39*(2), 367–376.

Graunke, S. S., Woosley, S. A., & Helms, L. L. (2006). How do their initial goals impact students' chances to graduate? An exploration of three types of commitment. *NACADA Journal, 26*(1), 13–18.

Gray, K. L. (2008, February 1). Dorm life may be the norm for OSU sophs. *The Columbus Dispatch.* Available from http://dispatch.com

Gray, K. S., Murdock, G. K., & Stebbins, C. D. (2002). Assessing study abroad's effect on an international mission. *Change, 34*(3), 45–51.

Green, M. F. (2007). Internationalizing community colleges: Barriers and strategies. *New Directions for Community Colleges, 138*, 15–24.

Grites, T. J., & Gordon, V. N. (2000). Developmental advising revisited. *NACADA Journal, 20*, 12–15.

Grotevant, H. D. (1992). Assigned and chosen identity components: A process perspective on their integration. In G. R. Adams, T. P. Gullotta, & R. Montemayor (Eds.), *Adolescent identity formation* (pp. 73–90). Newbury Park, CA: Sage.

Guay, F., Ratelle, C., Sevécal, C., Larose, S., & Deschênes, A. (2006). Distinguishing developmental from chronic career indecision: Self-efficacy, autonomy and social support. *Journal of Career Assessment, 14*(2), 235–251.

Gump, S. E. (2007). Classroom research in a general education course: Exploring implications through an investigation of the sophomore slump. *The Journal of General Education, 56*(2), 105–125.

Hagedorn, L. S. (2005). Square pegs: Adult students and their "fit" in postsecondary institutions. *Change, 37*, 22–29.

Hagstrom, S. & Schwartz, A. (2003). Sophomores: The next frontier. *Letters and Science Gazette, 5*, (pp. 1,3). University of California, Berkeley: Undergraduate Division, College of Letters and Science. (link: ls.berkeley.edu/undergrad/gazette/archives/ls_gazette_sp03 .pdf).

Hagstrom, S. J., Skovholt, T. M., & Rivers, D. A. (1997). The advanced undecided college student: A qualitative study. *NACADA Journal, 17*(2), 23–30.

Hakim, T. (1998). Soft Assessment of Undergraduate Research: Reactions and Student Perspectives. *CUR Quarterly, 18*(4), 189–192.

Hakim, T. (2000). *At the interface of scholarship and teaching: How to develop and administer institutional undergraduate research programs.* Washington, D.C.: Council on Undergraduate Research.

Hamilton, S., & Kahn, S. (2009, March). Demonstrating intellectual growth and development: The IUPUI e-portfolio. In D. Cambridge, B. Cambridge, & K. B. Yancey (Eds.), *Electronic portfolios 2.0: Emergent research on implementation and impact.* Sterling, VA: Stylus.

Hannigan, T. P. (2001). The effect of work abroad experiences on career development for U.S. undergraduates. *Frontiers, 7*, 1–23.

Hansel, B. & Grove, N. (1986, February). International student exchange programs—Are the educational benefits real? *NASSP Bulletin*, 84–90.

Hathaway, R. S., Nagda, B. A., & Gregerman, S. R. (2002). The relationship of undergraduate research participation to graduate and professional education pursuit: An empirical study. *Journal of College Student Development, 43*(5), 614–631.

Hawkins, J. G., Bradley, R. W., & White, G. W. (1977). Anxiety and the process of deciding about a major and vocation. *Journal of Counseling Psychology, 24*, 398–403.

Hess, G. (1983). *Freshmen and Sophomores Abroad: Community Colleges and Overseas Academic Programs.* New York: Teachers College Press.

Hillman, N., Lum, T., & Hossler, D. (2008). Understanding Indiana's reverse transfer students: A case study in institutional research. *Community College Journal of Research and Practice, 32*, 113–134.

History of Overseas Study. (n.d.). Retrieved June 26, 2008, from http://www.indiana.edu/~over seas/basics/history.shtml

Hoffa, W. W. (2007). *A History of US Study Abroad: Beginnings to 1965*. Carlisle, PA: Forum on Education Abroad.

Holland, J. L. (1997). *Making vocational choices: A theory of vocational personalities and work environments* (3rd ed.). Odessa, FL: Psychological Assessment Resources.

Hoover, E. (2008, August 1). Campuses see rising demand for housing. *Chronicle of Higher Education, 54*(47). Available from http://chronicle.com/weekly/v54/i47/47a00103.htm

Hopkins, J. R. (1999). Studying abroad as a form of experiential education. *Liberal Education 85*(3), 36–41.

Houlden, R. L., Raja, J. B., Collier, C. P., Clark, A. F., & Waugh, J. M. (2004). Medical students' perceptions of an undergraduate research elective. *Medical Teacher, 26*(7), 659–661.

Howe, N., & Strauss, W. (2000). *Millennials rising: The next generation*. New York: Vintage.

Howland, S. J. (2008, February 13). Sophs go abroad in greater numbers. *Harvard Crimson*. Available from http://www.thecrimson.com/article.aspx?ref=521860.

Hu, S., & Kuh, G. D. (2002). Being (dis)engaged in educationally purposeful activities: The influences of student and institutional characteristics. *Research in Higher Education, 43*(5), 555–575.

Huba, M. E., & Freed, J. E. (2000). *Learner-centered assessment on college campuses: Shifting the focus from teaching to learning*. Boston: Allyn & Bacon.

Hubbs, C. (2006, March/April). The year of study abroad. *Transitions Abroad, 29*(5). Available from http://www.transitionsabroad.com/publications/magazine/0603/year_of_study _abroad.shtml.

Huber, M. T., Hutchings, P., Gale, R., Miller, R., & Breen, M. (2007). Leading initiatives for integrative learning. *Liberal Education, 93*(2), 46–61.

Hull-Blanks, E., Kurpius, S.E.R, Befort, C., Sollenberger, S., Nicpon, M. F., & Huser, L. (2005). Career goals and retention-related factors among college freshman. *Journal of Career Development, 32*(1), 16–30.

Hulstrand, J. (2006). Education abroad on the fast track. *International Educator 15*(3): 46–55.

Hunter, M. S. (2006). *Lessons learned: Achieving institutional change in support of students in transition*. New Directions for Student Services, *114*, 7–15.

Ingraham, E. C., & Peterson, D. L. (2004). Assessing the impact of study abroad on student learning at Michigan State University, *Frontiers 10*, 83–100.

Inkelas, K. K., Zeller, W. J., Murphy, R. K., & Hummel, M. L. (2006). Learning moves home. *About Campus, 10*(6), pp. 10–16.

Inside Higher Education. Available at http://www.insidehighered.com/news/2005/05/02/ grinnell

Iowa State website for learning communities. Available at http://www.lc.iastate.edu/lc.index .html

Ishitani, T. T. (2006). Studying attrition and degree completion behavior among first-generation college students. *Journal of Higher Education, 77*(5), 861–885.

Ishiyama, J. (2001). Undergraduate research and the success of first-generation, low-income college students. *CUR Quarterly, 22*(1), 36–41.

Ishiyama, J. (2002). Does early participation in undergraduate research benefit social science and humanities students? *College Student Journal, 36*(3), 380–386.

IUPUI DSRP. *Overview: The Diversity Scholars Research Program at Indiana University-Purdue University Indianapolis*. Available from http://www.dsrp.iupui.edu/index.asp

IUPUI Undergraduate Research Opportunities Program. Available at http://www.urop.iupui .edu/Intro.html

Jacobi, M. (1991). Mentoring and undergraduate academic success: A literature review. *Review of Educational Research, 61*(4), 505–532.

Jafari, A., & Kaufman, C. (2006). *Handbook of research on e-portfolios*. Hershey, PA: Idea Group Reference.

Jaschik, S. (2009, January 26). Articulation is not enough. *Inside Higher Education*. Available from http://insidehighered.com/news/2009/01/26/articulation

Jenkins, K., & Skelly, J. (2004). Education abroad is not enough. *International Educator, 13*(1), 7–12.

Johnson County Community College, Civic Honors Website. Available from http://www .jccc.net/home/depts.php/S00025/site/introduction

Jones, R. T. (2005, Spring). Liberal education for the 21st century: Business expectations. *Liberal Education, 91*(2), 32–37.

Jones, E. A., & Hoffman, S. (1995). *National assessment of college student learning: Identifying college graduates' essential skills in writing, speech and listening, and critical thinking: Final project report*. Washington, DC: National Center for Education Statistics.

Jones, S., & McEwen, M. (2000). A conceptual model of multiple dimensions of identity. *Journal of College Student Development, 41*, 405–414.

Josselson, R. E. (1987). *Finding herself: Pathways to identity development in women*. San Francisco: Jossey-Bass.

Juhasz, A. M., & Walker, A. M. (1988). The impact of study abroad on university students' self-esteem and self-efficacy. *College Student Journal, 22*, 329–341.

Juillerat, S. (2000). Assessing the expectations and satisfaction levels of sophomores: How are they unique? In L. A. Schreiner & J. Pattengale (Eds.). *Visible solutions for invisible students: Helping sophomores succeed*. (Monograph No. 31) (pp 19–29). Columbia, SC: University of South Carolina, National Resource Center for The First-Year Experience® and Students in Transition.

Junco, R., & Mastrodicasa, J. (2007). *Connecting to the net.generation: What higher education professionals need to know about today's students*. Washington, DC: NASPA, Student Affairs Administrators in Higher Education.

Kardash, C. M. (2000). Evaluation of an undergraduate research experience: perceptions of undergraduate interns and their faculty mentors. *Journal of Educational Psychology, 92*(1), 191–201.

Karukstis, K. K., & Elgren, T. E. (2007). *Developing and sustaining a research-supportive curriculum: A compendium of successful practices*. Washington, DC: Council on Undergraduate Research.

Kauffman, L. R., & Stocks, J. (2003). *Reinvigorating the undergraduate research experience: successful models supported by NSFs AIRE/RAIRE Program* Available http://www.cur.org/ publications/aire_raire/toc.asp

Kazanjian, V.H., & Laurence, P. L. (2002). *Education as transformation: Religious pluralism, spirituality, and a new vision for higher education in America*. New York: Peter Lang.

Kazis, R., Callahan, A., Davidson, C., McLeod, A., Bosworth, B., Choitz, V., & Hoops, J. (2007). *Adult learners in higher education: Barriers to success and strategies to improve results*. U.S. Department of Labor, Employment and Training Administration. Occasional Paper 2007–03.

Keeling, R. (Ed.). (2004). *Learning reconsidered: A campus-wide focus on the student experience*. Washington, D.C.: American College Personnel Association and National Association of Student Personnel Administrators.

Keen, C. H. (2002). Spiritual assumptions undergird educational priorities: A personal narrative. In V. C. Kazanjian and P.L. Laurence (Eds.), *Education as transformation: Religious pluralism, spirituality, and a new vision for higher education in America* (pp. 37–44). New York: Peter Lang.

Kegan, R. (1982). *The evolving self: Problem and process in human development.* Cambridge, MA: Harvard University.

Kelly, K. R., & Pulver, C. S. (2003). Refining measurement of career decision types: A validity study. *Journal of Counseling and Development, 81*(4), 445–455.

Kerr, K. G., & Tweedy, J. (2006). Beyond seat time and student satisfaction: A curricular approach to residential education. *About Campus, 11*(5), pp. 9–15.

Keup, J. (2002). The impact of curricular interventions on intended second-year re-enrollment. *Journal of College Student Retention: Research, Theory, and Practice, 7*(1–2), 61–89.

King, J. E. (2002). *Crucial choices: How students' financial decisions affect their academic success.* American Council on Education. Available from http://www.acenet.edu/bookstore

King, L. J., & Young, J. A. (1994). Study abroad education for the 21st century. *Unterrichtspraxis 27*(1), 77–87.

King, M. C. (2002). *Community college advising.* Available from NACADA Clearinghouse of Academic Advising Resources Web site: http://www.nacada.ksu.edu/Clearinghouse/Advising Issues/comcollege.htm

Klippenstein, S., & James, P. (2002). The residential nexus: A focus on student learning. *Talking Stick, 19* (6), 7–16.

Koch, C., & Johnson, W. B. (2000). Documenting the Benefits of Undergraduate Mentoring. *CUR Quarterly, 20*(4), 172–175.

Kohlberg, L., & Kramer, R. (1969). Continuities and discontinuities in childhood and adult moral development. *Human Development, 12*, 93–120.

Korbel, L. A. (2007). In union there is strength: The role of state global education consortia in expanding community college involvement in global education. *New Directions for Community Colleges, 138*, 47–55.

Koskinen, L., & Tossasvainen, K. (2004). Study abroad as a process of learning intercultural competence in nursing. *International Journal of Nursing Practice, 10*, 111–120.

Kramer, G. L. (2000). Advising students at different educational levels. In V. Gordon & W. Habley (Eds.), *Academic advising: A comprehensive handbook* (pp. 84–104). San Francisco: Jossey-Bass.

Kramer, G. L., Taylor, L, Chynoweth, B., & Jensen, J. (1987). Developmental academic advising: A taxonomy of services. *NASPA Journal, 24*(4), 23–41.

Kuh, G. D. (2007). *National Survey of Student Engagement — Experiences that matter: Enhancing Student Learning and Success Annual Report 2007.* Bloomington, IN: University of Indiana, Center for Postsecondary Research.

Kuh, G. D. (2008). Advising for student success. In V. Gordon, W. Habley, T. Grites, & Associates, *Academic advising: A comprehensive handbook* (2nd ed.) (pp. 68–84). San Francisco: Jossey-Bass.

Kuh, G. D., Chen, D., & Laird, T.F.N. (2007). Why teacher-scholars matter: Some insights from FSSE and NSSE. *Liberal Education, 93*(4), 40–45.

Kuh, G. D., English, A. M., & Hinkle, S. E. (2003). Student-centered academic services. In G. L. Kramer & Associates, *Student Academic Services* (pp. 391–410). San Francisco: Jossey-Bass.

Kuh, G. D., & Hu, S. (2001). The effects of student-faculty interaction in the 1990s. *Review of Higher Education, 2*, 309–332.

Kuh, G. D., & Kauffman, N. (1985). The impact of study abroad on personal development. *Journal of International Student Personnel, 2*, 6–10.

Kuh, G. D., Kinzie, J., Buckley, J., Bridges, B., & Hayek, J. (2007). Piecing together the student success puzzle: Research, propositions, and recommendations. *ASHE Higher Education Report*, *32*(5). San Francisco: Jossey-Bass.

Kuh, G. D., Kinzie, J., Schuh, J. H., Whitt, E. J., & Associates. (2005). *Student success in college: Creating conditions that matter*. San Francisco: Jossey-Bass.

Kuhn, T. L. (2008). Historical foundations of academic advising. In V. Gordon, W. Habley, & T. Grites and Associates, *Academic advising: A comprehensive handbook* (2nd ed.) (pp. 3–16). San Francisco: Jossey-Bass.

Lardner, E., & Malnarich, G. (2008). Assessing integrative learning: Insights from Washington Center's national project on assessing learning in learning communities. *Journal of Learning Communities Research*, *3*(3).

Lemons, L. J., and Richmond, D. R. (1987). A developmental perspective of sophomore slump. *NASPA Journal*, *24*(3), 15–19.

Lent, R. W., Brown, S. D., & Hackett, G. (1994). Toward a unifying social cognitive theory of career and academic interest, choice, and performance [Monograph]. *Journal of Vocational Behavior*, *45*, 79–122.

Leontis, A. (1995). *Topographies of Hellenism: Mapping the homeland*. Ithaca, NY: Cornell University Press.

Leppel, K. (2001). The impact of major on college persistence among freshman. *Higher Education*, *41*(3), 327–342.

Levy, S. R., Stroessner, S. J., & Dweck, C. S. (1998). Stereotype formation and endorsement: The role of implicit theories. *Journal of Personality and Social Psychology*, *74*(6), 1421–1436.

Lewis, T. L., & Niesenbaum, R. A. (2005, June 3). The benefits of short–term study abroad. *The Chronicle of Higher Education*, p. B20.

Light, R. J. (2001). *Making the most of college: Students speak their minds*. Cambridge, MA: Harvard University Press.

Lindholm, J. A., & Astin, H. S. (2008). Spirituality and pedagogy: Examining the relationship between faculty's spirituality and use of student-centered pedagogy. *Review of Higher Education*, *31*(2), 185–207.

Lindsey, E. W. (2005). Study abroad and values development in social work students. *Journal of Social Work Education 40*, 229–250.

Loevinger, J. (1976). *Ego development: Conceptions and theories*. San Francisco: Jossey-Bass.

Lopatto, D. (2004). Survey of Undergraduate Research Experiences (SURE): first findings. *Cell Biology Education*, *3*(4), 270–277.

Lopez, F. G., & Sujin, A. L. (2006). Predictors of career indecision in three racial/ethnic groups of college women. *Journal of Career Development*, *33*(1), 29–46.

Lopez, S. J., Snyder, C. R., Magyar-Moe, J. L., Edwards, L. M., Pedrotti, J. M., Janowski, K., Turner, J., & Pressgrove, C. (2004). *Strategies for accentuating hope*. In P. A. Linley & S. Joseph (Eds.), *Positive psychology in practice* (pp. 388–404). Hoboken, NJ: Wiley.

Louis, M. (2008). *A comparative analysis of the effectiveness of strengths-based curricula in promoting first-year college student success*. Unpublished doctoral dissertation, Azusa Pacific University.

Lowman, J. (1994). Professors as performers and motivators. *College Teaching*, *42*, 137–141.

Lundberg, C. A., & Schreiner, L. A. (2004). Quality and frequency of faculty-student interaction as predictors of learning: An analysis by student race/ethnicity. *Journal of College Student Development*, *45*(5), 549–565.

Lundquist, C., Spalding R. J., & Landrum E. R. (2002–2003). College students' thoughts about leaving the university: The impact of faculty attitudes and behaviors. *Journal of College Student Retention, 4*, 123–133.

Luzzo, D. A. (1999). Identifying the career decision-making needs of nontraditional college students. *Journal of Counseling & Development, 77*, 135–140.

Maki, P. (2004). *Assessing for learning: Building a sustainable commitment across the institution.* Sterling, VA: Stylus.

Marcia, J. E. (1993). The ego identity status approach to ego identity. In J. E. Marcia, A. S. Waterman, D. R. Matteson, S. L. Archer, & J. L. Orlofsky (Eds.), *Ego identity: A handbook for psychosocial research* (pp. 3–21). New York: Springer-Verlag.

Margolis, G. (1976). Unslumping our sophomores: Some clinical observations and strategies. *Journal of College Health, 25*, 133–136.

Margolis, G. (1989). Developmental opportunities. In P. A. Graysen & K. Cauley (Eds.), *College psychotherapy* (pp. 71–91). New York: Guilford Press.

Markus, H., & Nurius, P. (1986). Possible selves. *American Psychologist, 41*, (9), 954–969.

Marion, P. (1980). Relationships of student characteristics and experiences with attitude changes in a program of study abroad. *Journal of College Student Personnel 21*, 58.

Marymount College. (n.d.). Available at http://www.marymountpv.edu/academics/advise Srvcs.asp

Mateja, J. (2006). Undergraduate research: Needed more today then ever before. *CUR Quarterly, 27*(1), 27–32.

Mau, W. (2000). Cultural differences in career decision-making styles and self-efficacy. *Journal of Voctional Behavior, 57*(3), 368–378.

McClenney, J., & O' Brien, C. (2006). Exploring relationships between student engagement and student outcomes in community colleges. Available from http://www.ccsse.org/publications%20Paper%20on20Validation%20Research%20December%202006.pdf

McDonough, P.M. (2004). *The school-to-college transition: Challenges and prospects.* Washington, D.C.: ACE.

McEwen, M. K. (1996). Enhancing student learning and development through service-learning. In B. Jacoby (Ed.), *Service-learning in higher education: Concepts and practices* (pp. 53–91). San Francisco: Jossey-Bass.

McGrath, M., & Braunstein, A. (1997). The prediction of freshman attrition: An examination of the importance of certain demographic, academic, financial, and social factors. *College Student Journal, 31*, 396–408.

McPherson College. (2007). 2007–2008 Catalog. (p. 153). Available from http://www.mcpherson.edu/academics/0708catalog.pdf

Medina-Lopez-Portillo, A. (2004). Intercultural learning assessment: The link between program duration and the development of intercultural sensitivity. *Frontiers, 10*, 179–199.

Meyer-Lee, E., & Evans, J. (2007). Areas of study in outcomes assessment. In M. C. Bolen (Ed.), *A guide to outcomes assessment in education abroad* (pp. 61–70). Carlisle, PA: The Forum on Education Abroad.

Mezirow, J. (1991). *Transformative dimensions of adult learning.* San Francisco: Jossey-Bass.

Michaelson, L. K., Knight, A. B., & Fink, L. D. (2002). *Team-based learning: A transformative use of small groups.* Santa Barbara, CA: Praeger.

Moltz, D. (n.d.). Look who's living on campus. Available from http://InsideHigherEd.com/layout/set/print/news/2008/06/27/housing

Montrose, L. (2002). International study and experiential learning: The academic context. *Frontiers, 8*, 1–15.

Mustakova-Possardt, E. (2004). Education for critical moral consciousness. *Journal of Moral Education, 33*(3), 245–269.

Nagda, B. A., Gregerman, S. R., Jonides, J., von Hippel, W., & Lerner, J. S. (1998). Undergraduate student-faculty research partnerships affect student retention. *Review of Higher Education, 22*(1), 55–72.

Nash, D. (1976). The personal consequences of a year of study abroad. *Journal of Higher Education 47*(2), 191–203.

National Association of Colleges and Employers (NACE). (2006). *Job outlook 2007*. Available from http://www.naceweb.org/

National Collegiate Athletic Association. (2006). *2006–07 guide for the college-bound student-athlete*. Indianapolis, IN: NCAA.

National Conferences on Undergraduate Research (NCUR). (n.d.). Available from http://www.ncur.org

National Resource Center for The First-Year Experience® and Students in Transition. (n.d.). Sophomore year resources. available from http://www.sc.edu/fye/resources/soph/index.html

National Science Foundation Publications website. (2008). Alliances for Broadening Participation in STEM (ABP). Available from http://www.nsf.gov/publications/pub_summ.jsp?ods_key=nsf08545

National Science Foundation SRS Report. (2001). *Characteristics of recent science and engineering graduates: 2001, NSF 04–302; National Science Foundation, Division of Science Resources Statistics* Available from http://www.nsf.gov/statistics/nsf04302/pdfstart.htm

National Science Foundation URC website. Available from http://www.nsf.gov/news/news_summ.jsp?cntn_id=104533

National Survey of Student Engagement (NSSE). (2000). *National benchmarks of effective educational practice*. Bloomington, IN: Indiana University Center for Postsecondary Research.

National Survey of Student Engagement (NSSE). (2006). *Engaged learning: Fostering success for all students*. Bloomington, IN: Indiana University Center for Postsecondary Research.

National Survey of Student Engagement (NSSE). (2008). *Annual Report*. Available from http://nsse.iub.edu/index.cfm

Nauta, M. M., & Kahn, J. H. (2007). Identity status, consistency and differentiation of interests, and career decision making self efficacy. *Journal of Career Assessment, 15*(1), 55–65.

Nealy, M. (2005). Key to student retention—strong advising. *Diverse Issues in Higher Education* (formerly *Black Issues in Higher Education*), *22*(14), 12.

Newman, J., Gray, E., & Fuqua, R. (1999). The relation of career indecision to personality dimensions of the California Psychological Inventory. *Journal of Vocational Behavior, 54*(1), 174–187.

Nilson, L. B. (2003). *Teaching at its best: A research-based resource for college instructors*, (2nd ed.). Bolton, MA: Anker.

Nnadozie, E., Ishiyama, J. T., & Chon, J. (2001). Undergraduate research internships and graduate school success. *Journal of College Student Development, 42*, 145–156.

Noel, P. M. (2007). *Still making a difference in the person I am becoming: A study of students' perceptions of faculty who make a difference in their lives*. Unpublished doctoral dissertation, Azusa Pacific University.

Nora, A., Barlow, E., & Crisp, G. (2005). Student persistence and degree attainment beyond the first year in college: The need for research. In A. Seidman (Ed.), *College student retention: Formula for student success* (pp. 129–154). Westport, CT: American Council on Education.

Northeast Community College Web site: Available from: http://www.northeast.edu/PS/ Academic_Support_Services/Career_Planning/index.php

Obst, D., Bhandari, R., & Witherell, S. (2007). *Current trends in U.S. study abroad & impact of strategic diversity initiatives*. New York: Institute of International Education.

Office of Residence Life. (2005). *Second year at Emory* brochure.

Olcott, S., & Kotovich, R. (2007). *Sophomore retention plan—final report*. Winona State University.

Orahood, T., Kruze, L., & Pearson, D. E. (2004). The impact of study abroad on business students' career goals. *Frontiers, 10*, 117–130.

Orndorff, R. M., & Herr, E. L. (1996). A comparative study of declared and undeclared college students on career uncertainty and involvement in career development activities. *Journal of Counseling and Development, 74*(6), 632–639.

O'Toole, J., & Lawler, E. E. (2006). *The new American workplace*. New York: Palgrave Macmillan.

Paige, R. M., Stallman, E. M., & Josic, J. (2008). *Study abroad for global engagement: A preliminary report on the SAGE research project*. Minneapolis: University of Minnesota, Study Abroad for Global Engagement Research Project.

Palomba, C. A., & Banta, T. W. (1999). *Assessment essentials: Planning, implementing, and improving assessment in higher education*. San Francisco: Jossey-Bass.

Palmer, P. (1998). *The courage to teach: Exploring the inner landscape of a teacher's life*. San Francisco: Jossey-Bass.

Parker, B., & Dautoff, D. A. (2007). Service-learning and study abroad: Synergistic learning opportunities. *Michigan Journal of Community Service Learning, Spring 2007*, 40–53.

Parks, S. D. (2000). *Big questions, worthy dreams: Mentoring young adults in their search for meaning, purpose, and faith*. San Francisco: Jossey-Bass.

Pascarella, E. T. & Terenzini, P. T. (1991). *How college affects students: Findings and insights from twenty years of research*. San Francisco: Jossey-Bass.

Pascarella, E. T., & Terenzini, P. T. (2005). *How college affects students*, Vol. 2, *A third decade of research*. San Francisco: Jossey-Bass.

Pask-McCartney, C., & Salomone, P. R. (1988). Difficult cases in career counseling: III. The multipotential client. *Career Development Quarterly, 36*, 231–240.

Pasque, P. A., & Murphy, R. (2005). The intersections of living-learning programs and social identity as factors of academic achievement and intellectual engagement. *Journal of College Student Development, 46*(4), 429–441.

Pattengale, J. (2000). Policies and practices to enhance sophomore success. In L. A. Schreiner & J. Pattengale (Eds.), *Visible solutions for invisible students: Helping sophomores succeed* (Monograph No. 31) (pp. 31–47). Columbia, SC: University of South Carolina, National Resource Center for The First-Year Experience® and Students in Transition.

Pattengale, J. (2006, Spring). Student success or student non-dissatisfaction. *Growth, 6*, 13–25.

Pattengale, J. (2008). *Why I teach: And why it matters to my students*. New York: McGraw-Hill.

Pattengale, J. (2009). *The purpose-guided student: Dream to succeed*. New York: McGraw-Hill.

Pattengale. J., & Schreiner, L. A. (2000). What is the sophomore slump and why should we care? In L. A. Schreiner & J. Pattengale (Eds.), *Visible solutions for invisible students: Helping sophomores succeed* (Monograph No. 31) (pp. v–viii). Columbia, SC: University of South Carolina, National Resource Center for The First-Year Experience® and Students in Transition.

Paulsen, M. B., & St. John, E. P. (2002). Social class and college costs: Examining the financial nexus between college choice and persistence. *Journal of Higher Education, 73*(3), 189–236.

Pearson, C., & Dellman-Jenkins, M. (1997). Parental influences on a student's selection of a college major. *College Student Journal, 31*(3), 301–314.

Peng, S. S. & Fetters, W. B. (1978). Variable involved in withdrawal during the first two years of college. *American Educational Research Journal, 15*(3), 361–372.

Penn State Pulse (1998, March). Class of 2000 Sophomores. Available from http://www.sa.psu.edu/sara/pulse/45-c2ksoph.PDF

Perry, R. P., Hall, N. C., & Ruthig, J. C. (2005). Perceived (academic) control and scholastic attainment in higher education. In J. C. Smart (Ed.), *Higher education: Handbook of theory and research*, Vol. 20 (pp. 363–436). Dordrecht, The Netherlands: Springer.

Perry, W. G., Jr. (1970). *Forms of intellectual and emotional development in the college years: A Scheme.* Austin, TX: Holt, Rinehart, and Winston.

Peterson, C., & Seligman, M.E.P. (Eds.). (2002). *The VIA classification of* strengths and virtues. Available from http://www.viastrengths.org/ index.aspx?ContentID=34

Peterson, G., Sampson, J., Reardon, R., & Lenz, J. (1996). A cognitive information processing approach to career problem solving and decision making. In D. Brown, L. Brooks, & Associates (Eds.), *Career choice and development* (2nd ed.). San Francisco: Jossey-Bass.

Petkewich, R. (2006). Community colleges tackle research. *Chemical and Engineering News, 84*(42), 53–54.

Phinney, J.S., Dennis, J., & Osario, S. (2006). Reasons to attend college among ethnically diverse college students. *Cultural Diversity and Ethnic Minority Psychology, 12*(2), 347–366.

Piper, T. D. (1997). Empowering students to create community standards. *About Campus, 2*(3), pp. 22–24.

Pintrich, P. R. (2000). An achievement goal perspective on issues in motivation terminology, theory, and research. *Contemporary Educational Psychology, 25*, 92–104.

Poe, R. E. (1991). Developmental changes in vocational identity among college students. *Journal of College Student Development, 32*, 249–252.

Powers, E. (2008, January 31). Targeting "the lost year." *Insidehighered.com.* Available, from http://www.insidehighered.com/layout/set/print/news/2008/01/31/secondyear.

Pryor, J. H., Hurtado S., Saenz, V. B., Santos, J. L., Korn, W. S. (2007). *The American freshman: Forty year trends.* Los Angeles: Higher Education Research Institute, UCLA.

Purdue website for The Center for Authentic Science Practice in Education (CAPSiE). Available at http://www.purdue.edu/dp.caspie

Raby, R. L. (2007). Internationalizing the curriculum: On- and off-campus strategies. *New Directions for Community Colleges, 138*, 57–66.

Raby, R. L., Valeau, E. J. (2007). Community college international education: Looking back to forecast the future. *New Directions for Community Colleges, 138*, 5–14.

Rensselaer Polytechnic Institute Web site: http://www.rpi.edu/dept/cdc/SCE.html

Reynolds, P., Gross, J., & Millard, B. (2005). *Discovering life purpose: Retention success in a leadership course at Indiana Wesleyan University.* Bloomington: Indiana Project on Academic Success, Smith Center for Research, Indiana University.

Richmond, D. R., & Lemons, L. J. (1985). Sophomore slump: An individual approach to recognition and response. *Journal of College Student Personnel, 26*(2), 176–177.

Robbins, S., Allen, J., Casillas, A., Akamigbo, A., Saltonstall, M., Campbell, R., Mahoney, E., & Gore, P. A. (2009). Associations of resource and service utilization, risk level, and college outcomes. *Research in Higher Education, 50*, 101–118.

Robbins, S., Allen, J., Casillas, A., Peterson, C., & Le, H. (2006). Unraveling the differential effects of motivational and skills, social, and self-management measures from traditional predictors of college outcomes. *Journal of Educational Psychology, 98*, 598–616.

Robbins, S. B., Lauver, K., Le, H., Davis, D., Langley, R., & Carlstrom, A. (2004). Do psychosocial and study skills factors predict college outcomes? A meta-analysis. *Psychological Bulletin, 130*, 261–288.

Rueckert, L. (2008). Tools for the assessment of undergraduate research outcomes. In R. L. Miller, R. F. Rycek, E. Balcetis, S. T. Barney, and others (Eds.), *Developing, promoting, & sustaining the undergraduate research experience in psychology*. Society for the Teaching of Psychology, online book available at http://teachpsycho.org/resources/ebooks/ur2008/ur2008.php

Russell, S. (2006). Evaluation of NSF support for undergraduate research opportunities: Follow-up survey of undergraduate NSF program participants: Draft Report [Electronic Version]. Retrieved August 17, 2007, from http://www.sri.com/policy/csted/reports/university/index.html\#urosynthesis

Russell, S., Hancock, M., & McCullough, J. (2007). Benefits of undergraduate research experiences. *Science, 316*(5821), 548–549.

Ryan, R. M., & Deci, E. L. (2000). Self-determination theory and the facilitation of intrinsic motivation, social development, and well-being. *American Psychologist, 55*(1), 68–78.

Rybczynski, W. (2004, March 26). Good dorms make good friends. *Chronicle of Higher Education*. Available http://chronicle.com/cgi-bin/printable.cgi?article=http://chronicle.com/weekly/v50/i29/29b0

St. John, E. P. (1989). The influences of student aid on persistence. *Journal of Student Financial Aid, 19*, 52–68.

St. John, E. P. (1990). Price response in enrollment decisions: An analysis of the high school and beyond senior cohort. *Research in Higher Education, 31*, 161–76.

St. John, E. P., Cabrera, A. F., Nora, A., & Asker, E. H. (2000). Economic influences on persistence reconsidered. In J. M. Braxton (Ed.), *Reworking the student departure puzzle*. Nashville, TN: Vanderbilt University Press.

St. John, E. P., Hu, S., Simmons, A., Carter, D. F., & Weber, J. (2004). What difference does a major make? The influence of college major field on persistence by African American and White Students. *Research in Higher Education, 45*(3), 209–232.

St. John, E. P., Paulsen, M. B., & Carter, D. F. (2005). Diversity, college costs, and postsecondary opportunity: An examination of the financial nexus between college choice and persistence for African Americans and Whites. *Journal of Higher Education, 76*(5), 545–569.

Salter, C. (2007). A Sophomore Course on Methods in Chemical Research. In K. Karukstis & T. E. Elgren (Eds.), *Developing and Sustaining a Research-supportive Curriculum: A Compendium of Successful Practices*. Washington, D.C.: Council of Undergraduate Research.

San Antonio College. Available at http://www.accd.edu/sac/csd/tc/default.htm

Sanford, N. (Ed.). (1962). *The American college*. New York: Wiley.

Savickas, M. L. (1989). Annual review: Practice and research in career counseling and development, 1988. *Career Development Quarterly, 38*, 100–134.

Savickas, M. L. (2000). Renovating the psychology of careers for the twenty-first century. In Collin & R. A. Young (Eds.), *The future of career*. Cambridge, UK: Cambridge University Press.

Schaller, M. (2000). *A phenomenological study of the traditional-aged sophomore year experience at a four year, residential university.* (Doctoral Dissertation. Ohio University, 2000). Dissertations Abstracts International.

Schaller, M. (2005). Wandering and wondering: Traversing the uneven terrain of the second year of college. *About Campus, 10*(4), 17–24.

Schaller, M. A. (2007). The development of college sophomores. In B. F. Tobolowsky & B. E. Cox (Eds.), *Shedding Light on Sophomores* (Monograph No. 47) (pp. 1–11). Columbia: University of South Carolina, National Resource Center for The First-Year Experience® and Students in Transition.

Schaller, M. A., & Wagner, R. L. (2007) Indecision and an avalanche of expectations: Challenges facing sophomore resident assistants, *44*(1), Article 4. http://publications.naspa.org/naspajournal/vol44/iss1/art4

Schreiner, L. (1998, July). *Building community on college campuses.* Paper presented at the National Conference on Student Retention, New Orleans, LA.

Schreiner, L. (2007a, July). *The major factors that impact student retention—and how they affect you.* Paper presented at the National Conference on Student Retention, Orlando, FL.

Schreiner, L. (2007b, September). *Taking retention to the next level: Strengthening our sophomores.* Keynote address at the National Symposium on Student Retention, Milwaukee, WI.

Schreiner, L., & Pattengale, J. (2000). *Visible solutions for invisible students: Helping sophomores succeed.* Columbia, SC: National Resource Center for The First-Year Experience® and Students in Transition. Monograph No. 31.

Schreiner, L. A. (2006). *A technical report on the Clifton StrengthsFinder with college students.* Princeton, NJ: The Gallup Organization. Available from https://www.strengthsquest.com/Library/Documents/SQwebsiteversionofvaliditystudy.doc

Schreiner, L. A. (2009, February). *Positive psychology on campus: Measuring student "thriving."* Paper presented at the Institute for College Student Values, Tallahassee, FL.

Schreiner, L. A., & Anderson, E. C. (2005). Strengths-based advising: A new lens for higher education. *NACADA Journal, 25*(2), 20–29.

Schreiner, L. A., & Juillerat, S. L. (1993). *The Student Satisfaction Inventory.* Iowa City, IA: Noel-Levitz.

Schreiner, L. A., & Louis, M. (2006, November). *Measuring engaged learning in college students: Beyond the borders of NSSE.* Paper presented at the annual meeting of the Association for the Study of Higher Education, Anaheim, CA.

Schreiner, L. A., & Louis, M. (2008, November). *The engaged learning index: Implications for faculty development.* Paper presented at the annual meeting of the Association for the Study of Higher Education, Jacksonville, FL.

Schroeder, C. C., Minor, F. D., & Tarkow, T. A. (1999). Learning communities: Partnerships between academic and student affairs. In J. H. Levine (Ed.), *Learning communities: New structures, new partnerships for learning.* Columbia, SC: University of South Carolina, National Resource Center for The First-Year Experience and Students in Transition.

Schuh, J. H., & Associates. (2008). *Assessment methods for student affairs.* San Francisco: Jossey-Bass.

Schuh, J. H., & Upcraft, M. L. (2001). *Assessment practice in student affairs: An applications manual.* San Francisco: Jossey-Bass.

Schunk, D. H., & Zimmerman, B. J. (2003). Self-regulation and learning. In W. M. Reynolds & G. E. Miller (Eds.), *Handbook of psychology, Vol. 7: Educational psychology* (pp. 59–78). New York: John Wiley.

Science for Life. (2007). Available from http://hhmi.chem.ufl.edu/metadot/index.pl

Secretary's Commission on Achieving Necessary Skills. (SCANS) (1991). *What work requires of schools: A SCANS report for America 2000*. Washington, DC: U.S. Department of Labor.

Sell, D. K. (1983). Research on attitude change in U.S. students who participate in foreign study experiences: Past findings and suggestions for future research. *International Journal of Intercultural Relations, 7,* 131–147.

Seymour, E., Hunter, A.-B., & Laursen, S. L. (2004). Establishing the benefits of research experiences for undergraduates in the sciences: First findings from a three-year study. *Science Education, 88*(4), 493–534.

Sharma, M. P., & Mulka, J. S. (1993, March). *The impact of international education upon the United States: Students in comparative perspective.* Paper presented at Comparative and International Education Society, Kingston, Jamaica.

Shulman, L. (1999). Taking learning seriously. *Change, 31*(4), 10–17.

Slavin Miller, S., Schreiner, L. A., & Pullins, T. (2008, March). *Sophomore success: Engaging the "invisible" student.* Paper presented at the annual meeting of the National Association of Student Personnel Administrators, Orlando, FL.

Smith, D. C., & Gordon, V. N. (2008). *Family guide to academic advising* (2nd ed.). Columbia, SC: National Resource Center for The First-Year Experience® and Students in Transition.

Snyder, C. R., Harris, C., Anderson, J.R., Holleran, S.A., Irving, L.M., Sigmon, S.T., et.al. (1991). The will and the ways: Development and validation of an individual-differences measure of hope. *Journal of Personality and Social Psychology, 60,* 570–585.

Snyder, C. R., Shorey, H. S., Cheavens, J., Mann Pulvers, K., Adamas, V. H., III, & Wiklund, C. (2002). Hope and academic success in college. *Journal of Educational Psychology, 94* (4), 820–826.

Snyder, C. R., Wiklund, C., & Cheavens, J. (1999, August). *Hope and success in college.* Paper presented at the annual meeting of the American Psychological Association. Boston, MA.

Sophomore College. (2006). Stanford University. Available at http://ual.stanford.edu/OO/ soph_college/SocoCurrent.html\#SophomoreCollegeProgramInfo2007

The sophomore year experience: An evaluation of outcomes: Fall 2004 cohort. (2006, August). Unpublished report. Emory University.

Sophomores get chance to "reorient." (2007, November/December). *Carolina Alumni Review,* 8.

Sorcinelli, M. S. (2007). Faculty development: The challenge going forward. *Peer Review, 9*(4), 4–8.

Southern Illinois University, Edwardsville. (2007). Living and learning communities: Second-year experience program. Available from http://www.siue.edu/housing/livingandlearning /secondyearexperience.shtml

Steele, C. (1997). A threat in the air. *American Psychologist, 52*(6), 613–629.

Steele, G., Kennedy, G., & Gordon, V. (1993). The retention of major-changers: A longitudinal study. *Journal of College Student Development, 34,* 58–62.

Steger, M. F., Frazier, P., Oishi, S., & Kaler, M. (2006). *The Meaning in Life Questionnaire.* Assessing the presence of and search for meaning in life. *Journal of Counseling Psychology, 53*(1), 80–93.

Stitsworth, M. (1988). The relationship between previous foreign language study and personality change in youth exchange participants. *Foreign Language Annals, 21*(2), 131–137.

Stockenberg, J. (2007). The "sophomore jump" program at Colorado College. In B. F. Tobolowsky & B. E. Cox (Eds.), *Shedding light on sophomores: An exploration of the second college year* (Monograph No. 47) (pp. 63–74). Columbia, SC: University of South Carolina, National Resource Center for The First-Year Experience® and Students in Transition.

Student Affairs Leader (2006). First-year housing: Should we give students what they want, or what they need? *Student Affairs Leader, 34*(8), pp. 1–2.

Summer Undergraduate Research Opportunities at Carnegie Mellon. (2008). Available from http://www.cmu.edu/bio/undergraduate/research/cmustudents.shtml

Super, D. E. (1992). Toward a comprehensive theory of career development. In D. Montross & C. Shinkman (Eds.), *Career development: Theory and practice* (pp. 35–64). Springfield, IL: Charles C. Thomas.

Sutton, R. C., & Rubin, D. L. (2004). The GLOSSARI Project: Initial findings from a system-wide research initiative on study abroad learning outcomes. *Frontiers, 10,* 65–82.

Sutton, S. B., Cunningham, K., Straight, S., & Kinsella, J. (2007, May). *Anthropology and international education: Connecting the science of culture to intercultural education.* Panel presented at NAFSA Annual Meeting, Minneapolis.

Svanum. S., & Bigatti, S. M. (2009). Academic course engagement during one semester forecasts college success: Engaged students are more likely to earn a degree, do it faster and do it better. *Journal of College Student Development, 50*(1), 120–132.

Swanson, J. L., & Gore, P. A., Jr. (2000). Advances in vocational psychology theory and research (pp 233–269). In S. D. Brown & R. W. Lent (Eds.), *Handbook of counseling psychology* (3rd ed.). New York: Wiley.

Tagg, J. (2003). *The learning paradigm college.* Bolton, MA: Anker.

Tagg, J. (2004). Alignment for learning: Reorganizing classrooms and campuses. *About Campus, May/June,* 8–18.

Taris, T. W. (2000). *A primer in longitudinal data analysis.* London: Sage.

Taylor, K., & Bellani, R. N. (2007). The Sophomore-Year Experience (SYE) at Colgate University: A case study. In B. F. Tobolowsky & B. E. Cox (Eds.), *Shedding light on sophomores* (Monograph No. 47) (pp. 87–94). Columbia: University of South Carolina, National Resource Center for The First-Year Experience® and Students in Transition.

Teagle Foundation White Paper. Student Learning and Faculty Research: Connecting Teaching and Scholarship. Available from http://teaglefoundation.org/learning/pdf_acls_white paper.pdf

Teichler, U., & Steube, W. (1991). The logics of study abroad programmes and their impacts. *Higher Education,* 21, 325–349.

Terenzini, P. T., & Upcraft, M. L. (1996). Assessing program and service outcomes. In J. H. Schuh & M. L. Upcraft (Eds.), *Assesment in student affairs* (pp. 217–239). San Francisco: Jossey-Bass.

Texas Southern University. Available at http://em.tsu.edu/guac/secondmile/

Theophilides, C., Terezini, P. T., & Lorang, W. (1984). Freshman and sophomore experiences and changes in major field. *Review of Higher Education, 7,* 261–278.

Tiedeman, D., & O'Hara, R. (1963). *Career development: Choice and adjustment.* New York: College Entrance Examination Board.

Tinto, V. (1975). Dropout from higher education: A theoretical synthesis of recent research. *Review of Educational Research, 45,* 89–125.

Tinto, V. (1987). *Leaving college: Rethinking the causes and cures of student attrition.* Chicago: University of Chicago Press.

Tinto, V. (1993). *Leaving college: Rethinking the causes and cures of student attrition* (2nd ed.). Chicago: University of Chicago Press.

Tinto, V. (1998). Colleges as communities: Taking research on student persistence seriously. *Review of Higher Education, 21*(2), 167–178.

Tinto, V. (2006). Research and practice of college student retention: What next? *Journal of College Student Retention, 8*(1), 1–19.

Tobolowsky, B. F., & Cox, B. E. (2007a). *Shedding light on sophomores: An exploration of the second college year* (Monograph No. 47). Columbia, SC: University of South Carolina, National Resource Center for the First Year Experience® and Students in Transition.

Tobolowsky, B. F., & Cox, B. E. (2007b). Findings from the 2005 National survey on sophomore initiatives. In B. F. Tobolowsky and B. E. Cox (Eds.), *Shedding light on sophomores: An exploration of the second college year* (Monograph No. 47) (pp. 13–30). Columbia, SC: National Resource Center for The First-Year Experience® and Students in Transition.

Tobolowsky, B. F., & Cox, B. E. (2007c). Learning from the best: Recommendations for sophomore initiatives. In B. F. Tobolowsky & B. E. Cox (Eds.), *Shedding light on sophomores: An exploration of the second college year* (Monograph No. 47) (pp. 95–99). Columbia: University of South Carolina, National Resource Center for The First–Year Experience® and Students in Transition.

Tobolowsky, B. F., Mamrick, M., & Cox, B. E. (2005). *The 2003 national survey of first-year seminars: Continuing innovations in the collegiate curriculum* (Monograph no. 41). Columbia, SC: University of South Carolina, National Resource Center for The First Year Experience® and Students in Transition.

Torres, V. (2003). Student diversity and academic services. In G. L. Kramer & Associates, *Student Academic Services* (pp. 333–351). San Francisco: Jossey-Bass.

Townsend, B. K., & Wilson, K. B. (2006). The transfer mission: Tried and true, but troubled? In B. K. Townsend & K. Dougherty (Eds.), *Community college missions in the 21st century*. New Directions for Community Colleges, No. 136. San Francisco: Jossey-Bass.

Tracey, T.J.G., & Robbins, S. B. (2006). The interest-major congruence and college success relation: A longitudinal study. *Journal of Vocational Behavior, 69*, 64–89.

Tuttle, D. (2006). *Report by the upper class experience task force*. Retrieved August 1, 2007, from http://www.trinity.edu/departments/student_affairs/dean_of_students/Upperclass%20 Task%20Force%20Report%201.18.07.pdf

Union Scholars Program: The Sophomore Project. (2006). Available from http://www.union. edu/Scholars/sophfaq.htm

University of Central Florida. Available at http://www.sophomore.sdes.ucf.edu/missiongoals. html

University of Central Florida Student Success Center. Available at http://www.catalog.sdes.ucf. edu/current/sdes/adr/student_success_center/

University of Cincinnati website: http://www.uc.edu/csi/

University of South Carolina website: http://www.sa.sc.edu/tsi

University of Washington. Available at http://www.washington.edu/uaa/gateway/advising/ about/isap.php

Upcraft, M. L. (2005). Assessing the first year of college. *Challenging and supporting the first-year student: A handbook for improving the first year of college*. San Francisco: Jossey-Bass.

Upcraft, M. L., Gardner, J. N., & Barefoot, B. O. (2005). *Challenging and supporting the first-year student*. San Francisco: Jossey-Bass.

Upcraft, M. L., Ishler, J.L.C., & Swing, R. (2005). A beginner's guide for assessing the first college year. In M. L. Upcraft, J. Gardner, & B. O. Barefoot (Eds.), *Challenging and supporting the first-year student: A handbook for improving the first year of college*. San Francisco: Jossey-Bass.

Upcraft, M. L., & Schuh, J. H. (1996). *Assessment in student affairs: A guide for practitioners*. San Francisco: Jossey-Bass.

U.S. Department of Education. (2006, September). *A test of leadership: Charting the future of U.S. higher education*. (A Report of the Commission Appointed by Secretary of Education Margaret Spellings.) Washington, DC: Education Publications Center.

UW Milwaukee Sophomore Research Experience Web Site. (2007). Available from http://www4.uwm.edu/access_success/opportunities/sophomore_research.cfm

Vande Berg, M. (2004). Introduction to special issue on assessment of study abroad learning, *Frontiers, 10*, xii–xxii.

Vande Berg, M. (2007). Intervening in the learning of U.S. students abroad. *Journal of Studies in International Education, 11*(3/4), 392–399.

Vande Berg, M, Balkcum, A., Scheid, M., & Whalen, B. J. (2004). The Georgetown University Consortium Project: A Report at the Halfway Mark. *Frontiers, 10*, 101–116.

Van Manen, M. (1990). *Researching the lived experience: Human science for an action sensitive pedagogy*. State University of New York Press.

Varma-Nelson, P. (2006). Peer-led team learning. *Metropolitan Universities Journal, 17*(4), 19–29.

Vygotsky, L. (1978). *Mind in society: The development of higher psychological processes*. Cambridge, MA: Harvard University Press.

Walker, C. O., Green, B. W., & Mansell, R. A. (2006). Identification with academics, intrinsic/extrinsic motivation and self efficacy as predictors of cognitive engagement. *Learning and Individual Differences, 16*, 1–12.

Wallace, J. (2000). A popular education model for the community. *American Behavioral Scientist, 43*(5), 756–766.

Walsh, D. C. (2002). Transforming education: An overview. In V. C. Kazanjian & P. L. Laurence (Eds.), *Education as transformation: Religious pluralism, spirituality, and a new vision for higher education in America* (pp. 1–14). New York: Peter Lang.

Wanberg, C. R., & Muchinsky, P. M. (1992). A typology of career decision status: Validity extension of the vocational decision status model. *Journal of Counseling Psychology, 39*(1), 71–80.

Ward, K., & Wolf-Wendel, L. (2000). Community-centered service learning: Moving from doing for to doing with. *American Behavioral Scientist, 43*(5), 767–780.

Wayne State University Undergraduate Research and Creative Projects. (2008). Available from http://www.undergradresearch.wayne.edu/

Wehlburg, C. M. (2007). Closing the feedback loop is not enough: The assessment spiral. *Assessment Update, 19*(2), 1–2,15.

Wenzel, T. A. (2000). Cooperative Student Activities as Learning Devices. *Analytical Chemistry*, 293A-296A.

Whitt, L. (1996). Assessing student cultures. In J. H. Schuh & M. L. Upcraft (Eds.), *Assessment in student affairs* (pp. 189–216). San Francisco: Jossey-Bass.

Whyte, D. R. (1963). *Social alienation among college students*. Unpublished doctoral dissertation, Cornell University.

Wilder, J. S. (1993). The sophomore slump: A complex developmental period that contributes to attrition. *College Student Affairs Journal, 12*(2), 18–27.

Wilkinson, S. (1998). Study abroad from the participants' perspective: A challenge to common beliefs. *Foreign Language Annals 31*(1), 23–39.

Willenbrock, C. M. (2008). The evolving role of the resident advisor. *Talking Stick, 26*(2), 45–60.

William Jewell College. (2007). Sophomore-year experience. Available from http://jewell.edu/william_jewell/gen/william_and_jewell_generated_pages/SophYear_Exper_Home_p1933.html

Williams, R., & Woodruff, G. (2005). *2004–05 Sophomore survey of study abroad University of Minnesota responses*. Minneapolis, MN: University of Minnesota, Learning Abroad Center.

Williams, T. R. (2005). Exploring the impact of study abroad on students' intercultural communication skills: Adaptability and sensitivity. *Journal of Studies in International Education 9*(4), 356–371.

Wooster Sophomore Research Program Web Site. (2008). Available from http://www.wooster.edu/research/SophomoreResearch.html

Young, D. Y. (2004, May). Persistence at a Liberal Arts University and Participation in a Study-Abroad Program. Paper Presented at the meeting of the Association for Institutional Research, Boston, MA.

Zajacova, A., Lynch, S. M., & Espenshade, T. J. (2005). Self-efficacy, stress, and academic success in college. *Research in Higher Education, 46*(6), 677–706.

Zeszotarski, P. (2001). ERIC Review: Issues in global education initiatives in the community college. *Community College Review 29*(1), 65–78.

Zhao, C., & Kuh, G.D. (2004). Adding value: Learning communities and student engagement. *Research in Higher Education, 45*, (2), p. 115–138.

Zinbauer, B. J., Pargament, K. I., & Scott, A. B. (1999). The emerging meanings of religiousness and spirituality: Problems and prospects. *Journal of Personality, 67*(6), 889–919.

Zlotkowski, E., Duffy, D., Franco, R., Jones, S., Gelmon, S., Norvell, K., & Meeropol, J., (2004). *The community's college: Indicators of engagement at two-year institutions*. Providence, RI: Campus Compact.

NAMES INDEX

SUBJECT INDEX

A

Absolute knowing, 149
Academic, ability, 28
Academic advising, 40, 83–98; and
        academic planning, 87–93;
        and academic resources,
        94–95; and advisor
        development, 96–97; and
        choice of major, 84–87; and
        family issues, 94;
        recommendations for,
        97–98; and return to
        campus community, 92–93;
        and sophomore transfer
        issues, 93–94; three aspects
        of process of, 86–87; and
        transition to junior year,
        95–96
Academic engagement, 24
Academic Impressions, 223
Academic issues, 35–36
Academic planning, 87–93;
        immediate planning phase
        of, 89–91; and long-range
        planning, 91–92; review
        phase of, 88–89

Academic resources, 94–95
Academic self-efficacy, 17–19;
        defined, 18
Academic Self-Sufficiency Scale
        (Chemers, Hu, and Garcia),
        48, 51
ACT, 103–104
Active learning, 139–140
Adult Trait Hope Scale (Snyder et al.),
        48, 51
Adults, relationships with, 77
Advisor development, 96–97
Africa, 165
African American students, 26–27,
        138, 155; and satisfaction,
        23
Age, 27
Alliances for Broadening
        Participation (ABP) in
        STEM program, 184
Almanac Issue *(Chronicle of Higher
        Education)*, 2
Alverno College (Wisconsin),
        121
American Association for Higher
        Education (AAHE), 235,
        239

American Association of Colleges
        and Universities, 242
American Association of
        Community Colleges
        (AACC), 150, 154, 166;
        Horizons Program, 157,
        158; Service-Learning
        Clearinghouse, 157
American College Health
        Association, 38
American Council on Education,
        192
Amherst College, 38
Asian students, 26–27
Assessment, principles of good,
        267–269
Assessment of Learning (Maki), 241
Assessment spiral, 245
Assessment Update (Wehlburg), 245
Association of American Colleges
        and Universities, 117, 118
Authenticity, 143–144

B

Beloit College (Wisconsin), 14,
        109–110, 151–153, 228,